Meet Mayor Mamdani, a substantially expanded edition of Ted Hamm's widely acclaimed *Run Zohran Run!*, maps how a groundbreaking candidate and his dynamic campaign for New York City mayor toppled a Democratic Party dynasty and ran circles around MAGA.

34-year-old Zohran's straightforward, openly democratic socialist platform—a rent freeze, free buses, universal childcare, and city-run grocery stores—resonated across the increasingly unaffordable city.

But Mamdani's job wasn't assured after winning the primary against "prince of darkness" Andrew Cuomo and his billionaire allies. Trump enthusiasts targeted Zohran's heritage and support for Palestinian rights, unleashing a torrent of Islamophobic hate. Mamdani's canny instincts helped him outmaneuver local and national power players alike.

Mamdani expanded his June coalition by bringing aboard city unions and stumping with mainstream Democratic Party leaders like Tish James. Steered by NYC-DSA, the campaign's massive outreach operation saw over 100,000 volunteers interact with over three million New Yorkers. Zohran scored over 1.1 million votes, the highest total of any New York City mayoral candidate since John Lindsay in 1965.

As fast-paced and compelling as its subject, *Meet Mayor Mamdani* reveals how a charismatic candidate and a vibrant grassroots campaign stayed ahead of the competition and set the stage for democratic socialism at City Hall.

MEET MAYOR MAMDANI

MEET MAYOR MAMDANI

THE SPECTACULAR VICTORY OF A DEMOCRATIC SOCIALIST IN NEW YORK CITY

THEODORE HAMM

OR Books
New York • London

© Theodore Hamm 2026

Published by OR Books, New York and London

Visit our website at www.orbooks.com

All rights information: rights@orbooks.com

All rights reserved. No part of this book may be reproduced or transmitted in any form or by any means, electronic or mechanical, including photocopy, recording, or any information storage retrieval system, without permission in writing from the publisher, except brief passages for review purposes.

First printing 2026

The manufacturer's authorised representative in the EU for product safety is Authorised Rep Compliance Ltd, 71 Lower Baggot Street, Dublin D02 P593 Ireland (www.arccompliance.com)

Typeset by Lapiz Digital. Printed by BookMobile, USA, and CPI, UK.

OR Books
40 Loisaida Avenue
New York, NY 10009

paperback ISBN 978-1-68219-543-7 • ebook ISBN 978-1-68219-544-4

Contents

Introduction ix

Part One: *RUN ZOHRAN RUN!*

1. The City Turned Upside Down 3
2. Cold War, R.I.P. 17
3. Roots 35
4. Roti and Roses 49
5. The Message is a Mantra 61
6. Fast Start 79
7. A Spicy Mix 93
8. Dodge Charger 105
9. Sticks and Stones 121
10. A Creative Class 133
11. Buckle Up 145
12. It's Getting Hot 157
13. Five-Alarm Fire! 169
14. The Spoils of Victory 185

Part Two: *MEET MAYOR MAMDANI*

15.	Group Therapy	225
16.	Heavy Lifts	241
17.	Police and Thieves	255
18.	Autumn in New York	269
19.	Turn Signals	283
20.	Balls Out	297
21.	Hot Seats	317
22.	Strange Bedfellows	335

Acknowledgements 355

For Toni, Ellis, and the next New York City

Introduction

"I was elected as a democratic socialist and I will govern as a democratic socialist," New York City's new mayor vowed from the steps of City Hall on the frigid first day of 2026. Shortly beforehand, Zohran beamed when his hero Bernie Sanders inspired spirited audience chants of "Tax the rich!" in his introductory remarks. Chuck Schumer—a figure rather less enthusiastic about both Mamdani and his worldview—sat inconspicuously in the row behind his colleague from Vermont. Amid the festivities, outgoing mayor Eric Adams received a loud round of jeers.

Throughout Zohran's 23-minute inauguration address, an air horn blared, with a gaggle of pro-Israel protesters across the street seeking to disrupt the proceedings. Meanwhile, throngs of NYC-DSA members, myriad community activists, scores of elected officials, and sundry shivering enthusiasts of all ages cheered wildly for Mamdani both inside and outside the gates of City Hall. "C'mon now!" a 40-something supporter near the stage repeatedly exhorted as Zohran advocated for both "Black homeowners in St. Albans" and "Palestinian children in Bay Ridge."

Mayor Mamdani had officially taken the reins just after midnight on January 1, when Attorney General Tish James administered the oath of office at a grand but unused subway station beneath City Hall, an apt location for the public transportation-oriented city leader. Although there was uncertainty about whether he was now the city's 111th or 112th mayor (with new evidence from the 17th century clearly pointing to the latter), there was no dispute that he was the first Muslim to hold the title. At the swearing-in, Zohran's wife Rama Duwaji held a Quran that once belonged to Arturo Schomburg, New York City's legendary archivist of the African diaspora.

The location of the new mayor's first presser was also telling. 85 Clarkson Avenue in Flatbush is seven miles from City Hall, but the pro-tenant candidate was now ready for action. Residents of the 71-unit building had stopped paying rent to Pinnacle Group, their corporate mega-landlord that had long neglected its properties while filing for bankruptcy. After an enthusiastic welcome from strikers, Mayor Mamdani visited a unit with broken floor tiles and a banged-up bathroom. He advised reporters that his newly named chief legal officer Steve Banks, a veteran housing advocate, would pursue the matter. Zohran also announced that his longtime ally Cea Weaver would run his tenant protection office.

On January 2, the next-gen leader faced attacks from the Netanyahu regime, with Israel's Foreign Ministry accusing

Mamdani on X of "pouring antisemitic gasoline on an open fire." The hyperbolic outrage stemmed from the new mayor's day-one revocation of nine executive orders issued by his predecessor (dating back to Eric Adams' September 2024 indictment), two of which bolstered Israel's effort to muzzle its critics. The *New York Post* amplified the Foreign Ministry's incendiary claim amid its onslaught of attacks on Mamdani, who appeared on four of the tabloid's first five January covers. At the same time, the far-right outlet's social media posts included an upbeat 90-second video tracking the leftist leader's commute to City Hall, showing him cheerfully interacting with subway riders. For the *Post*, Zohran was both a fierce ideological foe and glamorous clickbait.

When the Trump administration launched its brazen assault on Venezuela's sovereignty on January 3, Mamdani spoke forcefully in defense of international norms. Zohran also conveyed his position directly to the president, explaining that he phoned Trump that morning and "registered [his] opposition" to "regime change." Unlike New York's veteran political leaders, the 34-year-old mayor's official position—"Unilaterally attacking a sovereign nation is an act of war and a violation of federal and international law"—minced no words. The NYC-DSA, which Mamdani had recently called his "political home," echoed the critique, calling an emergency organizing meeting.

Exposing bad landlords, challenging Israel's hegemony, mixing it up with the *Post*, blasting a bellicose president—as Zohran's first year in office kicked off, it appeared that

Meet Mayor Mamdani

the battles he fought during the 2025 campaign would rage indefinitely. The era of democratic socialism in New York City began in earnest.

—T. Hamm
Sunset Park, Brooklyn
January 5, 2026

Part One

RUN ZOHRAN RUN!

INSIDE ZOHRAN MAMDANI'S SENSATIONAL CAMPAIGN TO BECOME NEW YORK CITY'S FIRST DEMOCRATIC SOCIALIST MAYOR

CHAPTER 1

The City Turned Upside Down

On June 25, 2025, just after 12:15 a.m., a victorious Zohran Mamdani stepped on stage at a brewpub in Long Island City, Queens. A 33-year-old Muslim immigrant from Uganda, and an unapologetic democratic socialist, Mamdani had electrified New York City for the past several weeks.

Six months earlier, in mid-January, the Manhattan-based crypto-currency website Polymarket had given the newcomer an 8% shot at winning the mayoral Democratic primary, and although he had not yet become an official candidate, the disgraced former governor Andrew Cuomo—with 100% name recognition—led the pack at 44%. But by election day, Polymarket listed Mamdani at 55%, nine points ahead of Cuomo, who had remained the frontrunner since joining the race in March. The Wall Street crowd knows the trendlines.

In a hotel room near the brewpub, Zohran scrambled to update his remarks along with campaign manager Elle Bisgaard-Church, political director Julian Gerson, media strategist Morris Katz, and top aide Spencer Goldberg. Coming into the night, they knew that the results had spiked in their favor—but still expected the outcome to be determined after future rounds of ranked-choice ballot tabulations.

The insurgent candidate planned to give a talk along the lines of what a basketball coach tells the locker room after winning the quarter-finals—i.e. "great job everyone, but we're not there yet." But less than 90 minutes after the polls closed at 9 p.m., Cuomo conceded. As they adjusted the speech, Mamdani thought of his youth, when he'd lived in South Africa. He had a quote that he liked.

In his victory speech, which was broadcast live on local TV and across social media, Zohran invoked his native continent's favorite son (and fellow socialist): "Tonight," the candidate calmly began, "we made history. In the words of Nelson Mandela, 'It always seems impossible until it is done.' My friends, we have done it. I will be your Democratic nominee for the mayor of New York City."

Local TV reporters told their mostly older viewers that the upset win was "stunning" and "historic." At election-night watch parties across the city hosted by the Democratic Socialists of America (DSA), of which Mamdani has long been a member, Zohran's army of millennial volunteers went wild. Across the five boroughs—from Ozone Park, Queens, to Kensington, Brooklyn, to Westchester Square in the Bronx—South Asian and Muslim voters of all ages celebrated. Sundry social media platforms lit up.

From the city elite came wails of bewilderment and exasperation. "Terror. Fear. Panic," is how Kathryn Wylde, a ubiquitous spokesperson for the city's dubiously labeled "business community," summed up the collective reaction. As one of the city's largest landlords told the *New York Times*, "You want to have leadership that speaks to what New York is. It's the capital of capitalism."[1] So concurred the extreme-right *New York Post*, which had conducted a smear campaign against Mamdani throughout the primary. On election day, its front page had denounced the insurgent candidate as a "radical, antisemitic socialist." Its follow-up cover page was desperate: "NYC SOS," shrieked the influential tabloid. "Who will save our city after radical socialist batters Cuomo in Dem mayoral primary?" Throughout the city's corridors of power, Mamdani Derangement Syndrome reverberated.

Zohran's quote from Mandela provided his answer to the *Post*'s question. For democratic socialists, it is "we"—not a "she" or "he"—that wins elected offices. When early voting began on Saturday, June 14, Mamdani's massive ranks of volunteers, which surpassed 50,000 by primary day, provided an outreach operation far more genuinely committed to its candidate than that of any mayoral contender in recent New York City history.[2] A massive

---

1 For a rundown of similarly hysterical reactions, see *Hell Gate*'s "Morning Spew: Billionaire Meltdown Compilation" (6-26-2025).
2 From the mid-nineteenth century through 1960, Tammany Hall had large election-day operations, and the powerful Democratic Party

number of Muslim and South Asian voters, including many in the city's Bangladeshi enclaves, mobilized for the first time in a city election. Although union-friendly, Mamdani received support from only a few local labor leaders,[3] most of whom preferred not to upset the status quo. Zohran's coalition—voters under 50, multiracial, polyglot, pro-Palestine, unafraid to be called socialists—was nothing if not groundbreaking in New York City.

Alexandria Ocasio-Cortez and a diverse array of other local leaders joined Mamdani for a rally on Saturday night, June 14. The candidate and fellow speakers addressed an overflow crowd of mostly twenty-somethings at Terminal 5, a performance venue on Midtown Manhattan's west side. Exponentially more viewers caught clips on social media. "This victory," Zohran declared, "will be historic, not just for who I am—a Muslim immigrant and a proud democratic socialist—but for what we will do: make this city affordable for everyone."

*

Although he did not talk much about Uganda on the primary campaign trail, Zohran never tried to conceal

---

machines in Brooklyn and the Bronx followed suit through the 1990s. Labor unions historically have sent numerous members to help various campaigns. By contrast, Mamdani's volunteers joined based on their own personal motivations.

3   The membership of Local 9A of the UAW is relatively small when compared to other city unions, but it represents many graduate students and thus was quite active in the Mamdani campaign. On primary day, UAW president Shawn Fain issued a rousing video statement of support for Zohran.

his roots among the South Asian diaspora in Africa. On the weekend before the primary, he told an older Black audience at Reverend Al Sharpton's National Action Network headquarters in Harlem that his middle name was Kwame, in honor of Kwame Nkrumah, Ghana's first president and the father of African nationalism. Zohran's mother, acclaimed film director Mira Nair (b. 1957), joined him on the campaign trail, while his father, internationally renowned Columbia University professor Mahmood Mamdani (b. 1946), kept a low profile.[4]

Mahmood Mamdani is a leading scholar of decolonization. As Zohran told the Sharpton gathering, the elder Mamdani risked deportation when he first came to the U.S. by joining SNCC protests in Montgomery. With Spike Lee smiling at The Rev's side, the DSA candidate quoted a Sharpton observation from 2004. It was about the Democrats' long-standing pattern of relying on minority and working-class voters but not delivering anything meaningful in return.

Zohran's nearly 470,000 first-place votes in the primary made him, by vote count, the most popular U.S. politician who fully supports Palestinian rights.[5] On June 25, City University of New York (CUNY) journalism professor Peter Beinart connected Mamdani's success to shifts among younger Jewish voters regarding Palestine. He explained that "social movements often become part of mainstream

---

4 Mahmood Mamdani joined Mira Nair at both the June 14 rally with AOC and the primary night party.
5 While Bernie Sanders supports Palestinian human rights, he typically criticizes the Netanyahu regime—and does not mention political equality for Palestine.

politics." Until Zohran's successful primary run, the former *New Republic* editor noted, no leading New York City politician had taken a stand on behalf of Palestinian rights. Although "he was very progressive on many issues," Mayor Bill de Blasio (in office from 2014-2021) "made a clear exception regarding Palestine," stated Beinart.[6] Zohran has frequently referred to this stance as progressive except Palestine (or "PeP"). As the CUNY professor observed, even though campus protests in New York City were forcefully shut down by university brass and Mayor Eric Adams' NYPD, Mamdani was now bringing the activists' viewpoint into the electoral realm.

In the homestretch of the primary campaign, State Senator John Liu (b. 1967)—the first citywide Asian-American elected official, who competed against de Blasio for mayor as a left-wing populist in 2013—made a high-profile endorsement of Mamdani and served as one of the speakers at the AOC rally. Attorney General Tish James (b. 1958) similarly lent her influential backing, comparing the attacks on Zohran to the smears Barack Obama had once endured. Alas, the PeP label applies to both Liu and James.[7]

---

6   The evening after Beinart distributed his comments, de Blasio appeared on *Inside City Hall*, an influential nightly TV program hosted by Errol Louis. To his credit, the former mayor stressed that "disagreements with Israel do not make Mamdani 'antisemitic.'"

7   Amid the mass famine crisis in Gaza, in late July 2025 Liu and Tish James joined Brad Lander and several other New York elected officials in a statement demanding that Israel allow humanitarian aid into Gaza while calling for an immediate diplomatic resolution of the conflict.

The festive crowd at Mamdani's victory party included a roster of notable Cuomo foes, including James and third-place mayoral finisher Brad Lander (b. 1969), along with countless next-generation leaders.

Mingling within the crowd were anti-monopoly figureheads Lina Khan (like Zohran, a practicing Muslim) and Zephyr Teachout, who challenged then-Gov. Cuomo from the left in the 2014 primary. Actress Cynthia Nixon, who stepped to the plate against Cuomo four years later, continued to express robust support for Zohran.[8] Jamaal Bowman, the DSA Congressman ousted with the help of pro-Israel hawks, caught up with Rep. Nydia Velázquez. Actor and activist Kal Penn, a longtime Zohran pal (who starred in Mira Nair's 2006 film *The Namesake*), gave lots of hugs. Nair and her son's wife Rama Duwaji shed tears of joy. Antigun activist David Hogg, who had cut viral clips with Mamdani as primary day neared, was also in the mix, along with South Asian DSA organizers Jaslin Kaur and Ashik Siddique, respectively representing Queens and Brooklyn.

Two of Zohran's closest DSA allies in the state legislature, Jabari Brisport and Marcela Mitaynes, celebrated with city councilman Chi Ossé, a social media phenom and fellow leftist Brooklynite. At one point, Ella Emhoff, the pro-Palestinian stepdaughter of Kamala Harris, shared

---

[8] Earlier in the steamy early summer day, Nixon posted a clip of herself walking to vote. She sported a T-shirt reading "Do Not Rank Cuomo," a popular refrain among several mayoral contenders. "I've never been so happy to vote for anyone," the former Cuomo challenger said, unironically.

a crowded staircase with Ossé. Everybody in the room festively sang "Hey, Hey Good-bye" to Cuomo.[9]

*

Across the East River, at the Carpenters Union Hall in lower Manhattan, Cuomo's people exited the room quickly after the toppled frontrunner conceded.

The veteran Democrat's "Potemkin campaign" needed strong support on election day but never assembled the volunteer operation to help make that happen. The whopping numbers of young and new voters that turned out during the initial nine days that ballots could be cast clearly signaled trouble for the former governor. Cuomo counted on the party's traditional base. Melissa de Rosa, his longtime aide and confidante with many female enemies—especially among the disgraced figure's thirteen sexual harassment accusers—appeared rather lonely as she passed out campaign lit near a poll site at Co-op City in the Bronx. Amid scorching heat on election day, the powerful figure once roundly accused of sending nursing home residents to die during the pandemic obliviously advised voters, "It is warm—but not too warm" to go vote.

Team Cuomo, as next-gen Democratic political consultant Nick Smith explained to Errol Louis on *Inside City Hall* on the night before primary day, had banked on the conventional wisdom that young as well as first-time voters would not show up at the polls. It was by no means the only stale,

---

[9] *New York*'s David Freedlander (6-25-2025) labeled the supporters "Mamdaniacs."

cynical calculation made by Cuomo and his inept crew. At the union hall on Hudson Street, tragicomedy ensued. Shortly after the polls closed, Louis asked *Inside City Hall* reporter Ayana Harry if the people seen behind her seemed worn-out after doing election-day voter outreach in the heat. After thinking about it for a few seconds, Harry wryly observed that "their work was through writing checks."[10]

The downbeat mood at the Cuomo gathering was consistent with the dreary theme and messaging that the campaign had transmitted throughout the spring. According to the oh-so familiar candidate, New York City was experiencing a "crisis" of "disorder" that only someone with his decades of "experience" could "manage." A drop in crime numbers during the primary season undercut Cuomo's argument.

In his speech conceding the race, Cuomo's "thanks" to former mayor Michael Bloomberg, his leading billionaire backer, seemed sincere, but the former frontrunner's claims about his "special, talented" campaign staff rang hollow. With his three daughters—twins Cara and Mariah (b. 1995) and Andrea (b. 1997)—at his side, the aging pol (b. 1957) offered half-hearted praise for the "highly impactful campaign" run by his kids' peer. Mangling the pronunciation of Zohran's last name for the umpteenth

---

10   Northwestern University journalism professor Steven Thrasher, a former staff writer for the *Village Voice*, posted a video of the clip with him laughing hysterically at Harry's comment.

time, Cuomo acknowledged that "tonight is Assemblyman *Maan-donny*'s" night.[11]

When Cuomo asked the crowd to give Zohran a round of applause, a smattering of one-hand clapping echoed around the room.

*

Mamdani "is a communist at the highest level, and he wants to destroy New York," warned President Trump during a Fourth of July celebration in Des Moines, Iowa. "I love New York and we're not gonna let him do that," declared the Queens-born Don. As the U.S. celebrated its founding as a democracy, the second-edition president sounded like a vengeful, capricious monarch.

Earlier in the week, Trump—amplifying an incendiary attack made one month earlier by a far-right elected official from Queens—threatened to revoke Zohran's status as a naturalized U.S. citizen. When Councilwoman Vickie Paladino called for Mamdani's deportation in early June, the local response was notably muted. Led by candidates Brad Lander and Adrienne Adams, Mamdani's fellow contenders denounced Paladino, but the city's editorial boards and most other civic leaders remained silent.

---

11 After the first televised debate in early June, New York Communities for Change activist Pete Sikora, who fought various Albany battles against the former governor, equated Cuomo's mispronunciations of Mamdani to Republicans' distortions of Kamala Harris' first name. "It's bigotry and signaling," Sikora tweeted on June 6.

Was the silence because Zohran is young, Muslim, pro-Palestine, a democratic socialist, or all four? The venom was often hard to sort out. As Cuomo backers launched what one longtime centrist city politics observer called "the most negative campaigning I have ever seen in my life!" both the *Times* and *New York Post* fanned the flames.[12] Although neither outlet endorsed Cuomo, both tried to kneecap Mamdani.

Zohran nevertheless made it through this trial by dumpster fire. Until the final three weeks of the campaign, Team Mamdani fought the blazes with very little outside support, even from many leftist figureheads. Although Rep. Rashida Tlaib, the nation's most prominent Palestinian American politician, had been in Mamdani's corner for months, AOC and Bernie did not weigh in until June. It was Mamdani and his devoted followers who stood at the front lines, holding steady amid an onslaught of hate.

While Cuomo fizzled, Zohran sizzled. That is the story of the 2025 mayoral primary in a nutshell. The how and why merit further scrutiny. Did the deluge of attacks funded by Bloomberg, Trumper Bill Ackman, and their fellow 1%-ers backfire? Zohran's stance on Israel was a recurring target in the over $26.5 million of outside money spent on Cuomo's behalf. Yet as Beinart surmised, many liberal Jews in New York City, and large numbers of all Democrats, do not support Israel's destruction of Gaza.

---

12 J.C. Polanco's June 29 televised remark (on WCBS) came in response to a pro-Cuomo consultant's ridiculous claim that "no one went negative against Mamdani."

Just four years earlier, the *New York Post* had been instrumental in Eric Adams' victory, while the *Times* helped Kathryn Garcia, a not particularly charismatic novice politician, finish a very close second. This time around, the *Post* relentlessly trashed Mamdani, and the Bloomberg-allied *Times* treated the newcomer with absurdist condescension.

So who and what helped Zohran prevail? The roster is led by the DSA, which had propelled Mamdani's political career. Immediately after the October 7 Hamas attacks in Israel, powerful right-wing forces tried to crush the leftist group because of its robust support for Palestine. Less than two years later, a longtime DSA member defeated a very powerful mainstream Democrat. No explanation that minimizes the socialists' role in Zohran's success passes muster.

The list also includes activist groups such as Jewish Voice for Peace, Desis Rising, CAAAV, and NY Communities for Change. Millennial leaders like Asad Dandia, a Brooklyn-born Muslim with Pakistani roots, and numerous South Asian organizers such as Queens-based Felicia Singh helped mobilize their communities. From teenage first-time voters to AOC (b. 1989), Rep. Nydia Velázquez (b. 1953) and the socialist figurehead from Vermont (b. 1941), support for Mamdani spanned generations.

A former rapper, Zohran exuded plenty of charisma. His campaign's always stylish, often humorous use of social media made him a star. Mainstream outlets including the *New York Times*, *New York Post*, and *Politico* (New York) sought to shoot him down. But Zohran and company created their own stories, getting help from players not previously prominent in city politics, including the multi-platform media superstars Hasan Piker and Charlamagne Tha God.

As Zohran frequently phrased it before, during, and after primary day, his victory would close the books on the "politics of the past." The task of any historian is to explain how we arrived at a particular watershed moment. As we shall see, Mamdani succeeded largely because he represents a new generation of leaders—principled, uncompromising, and committed to innovative public policy—that knows how to craft their own narratives.

As our curtain rises, Eugene Debs—a.k.a. Bernie Sanders' hero—is about to step onto the stage.

CHAPTER 2
Cold War, R.I.P.

It's the middle of July 2024. Across the nation, the question is whether President Joe Biden will run for reelection. In New York City, local observers wonder if Mayor Eric Adams will face federal corruption charges. No matter whether that happens, the unpopular first-term mayor seems likely to face challengers in the June 2025 Democratic primary.

Committee members of the Democratic Socialists of America (DSA) chapter gather on a Saturday. According to journalist Peter Sterne, the activists "briefly discuss" something that has been "an open secret" within the DSA's ranks. One of the group's elected officials may challenge Adams. "DSA Assembly Member Zohran Mamdani is considering a run for mayor," announces the matter-of-fact headline in City & State, a publication read by political insiders.

By the end of the year, Mamdani is a social media star. As the race takes shape in the winter and spring of 2025, he consistently polls second in a crowded field. But the front-runner is not Mayor Adams, who—after cutting a deal with the Trump administration that ended the feds' corruption case—ducked out of the June Democratic primary in order to run as an independent in the general election.

Instead of an embattled incumbent mayor, Zohran now runs against a figure inextricably linked to a New York Democratic political dynasty. Although he had resigned as a thrice-elected governor amid a sexual harassment scandal in August 2021, Andrew Cuomo remains popular with older voters in the city. For many of Cuomo's key backers, the war in Gaza overshadows the problems faced by New York City. Mamdani's vocal support for Palestine becomes a lightning rod. Meanwhile, the genocide notwithstanding, Cuomo declares that he is "100% supportive of Israel."

Throughout the spring of 2025, Zohran's campaign gains growing momentum. The insurgent stands firm in support of Palestine and continues to call himself a democratic socialist. After his strong performance in the first televised debate, fellow DSA member Alexandria Ocasio-Cortez endorses Zohran, catapulting him into the national spotlight. Mamdani's sensational takedown of Cuomo in the second (and final) televised debate leads Brooklyn native Sen. Bernie Sanders, the elder statesman of democratic socialism in the U.S., to champion Zohran.

Mamdani handily defeats Cuomo in the June 24 primary. As the U.S. celebrates its 249th birthday, millions of younger voters no longer view socialism as un-American.[13]

*

In the first half of the twentieth century, socialism had plenty of currency in both national and New York politics. Starting in 1900, Eugene Debs ran for president five consecutive times, with four bids on the Socialist Party (SP) ballot line. In 1904 and 1908, his SP running mate was Ben Hanford, a labor leader in New York City.

In 1914, Debs' disciple Meyer London became the SP's second national member to win a seat in the House of Representatives,[14] defeating the powerful Tammany Hall (Democratic Party) candidate in a Lower East Side district. London, an outspoken opponent of President Woodrow Wilson's entry into World War I, served two terms until the Tammany machine candidate knocked him out in 1918. Two years later, London reclaimed his seat and served two more terms. London, a Jewish socialist, angered Zionists because he opposed "forcible annexation" in Palestine.

The 1920 election also saw five members of the Socialist Party win state assembly seats. As one historian explains,[15]

---

[13] Note: Henceforth, citation information will be provided only for specific historical references or interpretations, not for quotes, news stories, podcasts, or social media statements posted on the internet during the campaign.

[14] The first was Milwaukee's Victor Berger, elected in 1910.

[15] Henry M. Greenberg in *Judicial Notice* (Spring 2012). Greenberg is the namesake in Greenberg Traurig, a powerhouse Albany law

all came from New York City districts with large populations of Russian Jews. Although the Democrats' assembly leader sought to form a coalition with the Socialist cadre (August Claessens, Samuel DeWitt, Samuel Orr, Charles Solomon, and Louis Waldman), Republican majority leader Thaddeus Sweet went on the warpath.

Sweet, a reactionary businessman from the Syracuse area, refused to seat the five Socialists, linking them to Bolshevism and denouncing their opposition to World War I. A few years after pushing the left out of Albany, the red-baiter won election to the House of Representatives. In 1928, Sweet became the first sitting member of Congress killed in an airplane crash.

Starting that same year, Norman Thomas, the New York City-based leader of the Socialist Party, ran for president in six consecutive elections. A pacifist until Pearl Harbor, Thomas frequently clashed with FDR. In advance of the 1936 election, Roosevelt encouraged his ally Mayor Fiorello La Guardia to work with union leaders in forming the American Labor Party (ALP), which aimed to shift Thomas' votes to FDR. David Dubinsky, leader of the International Ladies Garment Workers, characterized the union's 400,000 members as "all socialists," with more than half residing in New York City.[16]

---

firm that worked closely with then-Gov. Andrew Cuomo in his unsuccessful effort to stop DSA candidates in the 2020 New York state elections.

16 Theodore Hamm, *Bernie's Brooklyn* (OR Books, 2020), pp. 26-27.

A (very) liberal Republican who once won a race for Congress on the Socialist Party ballot line,[17] Mayor La Guardia's alliances with left-wing leaders including Vito Marcantonio caused critics to denounce the mayor as a red. In the 1940s, two members of the Communist Party—downtown Brooklyn's Pete Cacchione and Harlem's Ben Davis—held seats in the city council. In 1949, Davis and eleven of his comrades were charged and convicted of conspiracy to overthrow the federal government under the Smith Act. Like elsewhere in the U.S., the Cold War crackdown on radicalism effectively removed socialism from mainstream politics in New York.

*

Although socialism was no longer on the map, social democracy prevailed in New York City for the first few decades after World War II. The public provisions that greatly expanded under La Guardia—led by universal access to CUNY (which charged no tuition), and a low-cost health care network—remained intact through the early 1970s. During the same period, the city's Democratic Party maintained its New Deal orientation, remaining closely allied with large public sector unions.

As historian Kim Phillips-Fein explained in *Fear City* (2017), in response to the city's near-bankruptcy in 1975, Wall Street municipal bond traders created a blueprint that Democratic Governor Hugh Carey helped implement. That neoliberal agenda rolled back the city's large social

---

17 See Joshua B. Freeman's *Jacobin* profile of La Guardia (4-23-2025).

spending and sought to rein in the power of public sector unions.[18]

Media mogul Rupert Murdoch bought the *New York Post* in 1976, turning the previously liberal outlet into a right-wing attack machine. In 1977, Murdoch's support helped "tough-on-crime" Democrat Ed Koch capture City Hall. In his three terms (1978-89), Koch's neoliberal administration catered to Midtown real estate developers including Donald Trump. The future president also became a large donor to Governor Mario Cuomo, who was first elected in 1982, en route to a twelve-year reign.

None of Koch's successors—Democrat David Dinkins[19] (1990-93), Republican Rudy Giuliani (1994-2001) or CEO Michael Bloomberg (2002-2013)—challenged the dominance of the FIRE (finance, insurance and real estate) sector. Bloomberg, a multi-billionaire, rose to influence as a FIRE product.[20] Outside of small leftist circles, socialism remained off the New York City political radar through the first decade of the 21st century.

In September 2011, Occupy Wall Street sprang up, with a large tent encampment remaining in the downtown

---

18 Kim Phillips-Fein, *Fear City* (Metropolitan Books, 2017).
19 David Dinkins was a member of the Democratic Socialists of America in the 1980s. During his first year in office, Mayor Dinkins gave introductory remarks at a DSA gathering. The era's economic climate made it difficult for Dinkins to champion socialism while at City Hall, however.
20 Robert Fitch's *The Assassination of New York* (Verso, 1996) remains the best work that examines the rise of the F.I.R.E.-dominated economy.

financial district for several weeks. The movement was driven by the anarchist principles of mutual aid and solidarity, not by socialist demands for state-led redistribution of wealth. But Occupy's signature phrase, "We are the 99%," lent itself to various efforts.

Bill de Blasio, then the city's Public Advocate, visited the Occupy encampment. In the 2013 race for mayor, de Blasio ran as a progressive Democrat who called for taxing the rich in order to pay for universal pre-kindergarten (thus providing an economic benefit for parents because it reduced childcare costs). According to local political media outlets, de Blasio was the "Occupy" candidate in the race—which the movement's activists disputed.[21]

"A tale of two cities," de Blasio's Dickensian campaign theme, spotlighted the growth of inequality during the Bloomberg years. Joe Lhota, the Republican candidate in the general election, was clearly the preferred candidate of the 1%. "Mr. de Blasio's class warfare strategy in New York City," warned Lhota, was "straight out of the Marxist playbook." In response, de Blasio quipped "It's 2013," suggesting that socialism was a thing of the past.

When de Blasio crushed Lhota, the win was viewed as a liberal rejoinder to Bloomberg's "luxury city" model.[22] Few saw the next mayor as the new Fidel Castro. Once in

---

21 Brigid Bergin, WNYC (9-17-13); and Joe Coscarelli, *New York* (9-17-2013).
22 As Julian Brash explains, Bloomberg's administration viewed New York City as a "luxury brand," marketing it to prospective global investors in high-end real estate. Julian Brash, *Bloomberg's New York* (Univ. of Georgia, 2011).

office, de Blasio nevertheless successfully implemented universal pre-k (UPK), the city's largest social program expansion in recent memory. Governor Andrew Cuomo, de Blasio's nemesis and a close ally of the 1%, used existing state revenue to fund UPK—thus undercutting de Blasio's left-leaning campaign call for a targeted tax hike on millionaires.

The strong economy of the mid-2010s, driven in large part by low oil prices, allowed the progressive mayor to push through three consecutive years of rent freezes for the city's one million rent-regulated units.[23] In addition to the widespread economic benefits for public school parents and many tenants, de Blasio expanded the city government workforce and negotiated favorable contracts for most of the city's public sector unions.

By pushing popular New Deal-style initiatives, de Blasio cruised to reelection. Standoffish and unloved personally, de Blasio's policies nonetheless created solidly progressive legacies.

*

Mid-way through de Blasio's first term, Bernie Sanders brought socialism back into the national conversation.

---

23 New York City's version of rent control is called rent stabilization. The mayor appoints members of the Rent Guidelines Board (RGB), which determines the annual increase. Spikes in the yearly cost of heating oil in large rent-stabilized buildings are often a main factor in landlords' push for a yearly hike. Because the RGB members answer to the mayor, the size of the increase is widely seen as a reflection of the mayor's preference.

Although he characterized himself as a democratic socialist, most of Bernie's policies simply aligned with the New Deal. Sanders reminded his enthusiastic supporters that FDR "implemented a series of programs that put millions of people back to work, took them out of dire poverty and restored their faith in government." But "almost every program" FDR initiated was derided by his critics as "socialist," Bernie noted.

As his insurgent campaign gathered steam in early 2016, Sanders took aim at the "greed of Wall Street" at a speech in Midtown Manhattan. Even so, his proposed solution that day was to restore the Glass-Steagall regulations on the financial industry enacted during the New Deal—and eliminated by Wall Street-friendly Democrats including Chuck Schumer, with support from the Clinton White House.

Ahead of New York's presidential primary in April 2016, massive, mostly youthful crowds came out to see the septuagenarian socialist. Over 27,000 people heard Sanders denounce Wall Street in Washington Square, and a similar number of enthusiasts flocked to a Bernie rally in Brooklyn's Prospect Park.

One of Hillary Clinton's leading local supporters at the time was a rising star in the Democratic Party. In the words of Rep. Hakeem Jeffries, Sanders was simply "a gun-loving socialist with zero foreign policy experience." New York's mainstream Democrats forcefully repelled the insurgency, with Clinton easily winning the state primary by racking up large margins in the city.

Meet Mayor Mamdani

The Sanders campaign nonetheless inspired a new generation of New York City leaders. "I started to call myself a socialist after Bernie's run in 2016," Zohran told *Jacobin*'s Liza Featherstone on the eve of his mayoral campaign launch.

Most New York City political observers paid little attention to Alexandria Ocasio-Cortez's primary challenge to longtime incumbent Queens congressman Joe Crowley in the spring of 2018. AOC, a member of the DSA, had volunteered for Bernie's 2016 campaign. Crowley, meanwhile, had served ten terms in Congress. He came from a well-known political family and was the leader of the large Queens Democratic Party organization.

Like most local media outlets,[24] the party establishment ignored the upstart campaign. When AOC pulled off the stunning upset in June, members of both camps attributed the win to the DSA's voter outreach strategy, which emphasized direct voter contact in the district that covers greater Astoria and Jackson Heights in Queens, and parts of the southern Bronx. "We knocked on their doors, we sent them mail, we knocked on their doors again, we called them," explained Corbin Trent, AOC's communications director at the time.[25]

AOC, like Bernie, advocated Medicare for All, free college tuition, and campaign finance reform. Along with the DSA,

---

24 *The Indypendent* was a notable exception. Its June 2018 print issue featured AOC on its cover and copies were widely circulated in Northwest Queens.
25 *City & State* (6-27-2018).

she would soon push for a Green New Deal, further illustrating the alignment between contemporary democratic socialists and FDR's legacy. AOC's mastery of social media soon made her a national figure. The Democratic Party's neoliberal leadership neither embraced the rising star nor championed any of her policies.

In the wake of AOC's surprise success, the local chapter of the DSA focused on New York races in the fall 2018 statewide elections. The first of the group's several wins also previewed the main conflict it would confront in the mid-2020s.

Like AOC, the DSA's Julia Salazar sought to topple an entrenched legislator. State Senator Martin Dilan had represented fast-gentrifying Bushwick, Brooklyn, for sixteen years. Rather than focus on Salazar's calls for universal rent control or sex worker rights, local media outlets highlighted her stance on Israel.

Salazar's support for BDS—the movement calling for boycotts and divestments from Israel, which Gov. Andrew Cuomo had tried to squash—and Palestinian rights produced a relentless stream of attacks, with questions raised about her Jewish identity. The insurgent campaign carried the backing of Jews for Racial and Economic Justice, a pro-Palestine group for which Salazar had worked for as an organizer.[26]

DSA ground troops helped propel their candidate to a comfortable victory (59-41%) in the September primary,

---

26 Charles Dunst, *Jewish Telegraphic Agency* (8-23-2018).

further angering Israel hawks. An opinion piece headline in the *New York Times* labeled Salazar as "the left's post-truth politician." The commentator, not surprisingly, was militant Zionist Bari Weiss.[27]

In the wake of Mamdani's triumph in the 2025 primary, NYC-DSA co-chair Grace Mausser noted that an unsuccessful 2019 campaign supported by the group actually paid long-term dividends. In the Democratic primary for Queens district attorney, Tiffany Cabán, a public defender in her early thirties running on a radical platform calling for decarceration, nearly defeated 54-year-old centrist Melinda Katz, the party machine candidate.

Zohran and many of his fellow future supporters worked on the Cabán campaign, which captured national attention because the race took place amid the peak of the criminal justice reform movement. After Cabán lost by only sixty votes in a borough-wide race, Mausser explained six years later, the city's DSA chapter realized that it had the potential to win big electoral prizes.[28] The DSA's Tascha Van Auken served as Zohran for NYC's field director, and the cadre's dedicated members spurred the campaign's dynamic field operation.

*

In the spring of 2019, Bernie Sanders launched his second presidential run with a kickoff event at Brooklyn College,

---

27 *New York Times* (9-14-2018).
28 "If we only had only knocked on 60 more doors...," Mausser lamented on a DSA post-primary Zoom call.

which he attended in the late 1950s before transferring to the University of Chicago. While reiterating his key policy proposals from the 2016 campaign, Bernie pledged to fight for "economic justice, social justice, racial justice, and environmental justice." He also praised New York City's rent control protections, explaining that they provided stability for his lower middle-class family while he grew up near Brooklyn College.

Although he simply advocated New Deal policies, Sanders' self-identification as a socialist continued to raise hackles. After Bernie became the early frontrunner, Joe Biden warned in a televised debate that the label of "democratic socialist" would hurt Sanders if he became the nominee. ABC moderator George Stephanopoulos, a longtime Clintonite, then asked the other candidates if they were "concerned about having a democratic socialist at the top of the ticket."

After the debate, MSNBC host Chris Matthews ludicrously compared Bernie to Fidel Castro and warned that a Sanders win would result in "executions in Central Park." Just before Super Tuesday, *60 Minutes* host Anderson Cooper grilled Bernie regarding his past praise of Castro. Meanwhile, Michael Bloomberg entered the race and started spending enormous sums (eventually exceeding $1 billion) of his own money in order to stop Bernie. The coordinated assault of Democratic Party leaders and their corporate media allies helped sink Sanders again.

2020 was nonetheless a banner year for DSA candidates in New York. In central Brooklyn, Jabari Brisport won a state senate seat, and Phara Souffrant Forrest toppled an incumbent Hakeem Jeffries-ally in the state assembly. Democratic socialist Marcela Mitaynes knocked out a veteran Cuomo-linked assemblymember in Brooklyn's Sunset Park.

In northern Queens, Mamdani and Jessica González-Rojas made it four wins for the insurgent group's assembly candidates. In a congressional district that included the northern Bronx and suburban Westchester County, DSA-backed Jamaal Bowman toppled 16-term incumbent Eliot Engel, one of the Democrats' leading Israel hawks. All of the 2020 democratic socialist winners cruised to reelection two years later.

Along with Cabán, who won a council seat in Astoria, Queens, the DSA's Alexa Avilés triumphed in Brooklyn's Sunset Park and Red Hook in the 2021 New York City races. Four years later, Mamdani and Avilés (b. 1973, making her about twenty years older than most of her fellow democratic socialist elected officials) frequently campaigned together, helping the incumbent councilwoman defeat a primary challenger funded largely by Bibi's backers.

After the October 7 attacks, Jamaal Bowman's statements in support of a ceasefire and Palestinian rights put him in the crosshairs. Democratic Majority for Israel, an AIPAC-aligned national organization, targeted Bowman, whose district had been redrawn to include more suburbanites. In the 2024 Democratic primary, George Latimer, a veteran nonentity from Westchester, captured the support of pro-Israel voters and defeated Bowman. The unseated Congressman played an active role during the final month of Zohran's primary campaign, helping Mamdani gain votes in the Bronx.

By 2025, the DSA's ranks of statewide elected officials included three senators and seven members of the state assembly. The national group was no longer allied with AOC, although the New York City chapter continued to back her. That conflict involved her statements regarding Israel, not questions about AOC's commitment to democratic socialism.

*

Like the rest of the Democratic Party establishment, Andrew Cuomo views socialism as a term of derision. In mid-May 2025, as the late June primary began to heat up, Cuomo explained his view of the DSA to the *Times of Israel*. "I don't consider them Democrats," the former governor said. "I consider them socialists."

Unnerved by Mamdani's momentum as primary day neared, the *New York Times* editorial board denigrated the candidate in two much-discussed opinion pieces. In summarizing the views of the mayoral candidates among the "experts" on a panel of fifteen influential New Yorkers, the board explained that Cuomo's "heavy baggage" and Mamdani's "image as a democratic socialist" accounted for why each received only two first-place rankings.

One member of the *Times* panel who supported Cuomo nonetheless was impressed by Mamdani. According to veteran NYU public policy professor Mitchell Moss, the

DSA candidate was "not speaking to just poor people; he's speaking to young people who are not poor, but they feel he's talking to them." "Unfortunately," Moss continued, Mamdani is "basically running a Bernie Sanders local version."

Four days after presenting the expert panel recommendations, the *Times* implored voters not to rank the insurgent. Mamdani, declared the editorial board, "is a democratic socialist who too often ignores the unavoidable trade-offs of governance."

Meanwhile, as Zohran's run gained steam earlier in the spring, the far-right *New York Post* called the DSA candidate's plan for free busses "something out of the Politburo." As I pointed out at the time in the *Indypendent,* the twentieth-century reference was likely only something that registered for the tabloid's longtime readers, many of whom ride the Staten Island Ferry back and forth to Manhattan for...free.

On Sunday, June 22, red-baiting figured prominently in Cuomo's last pitch to voters ahead of the Tuesday primary. At the Christian Cultural Center, a very large Black church in Brooklyn, the former governor warned an older audience that "there is a far-left movement taking over the Democratic Party," referring to the DSA. The city was at a "tipping point," he declared. Cuomo, unwittingly, was correct.

The jittery frontrunner also addressed the electrical workers union's Catholic Council in Midtown Manhattan that morning. Neither "the MAGA right" nor the "democratic socialist left" have agendas that "include us," Cuomo told a friendly crowd made up of aging white labor officials. The reactionary Democratic Party establishment was imploding.

On the day after his humiliating primary defeat, Cuomo spoke at length to his preferred reporter, WCBS-TV mainstay Marcia Kramer.[29] "'Everything free' sounds good— free busses, free groceries" is how the former governor caricatured Mamdani's appeal. A chorus of naysayers derided Mamdani's proposal for "government-run grocery stores" as some sort of Soviet-style rationing. Somehow the creation of low-cost (i.e. not free) supermarkets, an initiative seen in cities across the U.S., did not compute for lifelong New York Democrats like Cuomo.

Mayor Adams, a former Republican turned right-wing Democrat, piled on. On the day after the primary, he met with the *New York Post*'s far-right editorial board, which helped elect Adams four years earlier. The mayor dutifully labeled Mamdani a "snake-oil salesman" for a "socialist city."

A button-pushing bigot whose default move is to play the race card, Adams then unironically insisted that the "young, white voters" who support Mamdani "don't even know what socialism is."

---

29   Kramer, now in her mid-seventies, is generally the go-to reporter for the city elite and hostile to progressives. But when she sat down with Mamdani in March, her questions were not at all hard-hitting. One likely factor in Kramer's decision-making is that Cuomo was comfortably ahead in the polls at the time.

The final primary tallies showed that Mamdani scored over 50% more first-place votes than Adams received four years earlier. A millennial, Muslim disciple of Bernie Sanders completely flummoxed the New York City elite, which had long assumed that the twin pillars of their worldview—that capitalism is sacrosanct, and Israel must never be criticized—would remain unchallenged.

Whether Mamdani's proposals amounted to actual socialism or were simply extensions of New Deal liberalism was a debate too academic for the mayoral candidates or most mainstream media commentators to even consider. As we will see in the chapters ahead, Zohran upended the status quo in myriad ways.

For now, let's note that June 24, 2025, marked the full-fledged return of the S-word to mainstream New York City politics.

CHAPTER 3
Roots

"I am an Indian-Ugandan New Yorker," Zohran once said. "It's the hyphenated immigrant dream."[30]

Born October 18, 1991, Zohran Kwame Mamdani spent the first five years of his life in Kampala, Uganda's capital, which was then a modest-sized city with a population just under one million.

Mahmood Mamdani's ancestors were Gujarati Muslims who left the coastal region northwest of Mumbai in the late nineteenth century, journeying across the Arabian Sea through the Indian Ocean first to Tanzania, later moving to neighboring Uganda. By the end of the twentieth century, over two million people of Indian descent lived in Africa, mainly in the continent's southeastern nations.

---

30 Unless otherwise noted, the quotes from Zohran in this chapter come from two 90-minute interviews the author conducted with Mamdani in the early spring of 2025.

Meet Mayor Mamdani

Bhubaneswar, located in the northeast India state of Odisha, was a very small town (pop. under 50,000) when Mira Nair grew up there in the 1960s, in a Hindu household. After earning a B.A. from Harvard, Nair started making films in what was then called Bombay (now Mumbai). In 1988, she visited Uganda while doing research for *Mississippi Masala*, her 1991 Hollywood debut that starred Denzel Washington. While in Kampala, she met Mahmood Mamdani.

When nationalist dictator Idi Amin took power in 1972, he forced all South Asians to leave Uganda, sending the Mamdani family to refugee centers in London. "My grandfather was forever changed by the expulsion," Zohran explains. In Uganda, his grandfather had been a manager at a cotton ginnery and held other comparable positions while also writing poetry.

While in London, Zohran noted, his grandparents "would go to Gatwick every week and watch planes take off back to Uganda, wishing that they were on them. What was taken from them was a sense of self, a sense of stability, and a sense of belonging."

Among the insights that Zohran gained from his family's plight is that "It taught me the lasting impacts of being displaced—whether it's caused by an expulsion or an eviction."

In the 1970s, Idi Amin was a familiar presence in U.S. popular culture, quite memorably spoofed by Richard Pryor, the legendary radical comedian.[31] It's hard to imagine

---

31 *Saturday Night Live*'s Garrett Morris also played Amin in several skits in the late 1970s.

that anyone predicted at the time that Amin's legacy might one day influence New York City politics.

*

Mahmood Mamdani was among the small number of South Asians who returned after Amin's downfall in 1979. As he noted in a 2022 essay in the *London Review of Books*, after Amin was overthrown, Mahmood went back to Uganda, where he was a citizen. After first interning for a Christian organization, he next took a position at Kampala's Makerere University in 1980.

After spending his first five years in the Ugandan capital, Zohran lived for two years in South Africa, where his father taught at the University of Cape Town. This meant that in his youth, Zohran lived in a nation governed by South Africa's first democratically elected president, Nelson Mandela, who was in office from 1994 to 1999.

Zohran's family moved to the U.S. in 1999, when Prof. Mamdani was named the Herbert H. Lehman Professor of Government at Columbia University. An only child, Zohran lived with his parents in faculty housing near the Columbia campus in Morningside Heights. The family frequently traveled back to Uganda.

Upon moving to the city, Zohran attended Bank Street, a progressive private school near Columbia. Zohran fondly recalls his favorite teachers and said that Bank Street "provided a very nurturing and loving environment." On the morning of the September 11 attacks, a teacher named

Stephanie[32] pulled the 9-year-old aside and told him that if he got bullied because he was a Muslim, Zohran should let her know.

"That was the opposite experience of most Muslim kids in the city at the time," Zohran observes. "I was lucky to have the teacher that I did."

In general, Zohran does not recall many direct encounters with Islamophobia on the streets of New York City while growing up. However, in the spring of 2008, after his return from one of his trips to Uganda, Zohran said that he was detained at JFK and taken into a double-mirrored room with other Muslim men. Homeland Security agents then asked if he had visited a terrorist training camp.

It was a brief, but scary experience for the teenager. "I was terrified," Zohran recalls.

In the aftermath of his primary win, billionaire Bill Ackman, the pro-Israel zealot who helped fuel the crackdown on pro-Palestine protests at campuses including Columbia, distorted Mahmood Mamdani's explanation of Al-Qaeda's adherents in order make it seem like both Mamdanis support the 9/11 terrorist attacks. The *New York Post* amplified Ackman's smear.

As Muslims gain political power in the city, the disease of Islamophobia lingers.

*

---

32 In the New York City public schools, grade-school teachers (and paraprofessionals) are typically called "Miss" or "Mister" followed by their first name, but Bank Street had a more informal protocol.

"I would take the 1 train uptown to W. 231st Street, ride the BX10 bus, and yell 'back door!'" is how Zohran recalls his daily commute from Morningside Heights to high school in the northcentral Bronx. Along with Stuyvesant, Brooklyn Tech, and a handful of others, Bronx Science (or just "Science," as Zohran refers to it) is one of New York City elite public high schools, requiring a specialized admission test.

Zohran's favorite teacher at Science was Marc Kagan, a former transit workers union official who made a late-career transition to education. The older brother of SCOTUS justice Elena Kagan taught social studies. As Zohran recalled, "One of the lessons Kagan imparted is that intelligence means nothing without the application of it."

Kagan introduced students to pedagogy. Seniors in his Advanced Placement world history class taught a specific lesson to each of the three class years below them. Kagan thus "showed just how difficult it is to capture the imagination—let alone the attention—of teenage students," Mamdani explains.

It will come as no surprise that Zohran joined Science's prestigious debate team as a freshman. But he did not stay long because he wanted to play soccer, eventually becoming the school's goal-scoring team captain in his senior year. Mamdani's favorite player at the time was Thierry Henry, the graceful French forward who starred for Arsenal in the Premier League through 2007.[33]

---

[33] Zohran's favorite bands as a teen included Franz Ferdinand, Artic Monkeys and Kaiser Chiefs. In 2002, Mahmood and son saw

Meet Mayor Mamdani

As the mayoral contender informed *Vulture*'s Nicholas Quah, "I came up as a fan in the early 2000s, and it was my uncle who introduced me to the team. Arsenal was one of the first teams to have a number of African players: Lauren, Kolo Toure, Nwankwo Kanu, Emmanuel Eboue, Alex Song. As a Ugandan kid looking at this team, I was just so proud."

Zohran told me that he remains an "obsessive Arsenal fan." At a pre-canvassing rally in Bed-Stuy during the last month of the primary, Mamdani spotted an eleven-year-old boy named Vic wearing an Arsenal jersey. The candidate came over to chat with the lad about the pair's favorite squad, making Vic very excited about Zohran's run.

While at Science, Mamdani co-founded a cricket club, which soon became part of a citywide, twelve-team, public high school league. As the Science squad traveled across the city, Zohran recalled, "I was getting a tour of the South Asian diaspora—playing teams that were Bangladeshi, Pakistani, Guyanese, Trinidadian, etc."

When asked to describe his level of skill, Zohran laughs. "In cricket, typically a player either excels as a batsman or a bowler. I tried to do both. I was good but not great. But there are very few feelings like when you bowl someone out, or when you hit a four or a six—and these were thrilling moments in my high school career."

Egyptian legend Hakim perform with Algerian powerhouse Khaled at the Beacon Theatre.

As the son of a leading political theorist, Zohran was encouraged to pay attention to world affairs while growing up. During Obama's 2008 campaign, the teenager rode on a bus full of volunteer doorknockers to central Pennsylvania. The future politician recalls liking Obama at the time because of the candidate's opposition to the Iraq War.

In his junior year at Science, Zohran ran for vice president and lost by a wide margin. The bid marked his debut as a rapper, as he cut a video in support of his campaign. For his AP literature class in his senior year, Mamdani and a classmate traded lines over an instrumental version of "Still Dre." It would be an exaggeration to say that Zohran was a prodigy by the end of high school. But the worldly lad clearly had skills, potential, and plenty of ambition.

*

Shortly after his shocking win in the 2025 primary, the *New York Times* embarrassed itself by creating a scandal about Zohran's college application to Columbia. The teenager who grew up in an Indian household in Uganda checked the boxes for Asian and African American. That is not how Mamdani has identified himself since becoming a public figure, rendering the substance of the story minimal at most.

The controversy nevertheless lit up the internet over the Fourth of July weekend, with liberal *Times* columnist Jamelle Bouie siding with the paper's many critics. The sources of the hit piece were known eugenicists and white nationalist stalking horses. Breaking its own ethics rules, the *Times* used hacked documents without initially identifying the direct source of the info, even though that far-right figure was known to the outlet.

After his rejection from Columbia, Zohran attended Bowdoin College in Brunswick, Maine, where he majored in Africana Studies. His favorite professor was Brian Purnell, a leading scholar of Brooklyn during the civil rights era. One of Purnell's courses used David Simon's classic series *The Wire* (2002-2008) as a point of entry to discuss urban political economy. It was an eye-opener, according to Zohran.

Purnell recalls that Mamdani "enjoyed talking about discussions and debates from our courses outside of class time. He also had a wonderful sense of humor and brought joy and fun to the serious issues that we studied."[34] The future mayoral candidate's courses with Purnell covered subjects including the history of Reconstruction in the U.S. and the historical legacy of racial slavery. Bowdoin is 875 miles, but light years away, from Michigan's Hillsdale College, the center of MAGA-approved U.S. history.

Zohran's senior research project focused on Frantz Fanon's classic works *Black Skin, White Masks* and *The Wretched of the Earth*. As Purnell, his advisor, notes, Mamdani "compared Fanon's theories on colonialism and anti-colonialism to Rousseau and Enlightenment political philosophies on the 'social contract.'" In his favorite professor's view, the Fanon project "showcased how

---

34 Quotes are from Purnell's 7-7-2025 email to author.

dynamic and broad Zohran's mind was when he was an undergraduate student."

While at Bowdoin, Zohran co-founded a chapter of Students for Justice in Palestine. After his 2025 primary victory, the *New York Post* reported that in November 2013, the Bowdoin chapter invited radical Lebanese scholar As'ad AbuKhalil to speak at the campus. AbuKhalil's argument that the 9/11 attacks were blowback from the actions of the US is a perspective shared by a range of commentators, including ex-CIA consultant Chalmers Johnson. But the *Post*, predictably, presented this as tantamount to support for Osama bin Laden.

Zohran completed his undergraduate degree in 2014. "I don't think that Zohran's studies at Bowdoin had a direct influence on his political career," Purnell observes. "But without question they helped him develop deep ideas related to justice, democracy, and the common good, all of which shape his current approach to public service."

*

After college, Zohran went to Uganda, where he developed his rap career. "Young Cardamom" (YC), as he first called himself, teamed up with his childhood pal Hussein Abdul Bar, or HAB, a Black Ugandan. "Kanda (Chap Chap)," a video posted on YouTube in September 2015, shows the duo travel around the outskirts of Kampala in a small flatbed cart pulled by a motorcycle.

Alternately wearing casual and traditional African clothing, YC and Hab distribute free chapati (the "chap" repeated in the song), which is the same as roti but made with a Ugandan plantain called matooke. Just after the midway point of the 4-minute clip, the rappers switch into college graduation attire. They then lecture to—and dance with—a group of Black graduates who receive a rolled-up chapati as a diploma.

Upbeat and cross-cultural, Young Cardamom and HAB soon reached audiences across the globe. In 2016, *OkayAfrica*, the popular arts and lifestyle news site based in Brooklyn, interviewed the duo. As Zohran stated, "we rap in six different languages—Luganda, English, Hindi, Swahili, Runyoro, and Nubi. People don't associate all these languages with Kampala, but for the two of us, Kampala cannot simply be lived in Luganda or English."[35] Zohran's linguistic range surpasses that of Fiorello La Guardia, New York City's last polyglot mayor.[36]

When Mamdani discusses his music career in Kampala, he is often self-deprecating. "When you're the warm-up act to the warm-up act, you learn humility," he maintains. It seems more likely that he and his partner had at least a decent-sized following in Uganda.

The duo's prominence grew upon the release of Mira Nair's *Queen of Katwe*, which premiered at the Toronto Film Festival in September 2016. YC and HAB recorded

---

35 *OkayAfrica* (5-12-2016).
36 La Guardia (1882-1947) was raised in a Jewish-Italian household (in Greenwich Village) and spoke Yiddish, Italian, German, and Croatian. On the 2025 trail, Mamdani also made headlines by speaking fluent Spanish.

"Spice," the film's lead number, then released a video of that track featuring Kenya-raised actress Lupita Nyong'o, who was then en route to international stardom.

Now in his mid-twenties, Zohran was splitting his time between Kampala and Manhattan. In 2017, he started working in New York City politics. From his parents' home in Morningside Heights, Zohran rode the subway all the way to Bay Ridge at the southern end of Brooklyn. On a weekday, that's at least a one-hour ride, and on a weeknight it's closer to ninety minutes.

As many New Yorkers will unhappily remember, 2017 was known locally as the "summer of hell," when the MTA's aging infrastructure crumbled. It was more notable when any subway ride was *not* delayed. The resulting packed subway cars must have been especially challenging for people like Zohran, who describes himself as "quite claustrophobic."

How Mamdani dealt with the compounded hardship catalyzed his future success. During the unending delays, with the train cars stalled in the tunnels, the 25-year-old asked strangers around him on the subway cars for help. "I would start by telling people that I am claustrophobic and spiraling," he recalls. "Then I'd say, 'Would you mind if we chat for a few minutes until the train starts moving?'"

"People humored me," continues Zohran. "And they were very kind. It was a quite difficult time, but I still rode the subway every day. It was definitely a memorable experience." The budding leader found strength in his fellow city dwellers.

Solidarity among working people became the essence of Zohran's 2025 run. Candidates who drive to the office cannot directly relate to the shared experience of millions of subway commuters.

*

What brought Zohran to Bay Ridge was the inspired city council campaign of Khader El-Yateem (b. 1968), who was raised in Palestine. A Lutheran minister and DSA member, El-Yateem's candidacy mobilized voters in Bay Ridge's sizable Palestinian community. The candidate's life story, which included an arrest by Israel on political grounds, impressed Mamdani.

In the primary that September, progressive Democrat Justin Brannan defeated El-Yateem 39-31%, with three others in the race. "He is a principled fighter for human rights," Zohran said about El-Yateem, who has since moved to Florida.

Zohran returned to Bay Ridge in 2018, this time to manage left-liberal journalist Ross Barkan's run for a state senate in the Democratic primary. Barkan, who describes himself as an "Israel-skeptical Jew," recalled in a June 2025 Substack essay that Zohran put up a poster of Mo Salah, the Liverpool star, in their campaign office.

According to Barkan, his energetic campaign manager's "philosophy" was that "you did not sit down." Although the spirited bid fell short, Zohran was increasingly prepared to run for office.

Mamdani next went to work for Chhaya, an economic empowerment organization that serves South Asian and

Indo-Caribbean communities in Queens, with offices in Jackson Heights and Richmond Hill. As a foreclosure prevention counselor, Zohran's salary before he entered the state assembly was $47,000. He now moved into a rent-stabilized one-bedroom apartment in Astoria, which is still his residence. As of mid-2025, the rent was $2,300 per month.[37]

"Home," stated Zohran, "is a through-line of my work. At Chhaya, the question was 'how do we keep people in their homes'? Now, my campaign is asking 'how do we keep people in the city that they call home?'"

In his spare time while working at Chhaya, Zohran continued developing his music career. In 2019, Zohran recorded another memorable rap video. Now known as "Mr. Cardamom," the performer teamed up with popular South Asian actress Madhur Jaffrey (b. 1933, in Delhi). The song is called "Nani" (grandmother), with Jaffrey as the title character. Wearing an apron but shirtless, Mr. Cardamom raps from inside a crowded halal food truck.

When the video debuted, the *New York Times* gave it a favorable write-up in the outlet's popular food section (Jaffrey is also known for her cookbooks). Playful photos showed a beaming Zohran and the feisty actress in the aisles of Patel Brothers, a longstanding South Asian grocery store in Jackson Heights.

Six years later, the same powerful media outlet tried to burst Zohran's balloon.

---

37   The current salary for New York state legislators is $142,000.

CHAPTER 4
Roti and Roses

Zohran's journey to City Hall began in Astoria. In 2020, he unseated a Democratic incumbent in the state assembly district that covered the Northwest Queens neighborhood as well as adjacent Long Island City. By that point, non-DSA elected officials had already acknowledged that the leftist group held a firm grip on Astoria politics.

Soon after he started working for Chhaya, Zohran started volunteering for DSA-backed Tiffany Cabán's 2019 bid for Queens district attorney. Raised in a Puerto Rican household in Richmond Hill, a central Queens area in which Mamdani then worked as a foreclosure counselor, Cabán (b. 1987) was a public defender in Manhattan when she ran for DA as a first-time candidate.

At the time of Tiffany's campaign, Zohran, who grew up in upper-middle-class household, was helping struggling working-class families, while Cabán, who came from a working-class household, understood the hardships faced by underclass communities ensnared in the criminal justice system. Public school teachers and sundry nonprofit sector workers similarly filled the NYC-DSA's ranks, with many of the activists sharing Mamdani's socioeconomic background.

In order to win a race in a borough with 2.3 million residents, the socialist cadre needed to partner with community groups and leaders across Queens. In the process, the NYC-DSA built a network of allies for future campaigns, propelling both Zohran's 2020 run for state assembly and his bid for mayor five years later.

*

Via his work with Chhaya, Zohran became familiar with Jackson Heights, which had been known for decades as a South Asian neighborhood; and Richmond Hill, which has a fast-growing South Asian and Indo-Caribbean population. As he told *Jacobin*'s Hadas Thier two years later, Mamdani became "a DSA point person" for Cabán's campaign, serving as a field organizer in these locations.

In sync with the then-growing national movement for criminal justice reform, Cabán advanced a decarceral agenda that radically challenged the status quo. The AOC-backed candidate called for shorter felony sentences, vowed not to prosecute nonviolent offenses (including sex work), and pledged to hold bad landlords accountable.

The primary contest went into overtime, with ballots counted by hand and challenged in court. Zohran was a committed volunteer, observing the post-primary day proceedings on behalf of the campaign. Cabán's narrow defeat (by 60 votes) initiated a power struggle between the Northwest Queens-based DSA and Rep. Gregory Meeks, the Queens Democratic Party boss based in Southeast Queens, an area with many Black homeowners.

As Mamdani explained to Thier, a DSA colleague then encouraged him to run for the assembly seat held by progressive Democrat Aravella Simotas, a five-term incumbent whose Greek heritage corresponded with Astoria's previous neighborhood identity. Zohran criticized Simotas for being too close to the Queens Democratic Party brass, citing her support for county leader Joe Crowley during AOC's 2018 run. The incumbent also did not endorse Cabán.

Zohran's anti-machine messaging drew criticism from Assemblywoman Catalina Cruz, a liberal Democrat who represents the neighboring district. As Cruz told *City & State*'s Rebecca Lewis, the Meeks-led county organization "no longer had power" in Astoria. Cruz (b. 1979) backed Simotas (b. 1978) and neither figure seemed to grasp why Mamdani appealed to his fellow millennials.

The socialist candidate celebrated his Indian-Ugandan heritage, frequently wearing long South Asian shirts called kurtas and including his African middle name on the ballot. The former rapper's "roti and roses" platform playfully updated the old socialist slogan, matching a South Asian staple with the DSA's red flower symbol. The spicy insurgent toppled the bland Simotas by a margin of just under 425 votes.

Cynthia Nixon plugged Zohran in *The Nation* in late January 2020, introducing readers to Mamdani and the rest of the NYC-DSA's slate in that year's state elections. The roster included future State Senator Jabari Brisport and victorious assemblymembers Phara Souffrant Forrest and Marcela Mitaynes. *Jacobin* and the *Indypendent* also paid close attention to Mamdani's first run.

By the end of 2020, Zohran's political career was on the ascent. 8,410 primary voters in Astoria and Long Island City, including the candidate himself, had no idea how fast Zohran would rise. Five years later, nearly a half-million other New York Democrats came out in support of the next-generation socialist.

*

Scores of Cabán campaign volunteers played pivotal roles in Mamdani's outreach effort. Now a member of the Queens DSA Organizing Committee, Felicia Singh is a prominent community organizer in Ozone Park, a neighborhood close to JFK Airport with a large South Asian and Indo-Caribbean population. Now in her mid-thirties, Felicia grew up in Ozone Park. Her mother is a Guyanese Muslim and her father is a Punjabi Sikh—a distinctly "new Queens" mix.

As Felicia explains, after volunteering for Cabán, she went door-to-door as a 2020 Census taker. She then ran for City Council in 2021, winning the Democratic primary with a platform focused on education issues, transportation, and climate resiliency (low-lying communities in Queens have faced severe flooding in recent years). Because polyglot Ozone Park is in the same district as Howard Beach, a bastion of ethnic white conservatism, a Republican defeated Singh in the general election.

Singh led a number of canvass teams for Mamdani's 2025 primary campaign, covering Ozone Park, South Ozone Park, and adjacent Richmond Hill. Whether Sikh, Hindu, or Muslim, most South Asian voters identified with Zohran because "he looks like them," Felicia told me in early July.

"We really started laying the groundwork for Zohran's success in 2019," Singh added. As noted in earlier chapter, NYC-DSA co-chair Grace Mausser similarly viewed the Cabán campaign as a catalyst. In the 2019 campaign season with few other races on the ballot, the leftists' borough-wide candidate reeled in just under 35,000 votes, so winning a citywide contest remained a tall order. But in the wake of his successful assembly run, Mamdani's name recognition steadily grew.

After entering the state legislature, Zohran became a familiar presence at Palestinian solidarity events organized by Jewish Voice for Peace. In May 2021, the legislator addressed fifty or so activists gathered at Brooklyn's Grand Army Plaza, which is directly across from Sen. Chuck Schumer's home.

"I have been called a terrorist," stated a beardless Mamdani while holding a microphone and standing on the base of a flagpole. "I have been called an antisemite … [But] there is something we all know here that must be spoken: anti-Zionism is not antisemitism." As the crowd cheers him on, Mamdani then loudly declares, "In the anti-Zionism I believe in there is NO ROOM for antisemitism."[38]

It is not clear whether the powerful Israel ally who lives across the street from Grand Army Plaza heard Zohran that Friday evening. But soon after October 7, Mamdani returned—and Chuck was not at all thrilled to see him.

*

In the fall of 2021, Zohran impressed many South Asian city residents by joining a hunger strike on behalf of taxi drivers experiencing a debt crisis spurred by predatory lenders. Over the preceding few years, several bankrupted South Asian taxi medallion holders had committed suicide.

The crisis dated back to the Bloomberg administration, when the medallions required for licensed taxis reached inflated levels that required drivers to take steep loans. The city then allowed Uber and other for-hire vehicles to flood the streets, thus deflating the value of the medallions. The de Blasio administration faced a stream of criticism over its insufficient relief assistance to the indebted drivers.

Along with left-aligned assemblymember Yuh-Line Niou, who at the time represented nearby Chinatown, Zohran joined many drivers in a fifteen-day hunger strike outside City Hall starting in mid-October 2021. The legislators did so in solidarity with the Taxi Workers Alliance (TWA), which had been pushing a comprehensive debt relief

---

38 See video shot by Javier Soriano: https://www.youtube.com/watch?v=0wh1ds2Lwcg&t=2356s

plan for months. When the de Blasio administration finally agreed to enact the TWA plan in early November, Zohran, Yuh-Line, and drivers across the city celebrated.

"We can have a future!!" fellow hunger striker Augustine Tang texted to a *City & State* reporter. Tang also noted that he had been experiencing headaches, chills, and hunger pangs. Zohran told the same outlet that this was by no means his first time going without food.

"I'm Muslim, and I fast during Ramadan," Zohran noted. The activist-lawmaker noted that a date is the first thing he typically consumes at the end of the ritual. As the taxi worker protest concluded, Zohran, and Yuh-Line consumed a date and scoops of avocado.

Zohran added that breaking the fast outside of City Hall "alongside my elders [and] people who've been fighting this issue for years" gave him "a profound appreciation of the joys and the dignity of food. And I don't think I'll ever look at an avocado or a date the same."[39]

Less than four years later, Mamdani was ready to move inside the building.[40]

*

---

39 *City & State* (11-4-2021).
40 During Ramadan in March 2025, Zohran for NYC posted a well-received YouTube video in which Mamdani and Kareem Rahma, a popular Egyptian American Muslim comedian, discuss the candidate's advocacy for taxi workers with a cabbie from Côte d'Ivoire named Mouhamadou. Zohran and Mouhamadou participated in the hunger strike.

Although the events of October 7, 2023, occurred 5,700 miles away, shockwaves instantly rippled across New York City. The violent attack by Hamas was the first incursion ever by Palestinian forces into Israel-held territory. Nearly 1,200 Israelis were killed, including 736 civilians. Hamas seized roughly 250 hostages.

New York's disparate antiwar groups quickly called for a protest in Times Square on Sunday, October 8. Neither the national nor local DSA co-sponsored the event. But what happened that day caused pols and pundits to declare war on the pro-Palestine socialist group.

That fateful Saturday, the NYC-DSA posted an invitation on X to the Times Square demonstration. It urged people to attend the Sunday demo "in solidarity with the Palestinian people and their right to resist 75 years of occupation and apartheid," then ended with "FREE PALESTINE!" That day's violence against Israeli civilians was not mentioned at all.

On Sunday, October 8, the *New York Post* editorial board issued the first of several bombastic condemnations of the DSA. With uncanny foresight, the tabloid predicted that "Swastikas [would] do the talking" at the Times Square demo plugged by the democratic socialists.

At that afternoon's rally, the mood was jarringly celebratory, especially given the certainty of a massive counterattack by Israel. On the Musk platform, a pro-Israel counter-demonstrator posted a pic of an unidentified young man of color on the pro-Palestine side of the barricades flashing a Nazi symbol on his cellphone.

"Swastika on display as Dem Socialists in NYC declare support for Hamas in terror attack on Israel," blared the cover of the *Post* on Monday, October 9. For the tabloid, it was a conspicuously perfect feedback loop. The fires quickly raged.

"The NYC–DSA's viciousness will spell the end of whatever scant power it has gained in New York City over the past half-decade," declared Nicole Gelinas in the far-right *City Journal*. A columnist for the *Post* (and a frequent contributor to the ideologically indulgent *New York Times*), Gelinas then insisted that "There is no coming back from this."[41]

Eager to expand the circle of attacks, the *Post* soon ran a curious short item about a lesser-known Black minister in Harlem who denounced the DSA. Although several leading figures in the group anchored the pro-Palestine protests, Rev. Johnnie Green criticized only one: Zohran.

Several months before October 7, Mamdani and his DSA allies in the state legislature angered New York powerful pro-Israel networks by introducing the Not on Our Dime act, a measure that would strip the state-approved tax exemption from nonprofits that helped fund Israeli settlements in the West Bank.[42] Zohran also championed BDS.

---

41 Nicole Gelinas, *City Journal* (10-11-2023). The Manhattan Institute, which publishes *City Journal*, is a right-wing think tank that was particularly influential in local politics during the Giuliani administration (1994-2001).

42 In May 2024, AOC announced her support for the legislation, which now included any New York nonprofit that helped subsidize Israel's post-October 7 war crimes in Gaza. The act is still pending in Albany.

In the immediate aftermath of October 7, Israel's allies thought they could knock out the DSA. But just over a year and a half later, the group's insurgent candidate crushed the pro-Netanyahu figure backed by most of the New York City elite. Something happened.

*

On Tuesday, October 10, the NYC-DSA issued a statement expressing regret over the "timing and tone" of the chapter's since-deleted Saturday tweet. The press release was not at all apologetic about the group's stance towards the larger conflict, however.

"We unequivocally condemn all hatred and the killing of all civilians," read the NYC-DSA's concise statement. The group then forcefully denounced the Netanyahu's "complete siege" of Gaza—which had already cut off electricity, food and water in the occupied territory—as well as the "collective punishment" of civilians for the actions of Hamas. The chapter's two-paragraph statement closed by calling for "the end of U.S. military aid for occupation and apartheid."

The NYC-DSA's "sorry, not sorry" response in no way mollified the group's many foes, nor was it meant to do so. Bronx congressman Ritchie Torres, who became AIPAC's leading New York City social media influencer after October 7, clearly consulted a thesaurus before posting that the activist group's statement was "despicable, detestable, disgraceful and disgraced."

Mayor Eric Adams, whose ties to Turkey's authoritarian Erdoğan regime would eventually lead to federal corruption charges, soon weighed in on Israel's behalf. He told MSNBC host Joe Scarborough, "You had the DSA and others carrying swastikas and calling for the extermination of Jewish people." Shockingly, the mayor's lies went unchallenged.

Zohran was a prominent figure at many of the pro-ceasefire rallies that sprouted up across the city after Israel initiated its collective punishment of Gaza a few days after the Hamas attacks. Along with his DSA colleague Assemblywoman Marcela Mitaynes (who represents Brooklyn's Sunset Park), Zohran joined a large protest organized by Jewish Voice for Peace outside of Chuck Schumer's home on Prospect Park West on Friday night, October 13.

"Tonight we are on the brink of genocide of the Palestinian people," Mamdani told the gathering of over one thousand activists. "Following the horrific murders of Israelis, we are seeing that Israel intends to level Gaza," Zohran stated.

After he and Mitaynes joined scores of activists in getting arrested (for blocking traffic), Zohran was detained for four-and-a-half hours and received two summonses. "I plan to continue to speak out against this impending genocide of Palestinians and use every avenue available to me to make it clear that New Yorkers oppose this indiscriminate killing of civilians," Mamdani stated after his release. Mass slaughter "cannot happen on our watch, and it cannot happen on our dime."[43]

The following Friday night, Mamdani and Mitaynes were joined by a slew of other DSA elected officials at a Manhattan march. Along with leftwing Muslim councilmember Shahana Hanif (who represents Brooklyn's Park Slope, Windsor Terrace and her home turf in Kensington), Mitaynes and DSA state senator Jabari Brisport engaged in civil disobedience.

There were no Swastika sightings at either of the two large protests. But that didn't stop Israel hawks from linking the DSA to the Times Square rally and the random teenager who flashed the Nazi symbol in the direction of a militant Zionist.[44]

As seen by the post-October 7 actions of Zohran, his fellow DSA elected officials, and the group's defiant local chapter, when threatened by powerful opponents, the insurgents clearly assumed a far different stance than far larger, more longstanding institutions (e.g. Columbia University). Rather than cave in, Mamdani and his DSA comrades forcefully stood their ground.

One year before he announced his mayoral run, Zohran and company were battle-tested.

---

43 Qns.com (10-14-2023).
44 After Zohran's primary win, David G. Greenfield, an Orthodox Jewish nonprofit leader who regularly denounces pro-Palestine protests, revived the spurious DSA-Swastika link on *Inside City Hall* (7-7-2025).

CHAPTER 5
The Message is a Mantra

Eight days after Eric Adams took office on Jan 1, 2022, a massive fire broke out at Twin Parks, a high-rise apartment complex in the central Bronx. One unit's faulty space heater sparked the blaze, and a defective safety door-mechanism allowed it to spread. Seventeen people died (with dozens more seriously injured), many of whom were Muslim immigrants from the West African nation of Gambia.

Mayor Adams responded by advising the city's millions of apartment dwellers to "close the doors" when a fire started, thus ignoring the Twin Parks landlord's neglect. (In general, the use of space heaters suggests that a building's owners are not providing sufficient heat, as required by city law.) Along with housing advocates, the NYC-DSA sharply criticized Adams' response, tweeting that the mayor "blame[d] the victims, not the landlord."

Meet Mayor Mamdani

As the same DSA post further noted, the co-founder of Camber Property Group, whose many residential holdings included Twin Parks, was a member of Adams' transition team. Two and a half years later, a press release from the mayor's office quoted the Camber honcho's positive comments about an Adams housing initiative. The self-styled "blue-collar mayor" frequently rolled with the 1%.[45]

This was by no means the first clash between the billionaire-friendly mayor and the DSA. "'Running against a movement': Eric Adams declares war on AOC's socialists," declared a *New York Post* headline in July 2021. At a fundraiser for the general election in upscale Douglaston, a northeast Queens neighborhood near the Nassau County border, the center-right Democratic candidate circled the wagons against what he called the "DSA socialists," a slightly redundant term.

The leftist "movement," declared the self-aggrandizing future mayor, was "mobilizing to stop Eric Adams. They realize that if I'm successful, we're going to start the process of regaining control of our cities." The event was co-hosted by a Republican city councilmember.[46]

---

45 During his late-night hours, the flashy mayor notoriously frequented Zero Bond, a members-only club in Lower Manhattan where Wall Street hot shots and large real estate players cut deals.
46 Adams appointed that ally, Eric Ulrich, as his first commissioner of the city's notoriously corrupt Department of Buildings. In September 2023, Manhattan District Attorney Alvin Bragg indicted Ulrich on sixteen felony counts of bribery, leading to the commissioner's resignation.

During Adams' first year at City Hall, the DSA helped organize protests at public hearings held by the Rent Guidelines Board (RGB), which determines the yearly rates for the city's one million rent-stabilized units. The DSA's two city councilmembers, Alexa Avilés and Tiffany Cabán (both elected in 2021), held town hall meetings and encouraged their supporters to attend the board's hearings that spring.

After the Adams-appointed RGB approved a 3.25% increase in mid-2022, "Eric Adams Raised My Rent" became a DSA rallying cry. Zohran wore a shirt featuring that statement while running the November 2022 NYC Marathon. At a May 2023 RGB hearing, Cabán and three leftist city council allies (Shahana Hanif, Sandy Nurse, and Chi Ossé) stormed the stage to dramatize their objection to the board's hikes.

Outside of a June 2024 Manhattan RGB meeting, Zohran went one step further, joining housing activists in civil disobedience. A photo in *Gothamist* showed the assemblymember in handcuffs, shouting in unison with other demonstrators while surrounded by a phalanx of NYPD officers.

Prior to announcing his run for mayor, over the next few months Zohran met with tenant advocacy groups including CAAAV, which works with Asian communities across the city. Tenants PAC, led by veteran city housing activist Mike McKee, had strongly criticized Adams' pro-landlord RGB since 2022. So did the Community Service Society, one of the city's most longstanding anti-poverty organizations.

The main item on Zohran's 2025 platform—a call to "freeze the rent" for four years—thus stemmed directly from the activist work by the DSA in conjunction with various grassroots organizations. After three years of supporting his RGB's rent hikes (of 3.25%, 3%, and 2.75%), amid his reelection bid in June 2025 Adams called for the board "to issue the lowest increase possible."

When the RGB determined that there would be another 3% increase, Adams insisted that the board "exercised their independent judgment" and claimed to be "disappointed" by his appointees' decision. Without mentioning Zohran by name, a City Hall press release stated that "While freezing the rent may sound like a catchy slogan, it is bad policy, short-sighted, and only puts tenants in harm's way."

As Zohran highlighted during the primary, an RGB report released in late March showed that between 2022 and 2023 (the most recent year fully calculated), rent-stabilized landlords' profit margin went up by 12%. Adams went to bat for the private equity investors and real estate speculators that own most of the rent-stabilized buildings. Mamdani spoke on behalf of the roughly 2.5 million tenants living inside those apartments.

From day one of his campaign, Mamdani owned the rent freeze issue. The primary results proved it to be a winning position.

*

In his second term in Albany, Mamdani teamed up with State Senator Michael Gianaris, a former Aravella Simotas ally who represents greater Astoria. The two Democrats designed a pilot program for free buses. In a September 2024 joint piece in *The Nation*, the lawmakers explained that two major U.S. cities with progressive mayors—Boston (led by Michelle Wu[47]) and Kansas City (under Quinton Lucas)—had launched similar initiatives. Mamdani and Gianaris called their trial balloon a "resounding success."

That statement was not just two pols tooting their own horns. Starting in the summer of 2023, the New York state legislature funded a one-year experiment that saw one bus line in each borough allow riders to board for free. The MTA reported that the open access resulted in a sizable spike in ridership on each line, with the largest uptick among riders with a yearly income of less than $28,000, for whom the $2.90 cost per ride is an obstacle.

A transit workers union official informed the lawmakers that the "fare box is responsible for 50% of the assaults on my operators. Free bus service would make my bus operators' job much safer." Countless bus riders and drivers thus supported the Mamdani-Gianaris effort.

The Nation byline listed Zohran first, and it's easy to see his influence on both the program and the legislators' recap. "The cost of a ride is just one more example of a cost-of-living crisis," the story noted at the outset, hyperlinking to a United Way report finding that 50% of New York City residents were "struggling to cover their basic needs."

---

47 Asked at a televised debate in June to name the nation's "most effective Democrat," Mamdani chose Wu (b. 1985).

Unlike Kamala Harris, Chuck Schumer, and Hakeem Jeffries, in the summer and early autumn of 2024, Zohran paid close attention to the struggles faced by countless working-class people. While national Democratic Party leaders insisted that the Biden economy was strong, Mamdani focused on the everyday hardship that the Dem brass did not want to acknowledge.

After Adams' indictment in late September 2024, Mamdani discussed the charges on *Democracy Now!* As Zohran told Amy Goodman, "The same mayor who allegedly received over $100,000 in bribes was just last week praising New York police officers for opening fire on four New Yorkers at a subway station over the crime of stealing a $2.90 subway fare." The prospective mayoral candidate thus connected high-level corruption to policing and inequality, previewing the affordability agenda he would soon roll out.

On October 23, the day he officially joined the race, Zohran told Goodman and co-host Juan Gonzalez that in addition to freezing the rent, "We are going to make buses free and fast across this entire city." In their *Nation* article, Mamdani and Gianaris did not mention the increased speed of buses. But as the DSA candidate would explain many times on the primary trail, bus stops with lines of passengers paying the fare are the biggest reason for delays. As riders smooth out dollar bills and insert coins, the bus falls behind schedule.

As Mamdani told Goodman and Gonzalez, the third main component of his agenda was "universal childcare at no cost for all New Yorkers for children from the ages of six weeks to five years." Public daycare access was an issue central to progressive Maya Wiley's platform in her 2021 run in the Democratic primary for mayor. Wiley, a longtime civil rights activist, had been an official in the de Blasio administration, during which the rollout of universal pre-kindergarten access in the city's public schools saved parents' thousands of dollars in childcare costs for four-year-olds.

In his second term, de Blasio had pushed for kindergarten to include three-year-olds. For unclear reasons, Mayor Adams balked at supporting that expansion until his reelection year. Mamdani's more comprehensive childcare proposal promised to save parents with young children a significant amount of money.

From day one, Zohran's message was clear: *He would fight for an affordable city by freezing the rent, making buses fast and free, and providing universal childcare.* Or simply, *Freeze the rent. Make buses free. Provide childcare.* Along with the candidate, Mamdani's volunteers individually repeated the trio of pledges hundreds of times—and collectively did so in the millions—as they interacted with voters across the five boroughs. The trinity of proposals formed the campaign's mantra.

*

Throughout the primary, the DSA candidate's extensive policy ideas could be found via Zohran for NYC's website. One proposal that he rarely got a chance to discuss in-depth was his call for the creation of a new Department of Community Safety (DCS).

Zohran's plan enables the NYPD to retain its jurisdiction over violent offenses and property crimes. The DCS would address a wide range of antisocial behavioral issues that city residents regularly encounter. Any changes to the criminal justice status quo frightens the city's power elite, however. The *Post*, Cuomo, and other opponents repeatedly attacked Zohran for his past support for "Defund the Police," a call not included in Mamdani's 2025 platform.

As stated on ZohranforNYC.com, the DCS would adopt a "public health approach to safety," focused on mental health intervention teams, including community navigators supervised by licensed medical professionals. It also would contain offices addressing hate crimes and gender-based violence via therapeutic programming. The DCS plan incorporates and expands many proposals advanced by Tiffany Cabán in her 2019 bid for Queens district attorney.

When we spoke in early April, here is how Mamdani explained his rationale for the DCS:

> *Our goal is to figure out how we actually deliver public safety. So often, these words are invoked but what is put forward are the same ideas that we've heard for years. There is a reverse New York exceptionalism. We look at things that have worked elsewhere and we say they will never work here because this is New York City and every approach we take must be unique. Rather than genuine exceptionalism, what we often see is mediocrity and failure masquerading as exceptionalism.*

According to Alex Vitale, author of the influential work *The End of Policing* (2017), Bill Bratton, NYPD commissioner under both Giuliani and de Blasio, showed no interest in how other cities handled "quality of life" issues. While other police departments applied less punitive strategies, Bratton championed the Broken Windows-based crackdown on all forms of disorder, regardless of the consequences for low-level offenders.

As Vitale explained to the New York City Council's public safety committee this past February, a nearby municipality has already shown that alternatives to traditional policing can be successful. Over the last several years Newark mayor Ras Baraka initiated community mental health programs similar to those outlined in the DCS plan, leading to dramatic reductions in violent crime in New Jersey's largest city.

"We are looking at cities across the country for public safety initiatives that we can bring to New York City," Zohran told me, rejecting the city's exceptionalism. Vitale notes that in addition to Newark, cities including Baltimore, Minneapolis, Albuquerque, and Los Angeles have offices comparable to the one proposed by Mamdani.

In our conversation, Zohran praised Ras Baraka's forceful opposition to ICE raids in Newark. "I often think of his statement that 'we cannot fight extremism with moderation,'" the candidate noted. In early May, Mamdani joined fellow contender Brad Lander, DSA councilmembers Avilés and Cabán, and comptroller candidate Justin Brannan at a rally denouncing Baraka's arrest by federal agents while

Meet Mayor Mamdani

he protested outside an ICE detention center in Newark.[48] Meanwhile, Zohran for NYC's platform vowed to end any cooperation between the city and ICE.

*

John Catsimatidis (b. 1948) may not be a household name across the U.S., but he has been a prominent player in New York City politics for several decades. The Greek immigrant is a billionaire, making his fortune first with Manhattan supermarkets while investing in real estate. His portfolio now includes a Brooklyn oil refinery and ownership of WABC radio.

A longtime Republican, Cats (as he refers to himself) is not particularly revered by members of his own party, as illustrated by his loss to Joe Lhota in the 2013 mayoral primary. But the *Post* has him on speed dial, and when the businessman doesn't answer, Murdoch's crew just quotes one of the many hyperbolic assertions the supermarket mogul regularly makes on the *Cats Roundtable*, his Sunday morning radio program aired on the station he owns. NYPD brass enjoy chatting with the big fella.

When Zohran gained steam during the primary, Cats let it be known that he is militantly opposed to Mamdani's plan to open city-run grocery stores in each of the five boroughs. As the insurgent explained on the trail, his assembly district includes the Queensbridge Houses in Long Island City, the largest public housing complex in the U.S. The surrounding area is what advocates call a "food

---

[48] On the weekend before the primary, Baraka endorsed Mamdani.

desert," sorely lacking in fresh produce. Supermarkets run by the city would offer all items at cheaper prices, because of reduced rental costs and the elimination of marked-up prices.

"Billionaire John Catsimatidis threatens to close Gristedes chain if socialist Zohran Mamdani is elected NYC mayor," announced a *Post* headline during the last week of the primary. Other Murdoch outlets amplified the declaration. Cats' vow prompted much ridicule on social media, however. Neither Gristedes nor its partner D'Agostino supermarkets are widely revered.

Cats' chains have over two dozen combined stores, almost entirely in Manhattan. All of the locations in their home borough are below 110th Street, where uptown begins and a lot more low-income New Yorkers reside. While the "free market" economy has made him a billionaire, Cats has no business incentive to sell food to working-class people. Mamdani's modest plan would help fill the void.[49]

To a lesser degree than Israel-Palestine, Zohran's public supermarket plan generated disproportionate outrage, stifling the candidate's attempts to call attention to other items on his agenda. An outgrowth of his work for Chhaya, Mamdani advanced several ideas that would help both first-time buyers and long-time homeowners.

---

49 As *Gothamist*'s Ryan Kailath explained in late July, the Economic Development Corporation, a city-owned nonprofit, already runs six markets in four boroughs (not including Staten Island). Zohran did not make that point on the primary trail, however.

Joined by Brooklyn Borough President Antonio Reynoso and local councilmember Chi Ossé, the candidate addressed reporters at Von King Park in Bed-Stuy. Mamdani touted his pledge to create an Office of Deed Theft Prevention, a predatory scheme that has forced many Black homeowners in the area to lose their property and its equity. Only a few reporters attended. But coverage in the *Amsterdam News* informed older Black voters that Zohran was paying attention to their plight.

Like all of his fellow contenders, the Mamdani pledged to build a large amount of new and affordable housing. DSA-aligned housing specialist Cea Weaver helped create a detailed plan. Zohran's proposed number of units—200,000 over ten years—placed him in the more modest range among fellow contenders. Liberal Zellnor Myrie proposed one million (including both new and "preserved" units, a slippery metric) and billionaire Whitney Tilson promised two million.

In mid-April, the frontrunner's housing proposal attracted the most attention to the issue, but the mini-scandal that transpired did not help the former governor. "Andrew Cuomo Used ChatGPT for his Housing Plan," announced a *Hell Gate* headline on Sunday night, April 13. The worker-owned outlet's Max Rivlin-Nadler and Christopher Robbins explained that the first 27 of Cuomo's 29-page document were "fairly unremarkable." But on page 28, things came unglued.

As Max and Chris amusingly detailed, the last two pages were full of typos, gobbledygook, and material generated by ChatGPT, the generative A.I. writing tool. It was not hard for the two reporters to establish that humans did not create the material found on the final pages of Cuomo's plan. The URL link in a footnote ended with the company's name. After the campaign's ornery spokesman Rich Azzopardi first claimed that ChatGPT was simply "a research tool," Cuomo's team later blamed the foolishness on a campaign adviser, identifying that person by name.

Whether sincere or not, no candidate was able to speak in-depth about the city's dire housing shortage. There were too many contenders and the details of how to build affordable units are intricate.

*

In early March, Zohran made a bold move: He sat down for an interview with the *Post*. The insurgent knew he was giving Murdoch's crew something they would denounce. "Socialist NYC mayoral candidate wants to hike corporate taxes to pay for loads of freebies," the ensuing headline declared. Some readers no doubt were aghast. Many others were likely intrigued.

As Mamdani later explained to progressive YouTube host Jack Cocchiarella, "We told the *Post* reporters the same thing we tell everyone else: 'We will tax the most profitable corporations at the same rate as the radical socialist utopia of New Jersey and use those taxes to pay for things that'll improve the lives of every New Yorker.'" Zohran's cheeky reference to the Garden State got plenty of social media attention.

Zohran also announced that he would raise taxes on New Yorkers with incomes over $1 million per year. As Bloomberg.com reported in July, the latest data (from 2022) shows that the total number of city residents in that category is between 34,000-35,000, a mere fraction of the city's nearly 8.5 million people.[50] Both the *Post* and the *Times* nonetheless ran numerous stories questioning Zohran's harsh treatment of this embattled group.

New York City, however, does not have the ability determine to its own income and corporate tax rates. The state legislature needs to approve such changes, and Gov. Kathy Hochul, a centrist Democrat, assured the business elite that she would veto any tax hikes. As of the end of July, Hochul had not yet endorsed Mamdani.

As the primary race took shape, it was easy for Zohran's fellow contenders and media antagonists to dismiss his promises of free buses, universal childcare, and city-run grocery stores as unrealistic because of their cost.[51] The campaign coincided with the annual budget negotiations at City Hall. For the fiscal year that started this July 1, the city's spending outlay totaled over $115 billion, more than two times greater than the state budget of Illinois, which has four million more residents than New York City. Mamdani also proposed reallocating some of that very large pot to fund his initiatives.

---

50 When calculated by net worth, the number of millionaires surpasses 350,000. Nearly everyone who owns an apartment in Manhattan falls into that category. Zohran's proposal thus targets income.

51 A rent freeze is revenue neutral because the stabilized buildings are privately owned.

In 2013, Bill de Blasio campaigned on a pledge to fund universal pre-k via a tax on the rich. Gov. Andrew Cuomo, a reliable ally of the 1%, responded by moving money around in the state budget in order to finance UPK without tapping elite wallets. As de Blasio noted in June 2025, New York City's upper crust stood to reap hefty dividends from Trump's tax cuts. Meanwhile, the billionaires made a bad bet that Cuomo would win the primary.

At the outset of August, Mamdani clearly had the wind at his back, thus increasing his ability to force Gov. Hochul into supporting tax hikes on the ultra-elite. Hochul is up for reelection in 2026.

*

Before we return to the outset of Zohran's 2025 run, here are a few things to keep in mind:

1. New York City has a very generous campaign finance program that currently provides 8-1 matching funds, setting these ground rules for the mayoral race:

    - $10, the minimum amount that is supplemented, yields $90.
    - $2,100 is the maximum contribution. If a donor lives in the city, $250 becomes $2,250 (making the largest individual donation yield $4,350).
    - A candidate must obtain 1,000 discrete contributions from city residents in order to get the extra funds.
    - The 1,000 donations must total at least $250,000.
    - Donors must list their employers.

- The New York City Campaign Finance Board scrutinizes the contributions.

2. Since 2021, city primaries have followed a ranked-choice voting process, meaning:

    - Voters list their preferred candidates, starting with their first choice (1) through their fifth (5). A ballot with fewer than five selections still counts.
    - Candidates may cross-endorse each other in order to get second-place rankings.
    - Elected officials, unions, advocacy groups and others sometimes propose an initial slate to rank without listing a candidate as number one. Later in the campaign the same endorser may opt to make a candidate their top choice. In the following chapters, I only mention when Zohran became the number-one pick by various political players.

3. A few other points about how the story proceeds.

    - Although I mention several national media outlets' coverage of Mamdani's primary run, which expanded infinitely in June, I devote far more attention to local media. My aim is to capture how New York City voters gathered information about the race. National and international coverage certainly can contribute to local views, but candidates typically need to first gain traction in the five boroughs before they generate significant interest elsewhere.
    - As seen thus far, when I discuss stories from leading outlets including the *Times* and the *Post*, I

frequently do not name the reporters listed on the bylines. I chose not to do so in many cases because a large portion of anti-Zohran stories appeared to be strongly shaped by heavy-handed editors.

Without further ado, off we go...

CHAPTER 6
Fast Start

In the initial stages of the 2025 Democratic primary, Zohran and fellow candidates believed they would need to topple a hobbled incumbent. The long-swirling rumors that Mayor Eric Adams would face corruption charges became reality in late September 2024, when federal prosecutors announced a five-count indictment accusing the mayor of bribery and campaign finance offenses.

The purported wrongdoing dated back to Adams' tenure as Brooklyn borough president (2014-2021) and continued throughout his first term in City Hall. According to Damian Williams, lead prosecutor for the Southern District of New York (SDNY), Adams had received "illegal benefits" from Turkish officials, resulting in that nation's new high-rise embassy near the United Nations headquarters opening without passing the required fire inspection.

Jocelyn Strauber, Adams' appointee as head of the city's Department of Investigation, fully cooperated with the

SDNY and FBI. "As charged, this illegal conduct compromised [Adams'] integrity as an elected official," Strauber stated. The SDNY indictment marked the first time that a sitting mayor of New York City faced criminal charges. Over forty elected officials—including AOC, Zohran, and fellow DSA elected officials, along with many mainstream Democrats—quickly called for Adams to resign. Several high-ranking members of his administration departed, but Adams stayed in office.

"It is impossible for the mayor to perform his duties," Zohran told *Democracy Now!* host Amy Goodman a few days after the SDNY indictment. "The same mayor who allegedly received over $100,000 in bribes was just last week praising New York police officers for opening fire on four New Yorkers at a subway station over the crime of stealing $2.90 of a subway fare." The prospective candidate had been refining his messaging, connecting every issue to affordability.

When Zohran sat down with *Democracy Now!* co-hosts Goodman and Juan Gonzalez on the day his campaign launched (Wednesday, October 23), all three assumed that defeating Adams remained the goal. Mamdani explained that in his view, the mayor's pledge to focus on the federal charges would short-change "working-class New Yorkers." In the candidate's view, Adams had been "failing" to address the needs of city residents well before the indictment. The "true crisis," Zohran said, was the skyrocketing cost-of-living in the city.

Mamdani vowed that if elected he would impose a rent freeze, expand free bus transportation and enact universal childcare. The then-longshot's message was the same on October 23 as it would be when he unexpectedly won the primary the following June 24. Mamdani further assured Goodman that he was proud to belong to the "democratic socialist tradition."

When Gonzalez noted that Mamdani's position on Palestine was "not normally a plank" for a New York City mayoral candidate "but certainly will affect how people vote," Zohran reiterated his opposition to the "taxpayer-funded genocide." He did not have time to discuss the incumbent's stridently pro-Israel politicking. But most *Democracy Now!* listeners were surely aware that Mayor Adams wholeheartedly backed the NYPD's violent crackdown on pro-Palestine campus protests.

In a *Guardian* story published on October 23, Zohran told reporter Erum Salam that he would target "sets of voters that have been erased" from city politics—adding that some groups "have been persecuted by the political system in the city." Mamdani provided an example from the Astoria assembly district he represents. In the aftermath of 9/11, he noted, Steinway Street was where Mayor Bloomberg "created the demographics unit within the NYPD to illegally surveil Muslims on the basis of our faith. And now the representative of that street is going to run for the same position that created that [unit]." Mamdani's success illustrates how dramatically the city has changed in the past 25 years.

On the same day Zohran announced his run, his campaign posted a cutting-edge 100-second launch video. Wearing a thigh-length white South Asian shirt, Zohran walks down a residential street in Astoria while succinctly describing his main platform planks. Text across the screen introduces the candidate as Zohran Kwame Mamdani.

After highlighting Mayor Adams' corruption charges (and briefly weaving in a shot of then-Governor Cuomo during the pandemic), the up-tempo video mixes action shots of Zohran with statements from everyday New Yorkers describing the hardships they face. A woman wearing a keffiyeh while pushing a stroller states, "I want to raise my kid in New York." Zohran does not mention Palestine, but the scarf speaks loudly.

Zohran scripted the video with campaign manager Elle Bisgaard-Church, media strategist Morris Katz, and communications director Andrew Epstein. It was produced by Fight Agency, a Democratic consulting firm that employs Katz. Shortly after its release, I showed it to a focus group of a dozen undergraduate college students in Brooklyn, most of whom grew up in the city. The response was entirely favorable.

At the evening launch party in Long Island City, Cynthia Nixon lent her star power in support of the candidate she called "a movement person," and a diverse group of activists brought people power. Ashik Siddique, the national DSA's co-chair raised in a Bangladeshi Muslim household in Brooklyn, observed that "everybody I've talked to in the past few days is so hype for this."

Jaslin Kaur, a Sikh Punjabi activist who—running as a DSA candidate—lost a close Democratic primary race for city council in 2021 in the central Queens neighborhood in which she grew up, shared Siddique's enthusiasm. "I really don't want to get priced out of the city I love," said Kaur, "and I'm so excited that a South Asian, Muslim candidate is stepping up." Brooklynite Asad Dandia, a Muslim raised in a Pakistani American household in Brighton Beach, explained that he supported Zohran because "I'm simply tired that my rent is going up."

The campaign's Instagram recap included a twenty-something woman wearing a hijab stating that Zohran "is one of the only politicians who has stood up for Palestine." On a lighter note, one lad claims that he supports the DSA candidate because a halal plate of chicken with rice used to cost three dollars and now it's ten bucks—what the candidate would soon refer to as "halal-flation." "What the fuck?" asks the young brown man, who is wearing a Rosa Parks t-shirt.

Eight months later, many of the same opening-night attendees returned to Long Island City for an even bigger Zohran event.

*

Two days before the 2024 election, Zohran ran his second New York City marathon. In his first, in 2022, the DSA assemblymember wore a shirt reading, "Eric Adams Raised My Rent!" Two years later, the back of his jersey vowed, "Zohran Will Freeze It!"

Although he improved by 25 minutes over his performance two years earlier, Mamdani's 2024 marathon time of nearly five hours and 40 minutes meant that he finished the race in a rather distant 48,013th place. Nonetheless, "I'm outpacing all the mayoral contenders in the race," Zohran quipped along the route to reporter Jeff Coltin, of *Politico*'s New York Playbook.

In the *Democracy Now!* launch-day interview with Zohran, Juan Gonzalez mentioned the ongoing speculation that Andrew Cuomo would join the crowded field. But Mamdani instead focused on the Adams administration's inattention to the city's housing crisis. The former governor's candidacy did not become official until early March.

In the meantime, Adams further angered New York Democrats by cozying up to the White House. In the wake of his September 2024 indictment, the mayor started making overtures to Trump, repeatedly asserting (without evidence) that the DoJ's corruption charges resulted from his outspoken criticism of the Biden administration's immigration policies.

Although he endorsed Kamala Harris, Adams did not campaign for her. Nor did he criticize Trump as election day neared. At his late October rally at Madison Square Garden, Trump declared that Adams had been "treated very badly" because of the mayor's stance on immigration.

After Trump's share of the vote in New York City spiked from 23% in 2020 to 31% in 2024, some analysts called it a "red wave."[52] Political observers now questioned whether

---

52 The real story was the drop-off in Democratic turnout from Biden in 2020. Over 400,000 Biden voters did not cast ballots for Harris. Trump collected roughly 150,000 more tallies than four years earlier.

Adams, a Republican in the 1990s, might switch parties again and run as the MAGA candidate for mayor.

Trump's November 2024 victory also led to the first time Zohran's mayoral campaign caught fire on social media. Rather than question why some working-class voters now backed Trump or simply did not turn out for Harris from his armchair, the candidate hit the streets and asked many people directly.

Zohran chose two locations—Hillside Avenue in Jamaica, Queens, and Fordham Road in the central Bronx—that witnessed shifts towards the right in the last two presidential elections. A strikingly diverse range of working-class residents told Mamdani that they voted for Trump.

"They liked Trump because they don't want the Palestinian brothers killed," a middle-aged pharmacist observes regarding residents of Jamaica, a neighborhood known as "Little Bangladesh." A Black respondent in his thirties, a middle-aged South Asian man, and an elderly Latina explain that Trump may bring back "lower prices" for groceries.

As two Black women under forty tell Zohran, Palestine was the main reason many people they knew did not turn out for Harris. They and others fault the Democrats' neglect of pocketbook issues. Several people respond enthusiastically to Mamdani's bread-and-butter platform.

Over the next six months, Mamdani's tweet featuring the three-minute video would be viewed over 2.5 million times. The immediate splash after the post went up in mid-November caught the attention of media observers not aligned with mainstream Democrats.

"This is so good," tweeted Briahna Joy Gray, national press secretary for the 2020 Bernie Sanders campaign. In late November, former MSNBC host Mehdi Hasan led off his interview with Mamdani on *Zeteo*—a news site Hasan founded in 2024—by showing clips of Zohran's Trumpers-on-the-streets interviews. The host asked Mamdani whether Trump's gains in the city reflected a shift in the electorate away from a working-class agenda.

"Many politicians across New York City and New York State are using this as an opportunity to air their previously held positions about whether the left should be part of a governing coalition," Zohran observed. "But when I went out and spoke to New Yorkers directly, I found that their economic concerns are what's at the heart of a left economic program."

Although Trump's campaign pledges were "insincere and ridiculous," Zohran observed, the salesman-president at least offered voters "a promise" that prices of household goods would return to their pre-pandemic levels. Meanwhile, the Harris campaign paid scant attention to voters' struggles to pay their bills.

*

Mamdani created another social media sensation on New Year's Day. This time the splash was literal, with Zohran dipping into the ice-cold water at Coney Island as part of the Polar Bear Club's annual January 1 plunge.

As reporter Haidee Chu recounted in *The City*, a local nonprofit newsroom, the candidate was sporting a dark grey suit he had purchased for $30 at an Astoria thrift store. Zohran declared that he was "freezing your rent as the next mayor of New York City. Let's plunge into the details." He then did a running head-first dive into Lower New York Bay.

While locals of various ages and shapes frolicked in the water, Mamdani gleefully launches into a spiel about his rent freeze plan. Few fellow plungers appear to be thinking about the Rent Guidelines Board, but while toweling off, Zohran succinctly explains how Eric Adams' appointees had consistently raised rents during the mayor's first three years in office. He then quotes the landlord-mayor's absurdist assertion that "I am real estate."[53]

At once madcap and wonky, Mamdani's Coney Island video racked up over 800,000 views across various platforms by the time Chu's article came out three weeks later. "Humor often is far more effective at having someone open up to even consider you," the candidate observed.

As Andrew Epstein notes, it was Mamdani's idea to attend the New Year's Day event, and only the two of them went. After his dip, Zohran held their stuff while Andrew dived in, with the longshot mayoral contender shivering on the

---

[53] Adams' four-unit building in Bed-Stuy does not qualify for rent stabilization, which requires six or more units. In the homestretch of the 2021 primary, Adams faced swirling questions about whether he lived in the basement apartment of his building. Most observers believed he resided in Fort Lee, New Jersey (just across the George Washington Bridge).

beach in a very wet suit. He would not be standing alone for long in 2025.

The plunge was just one of several videos posted by Zohran on social media that had recently caught fire. In addition to the Trump voter conversations, Chu cited his amusing skit with Brooklyn comedian Cassie Wilson, in which the latter plays the role of the "naysayer." Mamdani also "intervened" in a satirical diner debate about between two older white New Yorkers, one who claims to like Adams while the other supports Cuomo.

Less-scripted postings that captured eyeballs featured the DSA candidate asking city food truck vendors about what Zohran dubbed "halal-flation," referring to rising prices at food trucks. By the middle of January, Zohran's top-flight social media game had put him on the mayoral map.

*

In early January, Zohran bounced across the city to various fundraisers timed to coincide with a Campaign Finance Board deadline.

In order to receive New York City's 8-1 matching funds, a mayoral candidate in the 2025 cycle needed to obtain a minimum of 1,000 donations from city residents, totaling at least $250,000. The filing deadline in order to receive the first 8-1 disbursements was Saturday, January 11, at 11:59 p.m.

While Zohran hopped around to various events, Andrew reached out to early donors, seeking volunteers to appear in a campaign video. Prior to receiving matching funds, Zohran for NYC was a scrappy, low-budget operation.

But the public finance system provided plenty of incentive. Candidates without existing funding networks need to attract as many donors as possible, and social media attention often yields dividends.

In mid-December, a jewelry designer in Staten Island contributed $50 to the campaign (which matching funds would turn into $450). In response to Andrew's inquiry, Jasmine and her husband Matt, a higher-ed administrator, invited Zohran to their home.

A few days later, the candidate visited the couple and their two grade-school age children at their place near the Ferry Terminal, the section of Staten Island that typically votes for Democrats. Zohran, Andrew and a two-person video crew spent 45 minutes or so there. The children took a liking to their friendly guests.

As Mamdani and his team were leaving, Jasmine and Matt's inspired seven-year-old son gave the candidate a Lego creation he made. It was of a mayor wearing a top hat. The boy had high hopes, and Zohran posted the gift on Instagram. The Staten Island home visit formed the basis of a video distributed by the campaign in mid-January.

Fueled by the DSA and other activist networks, Mamdani far exceeded the minimum number of required donors. On Friday, January 10 and the following day, over 1,800 people contributed to the campaign, mostly in the $25-50 range. Because the program requires donors to list their occupations, we know that scores of educators like Matt and numerous creative professionals like Jasmine were excited about Zohran.

Mamdani's first report to the Campaign Finance Board covered the period since he launched his campaign in the fall. He recorded nearly 8,300 donations that totaled over $640,000, crushing the numbers put up by the rest of the mayoral candidates then in the race.[54]

Zohran's January 11 fundraising tour brought him to Sunset Stoop, a recently opened bar and small performance space in Brooklyn's Sunset Park, home to a mix of working-class Latinos and Asians as well as middle-class white homeowners and renters. Since 2020, the area has elected two DSA members, Assemblywoman Marcela Mitaynes and City Councilwoman Alexa Avilés. The warm-up performers that night included a Coney Island sword-swallower.

When Mamdani, sporting a white kurta, took the stage, the candidate joked that upon arriving in the neighborhood, he was confused because he thought the event was actually taking place on someone's front stoop. The mostly 30-something crowd consisted of DSA activists, criminal justice reformers, and educators. After Zohran's brief stump speech, the friendly figure mingled with supporters.

The socialist candidate came to Sunset Park that Saturday evening from an earlier fundraiser in nearby Park Slope. The public transportation candidate assured me that he indeed had taken the B63 bus that connects the two neighborhoods.

---

54 In the three days before the January 11 deadline, Zohran took in $115,000. That included just one maximum contribution of $2,100 (from a Brooklyn physician) and a few others for $1,000. The remainder were less than four figures.

After departing Sunset Stoop, Zohran marched off to Manhattan for another event. As the fast-rising contender told *Hell Gate's* Christopher Robbins a few days later, "I got on [the subway] on Saturday night to go from my second fundraiser to my third fundraiser, and a woman yelled across the platform, 'I just donated to you!'"

As Mamdani explained to Robbins, the campaign's palpable success "is far bigger than any one person. It's about a deep desire to have the city that we all love be one that is affordable for working-class New Yorkers." While bouncing across the five boroughs, Zohran stayed on message.

*

Throughout the winter, Mamdani and his fellow candidates continued to pitch themselves as alternatives to Mayor Adams. The mayor's political future, however, remained in limbo because his federal criminal trial was scheduled for late April, two months before the June 24 primary.

But on Monday, February 10, Emil Bove, then the top deputy attorney general at the Department of Justice, told SDNY prosecutors they should drop the charges against Adams. Danielle Sassoon, the SDNY's lead attorney handling the prosecution, fought to preserve the case. Rather than drop the charges, Sassoon and others on her team resigned.

Amid the fireworks, Trump's extreme-right border czar sat down for a morning interview with Mayor Adams on *Fox & Friends*. With Midtown Manhattan as the backdrop, the crusty border czar and flashy mayor yucked it up while sitting next to each other on the couch. Even though

Bove had explicitly stated that the criminal case hindered Adams' ability to assist with ICE arrests, the mayor insisted that he had not offered anything to the White House in exchange for the dropped charges. Tom Homan quickly undercut Adams' claim.

"I came to New York City and I wasn't going to leave with nothing," Trump's deputy told the hosts. Homan explained that the mayor had indeed agreed to remove the restrictions on ICE access to Rikers Island imposed by the city council during the de Blasio administration. Homan crassly assured the Fox team that if Adams did not follow through on the agreement, he would "come back to New York City, but we won't be sitting on the couch. We'll be in his office, and I will be up his butt saying, 'Where the hell is the agreement we came to?'" Adams smiled nervously.

Many city Democrats were appalled by Adams' craven response to Homan that Friday morning. The cringeworthy exchange made national headlines. "Trump's Border Czar Tells NYC Mayor He'll be 'Up His Butt' if He Breaks Vow to Help ICE," announced NBC News. The following Monday, three prominent deputy mayors (Maria Torres-Springer, Anne Williams-Isom, and Meera Joshi) announced their resignations.

Although Adams would not announce his decision to bow out of the Democratic primary for another six weeks, the handwriting was clearly on the wall. Zohran and his fellow mayoral contenders needed to revise their game plans.

Somewhere in the suburbs, Andrew Cuomo plotted his next move.

CHAPTER 7
A Spicy Mix

"DSA eyes Israel foe for mayor," read a headline of a short news item on page 13 of the *New York Post* on Saturday, October 12, 2024. That Murdoch's minions were eager to restart their year-old battle against the socialist group was no surprise. But how veteran *Post* reporter Carl Campanile ended up with a DSA internal planning document is a head-scratcher.

The NYC-DSA's nomination process nonetheless matched Campanile's description. On Oct. 5, Zohran—labeled by the *Post* as an "Israel-bashing Queens assemblyman"—spoke to the organization's Citywide Electoral Working Group. Along with seven branches within the local chapter, DSA delegates, including the group's elected officials, voted over the next week.

As Campanile reported on October 20, Zohran captured 60% support from the branches and from 107 of 130 delegates. *Jacobin*'s Liza Featherstone explained at the time that dissenters within the ranks questioned Mamdani's electability, fearing that a big loss might weaken the group's various legislative initiatives. But as Zohran told Liza, he "wouldn't run" without the DSA's support.

Having unseated a Democratic Party incumbent in 2020, Zohran was a fast-rising figure among the growing left-wing organization both at the local and national level. In August 2023, Mamdani gave the keynote address at the national DSA convention in Chicago. Now he was the NYC-DSA's first candidate in a citywide race.

Given the outcome of the 2025 primary, it may be surprising that the city's DSA chapter only had approximately 6,600 active members in October 2024. As Zohran's campaign gained steam over the next eight months, the group's ranks grew to 8,800. After Mamdani's resounding triumph over Cuomo, the number quickly surpassed 10,000. Shortly after the primary, the victorious candidate sent out a recruiting statement inviting his legions of fans to join the socialist group.[55]

While the DSA anchored Zohran's dynamic field operation, members of many other activist groups made important contributions. In the summer and early fall of 2024, Zohran met with numerous leaders and organizations to solicit advice and present his vision. As the campaign launched,

---

55 Distributed as a NYC-DSA email blast, Zohran explained his work as a foreclosure counselor and slammed Wall Street for "preying upon" working people. "When the odds are stacked against working people," he said, "the only lasting solution is to come together and create a force big enough to deliver meaningful change."

the grassroots organizations Jewish Voice for Peace (JVP), NY Communities for Change (NYCC), CAAAV Voice (CV), and DRUM Beats declared their support for Zohran.

From day one, Zohran's initial coalition consisted of pro-Palestine activists (JVP and DSA), anti-poverty organizers (NYCC, CV, DRUM, DSA), and East Asian tenants (CV), along with South Asian and Indo-Caribbean city residents (DRUM, CV). Tens of thousands of campaign volunteers, largely from Queens and Brooklyn, shared an affinity with one or more of these viewpoints.

Mamdani's platform resonated with working-class voters across the five boroughs. As his primary campaign gathered steam, NYCC helped Zohran gain traction in the city's Black and Spanish-speaking communities. Mamdani's multicultural legions of foot soldiers were instrumental in making people aware of what the DSA candidate offered.

*

Northwest Queens has been NYC-DSA turf ever since AOC and Cabán's campaigns. Activists view the heavily East Asian neighborhoods around Flushing in northeast Queens as most dominated by Rep. Grace Meng, a moderate Democrat, but liberal State Senator John Liu also wields influence. Southeast Queens, which has a large Black population, continues to be the base for Rep. Greg Meeks, a centrist Democrat.

Although he is Joe Crowley's successor as the Queens Democratic leader, Meeks (b. 1953) by no means influences most political activity across the borough. The tri-partite power structure leaves large swaths of turf in central Queens unclaimed—including fast-growing South Asian neighborhoods bordering Meeks' terrain. Richmond Hill, for example, is home to "Little Guyana." And in November 2024, Zohran conducted post-election interviews with Trump voters in "Little Bangladesh," which runs along Hillside Avenue in northern Jamaica.

Jagpreet Singh is the political director of DRUM Beats, an offshoot of Desis Rise Up & Moving, a nonprofit promoting economic empowerment for South Asian and Indo-Caribbean communities. "Desis" is a Sanskrit term (meaning "country") that diasporic South Asians call themselves, but according to Jagpreet, it's not used by Guyanese, Trinidadian, or other Indo-Caribbeans. As Singh told me, the M.O. of mainstream Democratic leaders in Queens involves sending liaisons to chat up community leaders at various meetings and events. The organizer first worked with the future mayoral candidate at Chhaya from 2018 to 2020. Even prior to Zohran's official campaign launch, Jagpreet said that his role was to introduce Mamdani to many of the same community leaders that the party machine interacts with.

During the early fall 2024, Zohran and Jagpreet, a Sikh Punjabi, attended the Durga Puja festival at a Nepali Hindu temple in Ridgewood, Queens. Just after the campaign launched, the duo appeared at the large Diwali celebration held every fall by Hindus in Richmond Hill's Little Guyana. Two months before the primary, they traveled across the East River to the Sikh Day Parade in Manhattan.

Jagpreet noted that he and Zohran went to countless Bangladeshi events in neighborhoods from City Line in Brooklyn (at the border of Queens) through Hillside Avenue to Parkchester in the east Bronx. As primary day neared, twenty-something Aaron Narraph, one of the DSA's most prominent social media influencers, posted a pic of his Bangladeshi parents expressing support for Zohran.

On Sunday, June 22, Zohran attended a rally in Kensington, Brooklyn with leftist Councilwoman Shahana Hanif, a Bangladeshi Muslim targeted by Israel hawks. Bangladeshi voters helped Hanif crush her challenger, and across the city they helped Mamdani dethrone Cuomo.

*

When Mamdani's campaign launched, CAAAV's political arm announced that the group's "working class Asian immigrant and tenant members" backed Zohran primarily because of his rent freeze position. "We have seen what happens when electeds like Eric Adams take real estate money—year after year, rents go up while New Yorkers work longer for less," stated Alina Shen, organizing director for CAAAV Voice.

CAAAV formed two decades ago as advocacy group for tenants in Manhattan's flagship Chinatown. During the Mamdani campaign Shen led volunteer teams in Brooklyn's Chinatown, which now extends from Sunset Park into Bensonhurst. CAAAV also has a chapter in Astoria that works primarily with Bangladeshi renters.

On a brisk Sunday in early April, Zohran came to Sunset Park for a "freeze the rent" rally hosted by CAAAV Voice (CV). Brooklyn's large Chinatown starts near the actual park, bringing many older residents to the event, with CV organizers providing Cantonese and Mandarin translation. Plenty of younger Asian activists were also in the mix.

Zohran joined Shen and his fellow DSA figureheads Alexa Avilés and Marcela Mitaynes at the event. When his turn at the mic came, the candidate led the mostly Asian, Spanish-speaking and middle-class white gathering in a call-and-response refrain, with Mamdani belting out "freeze the–" and the crowd yelling "–rent!"

Beside me in the crowd stood two teens, both wearing CAAAV shirts. As Zohran spoke, one said repeatedly to the other, "He's so cool." The sentiment was shared by all ages in attendance.

Two days before the June primary, CV troops would return to Sunset Park to do a final door-knocking push, joining a pre-canvass rally hosted by Jewish Voice for Peace.

*

Zohran's massive, unprecedented ground game was run by the DSA's Tascha Van Auken, who started working in electoral politics in the 2008 Obama campaign. She later managed the successful runs of democratic socialist Julia Salazar in 2018 and Phara Souffrant Forrest two years later.

Helmed by field director Van Auken, Zohran for NYC's outreach operation was nothing if not culturally conversant. Multilingual volunteers spoke to voters in dozens of native languages, from Arabic to Vietnamese. They also distributed informational materials translated into several languages, and the campaign created videos in Urdu, Bangla, and Spanish.

As Van Auken detailed to DSA members in post-primary Zoom call (with over 600 attendees tuning in), by the end of June 24, Zohran's campaign had 30,000 active volunteers and 20,000 additional participants. Nearly 500 trained field leaders directed more than 3,000 canvasses in over 60 neighborhoods across the five boroughs.

One month before the primary, Zohran's team predicted that the campaign's volunteers would knock on over one million voter doors. By the end of June 24, Van Auken reported, the tally reached a whopping 1.6 million. Participants made over 2.3 million calls. During the homestretch, voters heard from prominent voices including Naomi Klein, who headlined a phone bank event.

All who participated in voter outreach, Van Auken observed, felt the sensation of "collective power" to varying degrees. That muscle memory, she forecasted, will contribute to innumerable future campaigns, regardless of whether they are led by the DSA.

On the afternoon of June 23, yours truly was at home in Sunset Park chatting about the book you're reading with OR publisher Colin Robinson. During our call my doorbell rang. Sure enough, it was a canvasser for Mamdani and Avilés visiting my apartment building, for at least the fourth time that primary season.

At a televised debate in June, a very rich but politically impoverished mayoral candidate ludicrously claimed that Zohran's momentum resulted simply from "cute videos." Some candidates needed to get out more.

*

"It's not just white kids," Iggy Sanchez said about his fellow Mamdani volunteers. Sanchez is a twenty-something raised in the Bronx now living in Brooklyn. "It's not just transplants," Iggy states. "It's moms. It's immigrants. It's just people who want a slightly more affordable city. That really moved me."

Sanchez's account is one of several post-primary reflections compiled by *Indypendent* publisher John Tarleton. Twenty-something Amanda Vender explains how she gained access to large apartment buildings in Northwest Queens: "When I had to choose which buzzer to ring first to enter a building, I consulted the MiniVAN app[56] on my phone and always went with a voter under 35 because I knew they'd be a likely [Mamdani] supporter and let me in."

"At one door in Sunnyside," recounts Vender, "two children around 6 and 8 years old answered the door. I introduced myself and asked for the parents. 'Our parents aren't home,' one said, 'but we want our parents to vote for Zohran!'"

---

56 MiniVAN is a database of Democratic voters used by many campaigns.

Jose Sanchez (who is not related to Iggy) is in his early thirties and identifies as a gay Afro-Puerto Rican. Jose told John that he first participated in politics when he took the train from his home in New Jersey to join Occupy Wall Street. The Occupy practice of mutual aid surfaced during Jose's voter outreach for Zohran. On the sweltering hot primary day, a woman at poll site in Crown Heights saw that Sanchez was drenched in sweat and poured water from her bottle into Jose's.

A veteran organizer with NYCC, Pete Sikora won over many of his neighbors in Brooklyn's Carroll Gardens, an upscale progressive area that Brad Lander formerly represented in the City Council. Pete said that he regularly sat on his front stoop for "an hour or three" persuading Lander supporters to back Mamdani. He "met a lot of neighbors" and someone even left a note on his building's door thanking Pete for his advice. "Don't ever let anyone tell you otherwise," Sikora told Tarleton. "One-to-one contact works!"

In the wake of Zohran for NYC's resounding grassroots victory, many future Democratic campaigns in the city and elsewhere surely will expand their direct outreach to voters. But Mamdani did not inspire thousands of volunteers to devote their leisure time to his campaign because he has some sort of guru-like appeal. "Zohran's message is really what set him apart," Ozone Park canvass leader Felicia Singh (no relation to Jagpreet) told me.

The campaign featured Mamdani's cost-of-living agenda on buttons with simple phrases like "Freeze the Rent," "Fast, Free Busses" and "Universal Childcare." Enthusiastic volunteers sporting those badges chatted with voters and handed them vibrant campaign materials that featured the same proposals.

Meanwhile, none of the other mayor candidates in the primary offered signature policy ideas that were easy to deliver. For example, Brad Lander's main plan was to convert city-owned golf courses into residential housing, a complex process that would take several years. Many voters had more immediate concerns.

Zohran rolled out his crystal-clear affordability agenda on day one, his volunteer army brought it to front doors across the five boroughs, and voters gave them a very friendly reception.

*

In addition to the campaign's ground game, Zohran's skillful use of social media helped him move into second place by early April. He was already well-known in both activist circles and among the city's South Asian communities, dating back to his advocacy for taxi drivers. Zohran was now about to become a celebrity in the eyes of young Muslims everywhere.

After the CAAAV rally in Sunset Park, Zohran and Andrew Epstein headed back to Astoria for an evening with Hasan Piker, a millennial media superstar with a massive fanbase among zoomers. On Twitch, a platform favored by teens, Piker has over 2.7 million followers, with roughly half that number of devotees on TikTok. On YouTube, which spans generations, he has over 1.4 million subscribers.

Hasan is a Turkish American Muslim from New Jersey who, like Zohran, was born in 1991. A *New York Times* style reporter recently characterized Piker's appeal as twofold. There is a "bro" dimension, as the story described: "He likes weapons, inhales supplements, uses nicotine pouches and ruminates endlessly on the legacy of LeBron James." "But unlike many of his contemporaries," the *Times* continued, "Mr. Piker [is] an avowed socialist."

Hasan and Zohran spoke for about an hour, a YouTube-friendly format that allows Piker's team to post clips across platforms. The conversation was far more in-depth than that found in many traditional media outlet interviews with Zohran. They started with his platform but the host then asked the DSA candidate about the MTA, the NYPD, and Rikers Island, with Zohran stating that he would follow through on the city's planned closure of the notorious hellhole.

Although they did not discuss Gaza in much depth, in its rampage against Mamdani the *New York Post* often linked him to Piker, who they referred to as a "sick online influencer" because he frequently criticizes Israel. Without any evidence, the tabloid declared that Hasan was pro-Hamas, thus smearing Zohran as guilty by association.

After the conversation, Piker's Twitch livestream followed the media superstar and the ascending city leader as they went out for a Bangladeshi meal in Astoria. As they walked the streets, numerous young South Asian fans of both figures shook their hands and asked for photos. Many Desis and most young Muslims do not live in the *Post*'s world.

*

Meet Mayor Mamdani

By early June, Zohran was lighting up the city. But it wasn't just young South Asians, DSA members, and pro-Palestine activists who created the buzz. A backyard gathering brought together a range of older fellow travelers. The neighborhood was Brooklyn's historic Fort Greene.

Poet Ken Chen (in his mid-forties) and editor Andy Hsiao (in his early sixties) invited a wide assortment of literati and activists to the latter's house, including many leading figures in New York's Asian community. CNN host W. Kamau Bell joined fellow comedian Hari Kondabolu, a longtime friend of Zohran. *Guardian* columnist Moustafa Bayoumi, a leading Muslim commentator, mingled with Moroccan poet Omar Berrada.

It was not Zohran's short remarks that stood out. Instead, it was the depth of his answers to questions. Joyce Yu, a Chinatown fixture in her seventies, asked the candidate how he would manage the city's Department of Education, which has an annual budget of over $40 billion. She expected the usual "platitudes" about "the importance of a good education," etc. Instead, Yu explained, she was "stunned" by the depth of Zohran's response. He went "line by line" in describing problems in the budget. "He demonstrated knowledge of the challenges of reining in corruption" and discussed how he would work constructively with the powerful teachers union. "He got my vote!" Yu told me.

On that pleasant early June evening in Fort Greene, it was clear to all that the kid had chops. But most dynasties do not end quietly. Over in Midtown East, Goliath revved up his engine.

CHAPTER 8
Dodge Charger

After Andrew Cuomo resigned as governor amid a sexual harassment scandal in August 2021, a simple question lingered: Where did he live?

While in the governor's office for the past decade, Cuomo resided at either the Executive Mansion in Albany or with Sandra Lee, a one-time TV star and Cuomo's second long-time partner, at the large Westchester County home she owned in tawny Mount Kisco, 40 miles north of New York City. The pair split up in 2019.

After Cuomo's resignation in August 2021, where he lived through March 2025 remained a mystery. He did store his stuff at the Westchester mansion owned by his sister Maria and her husband Kenneth Cole, the fashion industry titan. But despite a $250,000 salary and a $5 million book deal, Cuomo had not purchased any property, a curious move for a former Housing and Urban Development (HUD) secretary. In the fall of 2024, as talk of his mayoral run heated up, reporters learned that Cuomo had recently registered to vote from a luxury Midtown building overlooking the East River. One of his daughters, Cara Kennedy-Cuomo,[57] inhabited the swanky unit, which rented for an eye-popping $8,000 per month.

In November 2024, *Hell Gate*'s Adlan Jackson toured Cuomo's new Sutton Place digs, a 38-story tower called "The Oriana." The amply staffed building featured amenities including a cardio gym on the roof deck. "Sutton Place," Jackson observed, "is the New York everyone wants—that's only real in campaign ads and in bygone visions of the city. It makes sense that Cuomo would want to live here if he's revving up a mayoral campaign." By the following March, the former governor had fully moved in, sending Cara to Brooklyn.

Cuomo officially threw his hat into the ring on Saturday, March 1, setting the tone for his primary campaign by releasing a nearly 20-minute video. Unlike Zohran's dynamic 100-second opening ad, the instant-frontrunner's rollout statement was poorly produced and comically dull. Although watching someone speak directly into a camera for 17.5 minutes is generally less than tantalizing, the protracted announcement got plenty of traction on Facebook, the Baby Boomer-preferred site where Cuomo has over 300,000 followers. The instant-frontrunner's large fan club no doubt grew exponentially over the pandemic, when the then-governor delivered life-or-death

---

[57] From 1990-2005, Cuomo was married to Kerry Kennedy, RFK's daughter. The pair had three daughters. The divorce was notoriously acrimonious.

information. Zohran's numbers on Facebook lagged behind, at just over 120,000 followers, whereas his next-gen campaign is far more active on Instagram, TikTok, and X.

"Intellectually, I have mastered social media," Cuomo informed his favorite reporter, WCBS-TV's Marcia Kramer, two days before the primary. "Practically, I have not mastered it." While the first assertion requires more evidence, the second one was abundantly clear vis-à-vis his announcement video.

A few weeks after Cuomo's launch, Zohran held a presser outside of the Oriana, introducing himself to the former governor's fellow residents. Andrew Epstein had proposed doing the event in order to "disrupt the Rose Garden," referring to the frontrunner's already-evident plan to steer clear of both the public and the press.

Although the Sutton Place appearance captured only modest media attention, it showed that Zohran was unafraid to challenge Goliath on his purported home turf. The insurgent candidate soon began to regularly question the former governor's bona fides as a city dweller, urging his supporters to help "send Andrew Cuomo back to the suburbs," an effective line of attack that helped undercut frontrunner Andrew Yang four years earlier.[58]

It would be erroneous to suggest that Cuomo's time in Westchester or Albany meant that he was unaware

---

58   During the pandemic Yang lived in New Paltz, 80 miles north of New York City.

of what was happening in New York City. But the lens through which he viewed the sprawling metropolis was quite narrow. During the nearly fifteen years he spent as a statewide elected official, Cuomo presided over two large Manhattan offices. The attorney general often works from an outpost in the financial district, whereas the governor is frequently at 3rd Avenue near 41st Street, close to Grand Central Station.

When the primary entered the homestretch in June, the *New York Times* asked Cuomo when he last lived in New York City. The answer? The late 1980s.

*

A charmless, high-rise center of power, Midtown East suited the most recent Governor Cuomo, who cut deals with many Manhattan real estate titans from there. Until his first term in office, Donald Trump regularly resided at a nearby place from which he famously launched his initial presidential campaign.

The developer built Trump Tower (at 5th Avenue between 56th and 57th Street) in the early 1980s with plenty of assistance from Mayor Ed Koch. Two decades later, like most large players in New York City real estate, Trump helped fill Cuomo's coffers.

As Cynthia Nixon highlighted in her 2018 run against Cuomo, between 2001 and 2009 the developer's ante to Andrew was $64,000. Like most politicians, Cuomo indignantly asserted that the money did not influence his actions. "I am going to be deeply critical of [Trump] and keep the contributions," the governor declared, in response to Nixon.

The future president viewed his transactions with politicians differently. "When you give [money to pols], they do whatever the hell you want them to do," Trump observed in 2016.[59]

During Cuomo's reign as governor, New York State's campaign finance system remained far less progressive than New York City's. Sky-high limits on contributions enabled Trump's fellow real estate titans to drop large sums in the multiple campaign accounts controlled by Cuomo.

Between 2010 and 2018, Len Blavatnik, a business associate of Trump's 2016 campaign manager Paul Manafort, deposited over $350,000 into the governor's war chest. In 2013, a leading developer of "Supertall" luxury towers near Central Park gave Cuomo $100,000 (and the state Democratic Party account another $100,000), yielding legislation that provided favorable tax breaks.[60]

Trump (b. 1946) and Cuomo (b. 1957) may belong to different political parties, but the two Baby Boomers share plenty of attributes. Both were raised in upscale neighborhoods in eastern Queens, near the border of Long Island's Nassau County. Nepotism indelibly influenced their career paths. Trump inherited his father's real estate empire. Mario Cuomo's son extended a political legacy. Both

---

59 *Washington Post* (9-7-2016).
60 *NY Daily News* (8-9-2013).

Donald and Andrew are bullies who have faced frequent accusations of sexual misconduct.

Just before the June 2025 primary, Marcia Kramer asked the mayoral frontrunner to explain his common roots with the president. "I'm no one to be trifled with," Cuomo replied. "And Trump is no one to be trifled with." After Zohran toppled Cuomo, Trump praised his fellow Boomer, illustrating that the Queens dudes still got along fine.

In 1977, Andrew, then nineteen, cut his teeth in city politics while working on his father Mario Cuomo's dogged, but unsuccessful campaign for mayor. Seeking the law-and-order vote in response to widespread looting that summer, Democrat Ed Koch shamelessly called for the reinstatement of the death penalty, which the legislature had eliminated twelve years earlier. Mario, en route to becoming a leading Catholic politician of the late twentieth century (alongside his friend Joe Biden), remained a steadfast opponent of capital punishment. After losing to Koch in the mayoral primary, the elder Cuomo opted to run as the Liberal Party candidate in the general election. Koch won easily.

It was during their next showdown with Koch that the Cuomo duo began to forge deep alliances with Black leaders and voters across the city. After the 1977 primary, Harlem's influential Congressman Charles Rangel had endorsed Koch. During his first term, Koch angered many Black leaders, causing Rangel to back Cuomo in the 1982 race for governor. Along with many leading Black ministers, Al Vann, an African-American power broker based in

Bed-Stuy, was also a key Cuomo ally. Black voters catapulted Mario into the Executive Mansion.

The elder Cuomo served three terms as governor, before losing to an upstate Republican (George Pataki) who made restoring the death penalty his key issue. Andrew then took an executive position with HUD under President Bill Clinton, moving up to become a Cabinet secretary in the Arkansas Democrat's second term. Close ties to a president who received large support from Black voters certainly did not hurt the younger Cuomo's reputation. Two days before the June 2025 primary, Clinton endorsed the now-mayoral candidate.

Starting in 2006, in his four consecutive wins for statewide offices, Andrew racked up large numbers of votes in Black communities from Harlem through Central Brooklyn to Southeast Queens. Whether that reflected equal enthusiasm for both Cuomos is an open question, though.

Two weeks before the 2025 mayoral primary, an audience member at a Zohran event in Greenwich Village asked about Cuomo's support from many Black leaders across the city. "I've had many conversations, including with pastors, who've described their endorsement of Andrew Cuomo as an endorsement of Mario's son," Mamdani replied.

According to State Sen. Jabari Brisport, Zohran's DSA comrade, the city's older Black voters generally view "trust" as much more important than "promises" about what a candidate's platform will do for them. Having been "lied to" many times over, Brisport told me, this large swath of the city's electorate views big plans quite skeptically.

Brisport, whose district spans from Fort Greene and Clinton Hill through Bed-Stuy to Brownsville, observes that many Black voters over fifty supported Cuomo mainly because he was quite familiar to them. Scandals notwithstanding, the former governor's daily televised updates during the pandemic had provided forceful reassurance that Mario's son was looking out for their well-being. As the primary race took shape, Brisport brought Zohran to meet Black clergy and community leaders.

In late April, Zohran spoke to a large number of older Black voters at Medgar Evers College in Crown Heights. Sponsored by the Brooklyn Democratic Party, the event organizers cut a deal with their preferred candidate. Cuomo would indeed make one of his rare public appearances—provided that the format was individual interviews with contenders, not a forum with many figures on stage responding to each other's comments.

Zohran's turn came second, and he began by informing the largely Black audience of a few hundred people that his middle name honors Kwame Nkrumah. The fifteen-minute slot allowed the newcomer to explain his proposals regarding public safety and affordability in response to questions raised by host Ayana Harry from NY1. Although the crowd gave him a favorable round of applause, it was more like Zohran had hit a solid single than a home run.

The fireworks came at the end of the event, when the former governor took his turn. As he sat down with Harry, a group of youthful, racially diverse protesters charged onto the stage, chanting "Cuomo lies—New Yorkers die," referring to the nursing home scandal during the pandemic. Other than when he got up to shake hands with some supporters, the frontrunner sat passively during the disturbance, which was resolved by the NYPD.

After Cuomo dismissed the dissenters' outburst with a "people in New York City always disagree"-type comment, Harry asked him about his initial campaign theme:

> Harry: *NYPD statistics show that on many serious crimes, the numbers are coming down. The city seems to be getting safer, but a lot of New Yorkers don't feel safer. How do you address that perception issue—and help folks just feel safer?*
>
> Cuomo: *I don't believe it's a perception issue. If I don't feel safe, I don't feel safe. And you saying to me, "You should feel safe because the statistics say I'm safer," that doesn't work for me. Don't tell me that my feeling is wrong, right? My feeling is legitimate because that's what I feel.*

To emphasize the point, the former governor stated that the "random assaults by mentally ill homeless people are one of the prime movers of this feeling of anxiety," which few people would dispute. But his only solution was greater NYPD presence below ground—not the mental health intervention teams Zohran and criminal justice activists advocate.

More problematic was what Cuomo called two "horrendous" incidents that recently happened on the subway— "people getting burned, people dying on subways and then being violated." The high-profile events involving an arson-murder and necrophilia were indeed eye-popping, but they were isolated cases, not indicative of a terrifying pattern.

Like many older voters (of all backgrounds) in the city, Cuomo's view of crime flows directly from the *New York Post*, which sets the table for local TV and radio news. Depending on location, severity, and the backgrounds of the people involved, a single violent incident can create shockwaves across the city.

Prior to joining the race, the suburban candidate clearly ingested plenty of scary headlines. "Dire is the vibe" is how *City & State*'s Holly Pretsky characterized Cuomo's protracted March 1 video statement. "The anxiety rises up in your chest as you're walking down into the subway," claimed the veteran Democrat. "You see it in the empty store fronts, the graffiti, the grime, the migrant influx, the random violence. The city just feels threatening, out of control."

As Ayana Harry mentioned at the Medgar Evers forum, the city's most important crime number had been trending downwards since Cuomo entered the field, with murders dropping by more than 40 percent from mid-March through mid-April. The frontrunner had banked on the "perception" that the city was besieged by violence. Mario's son wanted voters to fear killers, arsonists, and predators of all kinds so they would view him as their Dark Knight.

Tough luck, Batman.

*

After Cuomo cruised to reelection in 2018, there was chatter among pundits that he might run for president. The governor's closest aide later noted that Mario's pal Joe Biden talked him out of it, with the latter arguing that two moderate candidates would create an opening for a left-winger (either Bernie Sanders or Elizabeth Warren). When the pandemic struck in March 2020, Cuomo seized the national spotlight, scoring an Emmy Award for his daily televised press conferences. Less than eighteen months later, he would resign in disgrace, with the Emmy rescinded.

The downfall started in December 2020, when Lindsey Boylan, a former high-ranking staffer in the Cuomo administration, accused the governor of sexual harassment. According to Boylan, who was in her mid-thirties, Cuomo, then in his early sixties, frequently made comments about her "looks" and unexpectedly kissed her on the lips.

A flurry of accusations from present and past Cuomo staffers ensued. Charlotte Bennett, then in her mid-twenties, accused the governor of asking inappropriate questions about her sex life. Bennett's peer Brittany Commisso said that the state's top executive had fondled her. Karen Hinton, who worked as a HUD press aide for Cuomo, recalled that in 2000, Mario's son made "unethical" physical contact.

In early March 2021, Zohran and his five fellow DSA state legislators were among the early voices calling for Cuomo's resignation. AOC soon followed suit, as did Chuck Schumer, Kirsten Gillibrand and dozens of other mainstream Democrats.

That summer, Attorney General Tish James released a damning report confirming the accusations of eleven women against Cuomo. (A DOJ investigation later brought the number to thirteen.) The governor, the AG's investigators concluded, had engaged in "unwanted touching" that the women viewed as "deeply humiliating and offensive." Rather than face impeachment proceedings, Cuomo opted to resign a few days after James released her report. In a televised address on August 10, the guy who had micro-managed Albany for the past decade stated, "Given the circumstances, the best way I can help now is if I step aside and let government get back to government."

Cuomo apologized to his accusers and to his three daughters, telling the latter that "Your dad made mistakes." The governor's offspring were by no means the only people he cared about. however. "I love New York, and I love you," he assured viewers.

*

The loud calls for Cuomo's resignation did not stem just from the harassment scandal. Early in the pandemic, questions began to swirl about the high rate of deaths in the state's nursing homes. An eleventh-hour provision had been mysteriously inserted into the state budget (due April 1 each year) specifically granting those facilities immunity from pandemic-related lawsuits.

Cuomo, unsurprisingly, had collected significant campaign contributions from the nursing home industry during his time in Albany.[61] The state's large network of elder-care residences already had a checkered reputation—but the pandemic now turned the spotlight on their deadly practices.

In late March 2020, the State Department of Health (which answers to the governor) issued a directive instructing nursing homes to accept and readmit patients diagnosed with Covid-19. This meant that hospitals were sending vulnerable elders back to the shared living facilities, a recipe for disaster. After the lethal impact of the state order became clear in mid-April, Cuomo implausibly claimed that he did not know who issued it. He then declared that nursing homes did not "have the right to object" to the command.

Over 15,000 seniors ultimately died in New York's nursing homes during the pandemic, with over 40% of the fatalities at locations in the city, primarily in Queens, Brooklyn and the Bronx.

Even as Cuomo's daily TV presence elevated his status throughout 2020, critics across the political spectrum blasted his administration's nursing home policies. Janice Dean, a meteorologist on *Fox & Friends* who lost both her in-laws in elder care facilities during the pandemic, relentlessly denounced Cuomo on social media. Queens assemblyman Ron Kim, a Democrat who lost his uncle, had a high-profile showdown with Cuomo, with the legislator accusing the governor of verbal threats. "No man has ever spoken to me like that in my entire life," Kim told CNN.

---

61 *The Indypendent* (4-23-2020).

Meet Mayor Mamdani

As journalist Ross Barkan explains, the public thus witnessed two competing narratives regarding Cuomo during the pandemic. The governor and his allies (especially his younger brother Chris, then a CNN nightly host) created a "mythos of Cuomo [as] coronavirus conqueror." That competed with the "Cuomo killed grandma" charge amplified by Murdoch media outlets.[62]

It was up to the millions of New Yorkers trapped at home, with both traditional and social media as their main connections to the world, to decide which story to believe. With boosts from local celebrities including Rosie Perez and Chris Rock (both raised in Brooklyn), Cuomo convinced many people that he would shepherd them out of a very scary crisis.[55]

As Zohran and his team realized, their task was to show that regardless of what happened four years earlier, Cuomo was oblivious to voters' everyday concerns in 2025. Starting with the March presser at Sutton Place, Mamdani demonstrated that he was unafraid to challenge Goliath. In both style and substance, there was also a monumental gap between the two candidates.

Zohran is just under half Cuomo's age but has at least four times more energy. The smiling young guy took the subway, ran the marathon, chatted with voters while walking on city streets, and cheerfully shared playoff fever with excited Knicks fans.

---

62 Ross Barkan, *Cuomo: Return of the Dark Prince* (OR Books, 2025).

Meanwhile, a scowling old dude drove around in his beloved black Dodge Charger, a muscle car favored by suburban teenagers in the 1970s. And the only place Mario's kid seemed comfortable chatting was on the couch in Marcia Kramer's WCBS-TV studio.

*

Zohran joined Brad Lander and seven other candidates at a late March event in Cobble Hill, Brooklyn, near a wall with photos of loved ones who perished in nursing homes. But in general, Cuomo's role in that crisis did not receive much attention during the primary.

That was not the case for the accusations of sexual harassment, however. Lindsey Boylan, the former governor's initial accuser, remained particularly vocal in her condemnation of her former boss. From the day Cuomo entered the race through June 24, Boylan provided constant social media reminders about the misconduct accusations that caused Cuomo to resign.

Cuomo enthusiasts stood by their man, with one ubiquitous agitator slurring Boylan in front of her adolescent daughter on the weekend before the primary. Boylan nonetheless seemed hopeful that her efforts would pay off. On June 23, she advised her daughter that "I and every person I respect is doing all they can to beat this monster and that we are very hopeful today."

Two days earlier, Boylan's fellow Cuomo accuser Charlotte Bennett joined her at a press conference with Lander. As several candidates spotlighted, the former governor's hyper-aggressive legal team, led by powerhouse corporate attorney Rita Glavin, had collected over $60 million in taxpayer-funded legal fees.

Glavin crossed the line for many Cuomo critics by suing to obtain Bennett's gynecological records. That action contributed to Zohran's viral attack on Cuomo at the second televised debate.

Although there were countless mayoral forums held across the city through the winter and spring, Cuomo almost never bothered to attend. While he was required to participate in the two televised debates in June, the veteran pol hardly seemed thrilled to join the discussion.

More surprising is that after four years to workshop his explanations of the nursing home and harassment scandals, Cuomo's answers were meandering and lawyerly.

Goliath may drive a fast car, but he isn't very quick on his feet.

CHAPTER 9
Sticks and Stones

Although Kamala Harris and Chuck Schumer steered the Democratic Party away from Gaza during the 2024 election, Zohran and the DSA continued to pay plenty of attention to the humanitarian nightmare. As Liza Featherstone noted in her *Jacobin* interview with Mamdani at the time of his mayoral launch, Zohran "has been a stalwart supporter for justice in Palestine at a time of immense pressure for elected officials like him to keep their mouths shut on the ongoing genocide there." At the post-October 7 protests, the DSA legislator also had no qualms using the term "genocide" when criticizing Israel and the funding it receives from the U.S.

Prior to his entry into the 2025 race, the candidate told Featherstone, Gaza had already become an issue because of Eric Adams and the NYPD. In early May 2024, following the advice of deep-pocketed Zionists, including hedge-fund billionaire Dan Loeb, the NYPD stormed the Columbia University campus in order to break up a pro-Palestine protest. The police conducted a Fallujah-style door-to-door search in the activist-occupied Hamilton Hall, which the student leaders had renamed Hind's Hall in honor of Hind Rajab, a six-year-old Palestinian girl killed by the Israeli military in Gaza. In the process, a cop fired his weapon into an empty office. The NYPD said it was an accident.

"We could have seen students killed," Mamdani warned Featherstone. Mayor Adams, he continued, "has used his bully pulpit to erase an entire people's humanity, denying calls for a cease-fire. A *cease-fire*," Zohran repeated incredulously.

As journalist Peter Beinart argued the day after Mamdani's primary victory, leading Israel allies such as Loeb and Bill Ackman will lend their considerable financial support to any candidates who pledge "unqualified support" for Israel. Both Cuomo and Adams have no qualms about defending mass slaughter if it helps their political careers. Mamdani and the DSA showed that the next generation of New York City's political leaders would no longer remain silent about Palestine.

Even as Zohran's campaign gained momentum in early 2025, the insurgent's stance on Israel was treated by the media as somehow scandalous. The *New York Post* led the charge, running scores of news stories and opinion pieces that pounced on any past or recent utterance by Zohran that could be construed as antisemitic. The *Post*'s sundry cranky columnists were joined by special guest fellow travelers, including a well-known pro-Israel college basketball coach who visited New York City and took offense at Mamdani's pledge to carry out the International Criminal Court arrest warrant for Bibi Netanyahu.[63]

Cuomo, meanwhile, had joined the legal team defending Netanyahu. As I detailed in *Drop Site News*, the former New York attorney general announced that he would join the Alan Dershowitz-led retinue in late November 2024, at a Manhattan gathering of Chabad-Lubavitch movement, a powerful ultra-Orthodox Jewish group with close ties to Trump and Israel's current regime. Although the *Post* shared Cuomo's deference to Netanyahu, Rupert Murdoch's house organ did not support Mario's kid, for reasons discussed below.

In sync with the Trump White House, the *Post* cheered on the early March arrest and detention of Columbia University graduate student Mahmoud Khalil, which separated the pro-Palestine leader from his pregnant wife. The Trump administration invoked a McCarthy era-statute that allowed for the revocation of student visas for people deemed to be foreign policy threats.

When border czar Tom Homan, who supported Khalil's arrest, came to Albany a few days afterwards, Zohran angrily confronted him. "Do you believe in the First Amendment?" the assemblyman shouted, garnering

---

63 In criticizing Mamdani "divisiveness," Auburn University's Bruce Pearl offered (on July 3) the highly questionable contention that Alabama "provides an alternative vision: Cherishing faith and country fosters a healthy pluralism that represents America at her best."

national attention. The ACLU, Writers against the War on Gaza, and ousted Columbia Law professor Katherine Franke (an early Zohran for NYC donor) joined Mamdani in denouncing the Trump administration's capricious actions.

The day after his arrest, a *Post* story falsely connected Khalil to Hamas. Two weeks later, the tabloid claimed that the activist had been the "political affairs officer" at UNRWA, the relief agency Israel painted as pro-Hamas. In truth, Khalil had merely done an internship at the large organization, and UNRWA did not have a political affairs officer. The tabloid's approach to Zohran's rise was similarly hostile, with accuracy again viewed as an incidental concern.

*

Zohran's initial appearance on the *Post*'s cover[64] came in early April, by which point the insurgent was polling in second place. "Dangerous Mam," read a large *Post* front-page headline on Wednesday, April 2, which was placed next to an action shot of Zohran running. "They usually have a better pun game," Mamdani told me with a smile when we spoke shortly after his cover debut. "I'm not sure what that one even means." Although the DSA insurgent was still 20-25 points behind Mario's son, he was gaining ground, and the former's support for Palestine was not holding him back.

---

64 Although the *Post*'s website has exponentially more readers than the print edition, the tabloid's front page is still viewed by many within New York City's local political media as an agenda-setter, often influencing local TV news coverage.

Along with the large "Mam" headline and action shot of Zohran, the Murdoch rag included a small pic of Rep. Rashida Tlaib, adding a screenshot of Palestine flag emojis posted in response to the Squad member's recent Zoom call discussing Mamdani's campaign. Veteran columnist Michael Goodwin, a hardcore Trumper, denounced Zohran's support from Brooklyn's prominent Palestinian activist Linda Sarsour and Tlaib. The newspaperman smeared them as "two notorious antisemites," but did not make the same claim regarding Zohran. After the primary, however, Murdoch's hatchet man called the winner "a nepo baby who is a socialist antisemite." Unlike the *Times*, the *Post* minces few words.

In early May, Rupert's crew took aim at Ella Emhoff, another prominent Mamdani backer who is Kamala Harris' stepdaughter and lives in Bushwick. In the *Post*'s view, Emhoff is an "insanely rich nepo-baby" and a hypocrite for supporting a socialist. On Sunday night, May 4, the fashion designer attended a large Mamdani rally at Brooklyn Steel, a music venue in her neighborhood. Ella then shared a clip from the event on Instagram in which she declared her support for Zohran.

In their trash-spewing tirade, Murdoch's deputies declared that Emhoff's support showed that "Zohran 'Man of the People' Mamdani continues to win the hearts of nepo babies and Jew-haters." "To be fair," the editorial claimed, "Emhoff *does* represent a key Mamdani demographic: rich kids from out of town posing as gritty, tough native New Yorkers" (emphasis original). Support from Emhoff—who has advocated for Palestinian causes—illustrated what the *Post* claimed was "central to" Zohran's campaign and to the "coalitional politics of the modern left: rabid antisemit[ism]."

This unhinged attack made me curious about its origins. I asked Michael Benjamin, a member of the *Post* editorial team, whether he wrote the statement. He said no but clarified that "editorials are unsigned but represent the sentiment of the board."

"Why do you ask?" Benjamin queried.

"I'm wondering if my opposition to Israel's war crimes makes me an 'antisemite,'" I replied.

"What war crimes?" Benjamin responded. "War should be brutal and short. Antisemites don't believe in Israel's right to exist."

I was taken aback, but rather than prolong the exchange, I opted to send Benjamin a link to former Human Rights Watch figurehead Kenneth Roth's most insightful June 2024 *New York Review of Books* rundown of Israel's manifold violations of international law. Benjamin acknowledged receipt.[65]

---

65 The day after Zohran's October 23 launch party, Benjamin responded to Asad Dandia's enthusiastic X post about the event by stating "Is it true that no pagers were allowed?" referring to Israel's deadly assaults in Lebanon and Syria in September 2024. As *Semafor*'s Max Tani documented in a post-primary recap, Murdoch's guy later made another pager reference on X regarding Mamdani. According to Andrew Epstein, Zohran frequently brought up Benjamin's "jokes" when speaking to Muslim audiences.

By the end of May, Zohran clearly had the wind in his sails, causing the *Post* board to claim that "antisemitism may be the main reason why Assemblyman Zohran Mamdani is doing so well."

I checked in again with Benjamin, sending him a tweet from *Jewish Daily Forward* reporter Jacob Kornbluh showing Mamdani getting 20% support from the city's Jewish voters in a recent poll (placing Zohran only 11% behind Cuomo, and slightly ahead of Brad Lander). I asked whether such enthusiasm undercut the antisemitism charges against Zohran.

Benjamin responded by calling the 20% of Jews supporting Zohran as the "self-hating ones, who are oversampled" in the poll.

"The 'self-hating ones' who don't like war crimes?" I asked.

"What war crimes?" Benjamin reiterated.

Benjamin (b. 1958, in the Bronx), who is Black and Protestant, thus deployed a twentieth-century slur against liberal Jews. While Mamdani supporters (including yours truly) may find his views appalling, Benjamin, like the rest of his colleagues at the *Post*, at least does not try to hide his opinions.

*

Although the *Post* relentlessly thrashed Mamdani throughout the primary (and well into the summer), Murdoch's team showed no love for Cuomo. Had the powerful outlet backed the former governor, it's conceivable that the race would have been closer.[66]

On Saturday, March 1, the day Cuomo formally launched his mayoral run, the *Post* editorial team deemed him to be "the biggest liar in New York." The board certainly did not like the former governor's handling of the pandemic, particularly the nursing home scandal. Written as a sarcastic piece of advice, the statement further warned young women that Cuomo will "grope you."

What seemed to bother Murdoch's crew most of all was that although he governed as a centrist, Cuomo on occasion tacked left (if he saw the wind blowing that direction). As the editorial mentioned, Cuomo banned fracking and signed progressive criminal justice legislation, including bail reform. Any leftward shifts are anathema to the *Post*, the de facto mission of which is to aid the 1% by keeping the 99% at war with each other. In April, the *New York Times* reported that the former governor was so frustrated with the tabloid's unfavorable coverage that he sought to meet with Rupert Murdoch (b. 1931) to clear the air.

It's not certain whether Cuomo ever got a chance to pull on the Fox patriarch's ear, but he didn't get much favorable treatment from the tabloid down the stretch. As soon as the June 24 primary ended, the *Post* unsuccessfully

---

66 As the eminent U.S. historian Eric Foner has observed, "The great thing about counterfactual (i.e. 'What if...') questions is that there are no wrong answers." Given that the *Post* helped propel Adams in 2021, any show of support from the Murdoch outlet may have helped motivate Cuomo's older voter base.

tried to force the toppled frontrunner into removing his name from the general election ballot. Meanwhile, on Wednesday, June 25, Mayor Eric Adams visited the *Post*'s headquarters in Midtown. The mayor had just denounced Zohran as a "snake-oil salesman for socialism" on *Fox & Friends*, so he was in Murdoch's neighborhood.

*

"Zohran Mamdani is an antisemite!" "His father is antisemitic!" So came the repetitious onslaught of slurs from an extremely aggressive antagonist at a Sunset Park rally on an otherwise beautiful spring afternoon at the beginning of June.

The heckling came from a man who was previously known for waving huge Trump flags at campus protests. RR[67] had recently harassed staffers at an Alexa Avilés campaign event in late May. Zohran, who had been receiving death threats, now had a bodyguard who came with him to Sunset Park.

RR's M.O. is to record video of himself while he gets into people's faces, brushes up against his targets, then tells opponents that they will get arrested for pushing him. It's W.W.E.-type theater, except that RR's venom is not fake.

Zohran had traveled back to scenic Sunset Park, which offers a panoramic sweep of the Statue of Liberty and the downtown Manhattan skyline, in order to give a

---

67 Although RR's name is well-known to the activists he has confronted, it merits no mention here.

pre-canvass pep talk. As scores of volunteers eager to knock on doors for Mamdani and Avilés looked on from the hillside grass, a phalanx of staffers for both campaigns sought to restrain RR while he spewed venom and tried to move toward Zohran.

Clad in combat gear while wearing a black MAGA baseball cap, RR pushed a brave but diminutive young woman out of the way and then mixed it up with a beefier, male Avilés staffer he had previously baited at the May event. After several minutes of skirmishing, the DSA antagonist went to the other side of a fence.

When RR reached into a duffel bag, many of us feared that he was pulling out a gun. Instead, it was a megaphone, enabling the loudmouth to amplify his vitriol. "You're all a bunch of socialists!" was one of the few accurate things RR shouted, provoking a few chuckles. "God bless Trump!" he screamed.

It was clear to everyone on-hand that RR was almost certainly a habitual consumer of Murdoch bile. At the event I asked the candidate about an article that had been on the *Post* site since the previous afternoon. Zohran's answer surprised me.

"Did you see the story about Stringer's call for the NYPD to partner with the ADL?" I inquired, referring to one of his competitor's flailing attempts to score points with conservative Jewish Democrats by letting the far-right ADL decide which social media posts are antisemitic and may pose imminent danger.

"Really? I haven't seen it," Zohran replied, leading me to surmise that, unlike most candidates, Mamdani's morning routine did not include checking out who Murdoch's minions were bashing or hyping that day.

According to Andrew Epstein, Zohran's news consumption during the primary followed no clear pattern. Sometimes he knew very specific details buried deep in stories from an assortment of outlets. Other times he was unaware of coverage that many in his inner circle followed closely. Because "the volume of *Post* stuff about Zohran was so intense," Andrew explains, "we often opted not to call his attention to the latest attack." Although Mamdani sometimes looked at the *Post,* Epstein says the candidate did not do so "obsessively."

Other than denounce Zohran, it's not clear what the DSA hater had hoped to accomplish that Sunday afternoon in Sunset Park. Although his attacks surely could be heard in areas surrounding the park, RR directed them towards Mamdani and Avilés volunteers who had decided to spend their weekend leisure time knocking on voters' doors.

As RR continued to harangue, I asked a thirty-something male canvasser wearing a patterned short-sleeve button-down shirt the following question: "Do you think this dude reads the *New York Post*?"

"I think he writes it," the millennial quipped, without missing a beat.

CHAPTER 10
A Creative Class

A successful long-shot election campaign in a sizable race requires six major ingredients: a compelling candidate, a timely message, the necessary funding, a strong field operation, media savvy, and an innovative creative design team.

Zohran clearly had chops, and his agenda met the moment. Although he was not the only candidate with substantial funds, Mamdani's volunteer army was unmatched. From day one, no rival contender came even remotely close to matching Zohran for NYC's overall media game. Zohran's marketing crew was also nothing if not state of the art (or craft). Meanwhile, in sync with its candidate, Team Cuomo's campaign materials were extremely yesterday.

One day after Mamdani's primary triumph, *New York* magazine's city editor Christopher Bonanos assessed the winning campaign's graphic design output. The veteran journalist heaped praise on Mamdani's team. By contrast,

Meet Mayor Mamdani

Bonanos observed, "I cannot for the life of me tell you what Andrew Cuomo's logotype looks like."

Whereas Cuomo's logo stuck with the familiar red, white and blue scheme, Zohran's palate was far from "conventional," explained Bonanos. Mamdani's main signage discarded the first two parts of the trinity altogether, and—according to designer Aneesh Bhoopathy—the campaign's most-used blue backdrop verged slightly toward violet.

A former Queens resident (now living in Philly), Bhoopathy told Bonanos that his firm's "mood board was definitely New York iconography: taxicab yellow, MetroCard primary colors, bodega awnings, stuff people are familiar with in the New York street." The "ZOHRAN" lettering in the logo found on the campaign's posters, buttons, and bandanas was hand-drawn, paying homage to a typeface named Boheld. Set against the blue backdrop, the orange-lined yellow lettering was eye-catching, with the mustard tinge within the body of each letter enhancing the appeal.

Zohran was an early teen when social media first debuted. Many of his younger followers have grown up in a world in which images vastly outweigh the power of the written word. While it would be shocking if a millennial mayoral candidate did not have compelling graphics, it's not at all surprising that Cuomo ignored the importance of his campaign's visual appeal, or lack thereof.

Bhoopathy, meanwhile, hit what many in the U.S. would call a home run, although cricket devotees might refer to it as a "sixer."

*

Rather than send out several rounds of glossy mailers to likely primary voters, Mamdani's legions of volunteers aimed to make direct contact with them. And if no one answered, the door-knocker would leave campaign lit. At my co-op apartment building in Sunset Park, I returned home at least four times and found materials for Mamdani and/or DSA Councilwoman Alexa Avilés either on my doorknob or under my front door. Such direct outreach creates a far greater chance that the prospective voter will actually look at the material. When oversized materials get stuffed into small mailboxes, they simply create clutter. Only politics geeks like me are likely to pay attention to the declarations for or against countless candidates.

Zohran's lit left by canvassers also stood out for its stellar design. One door-handle piece featured an action pic of the candidate holding a microphone, placed above the campaign's stylish logo in orange against a solid blue background (the color scheme of the New York Mets). In yellow, the statement encouraged voters to "Rank Zohran #1 for a city you can afford," with the final word in red.

The handbill further listed Zohran's key platform planks, then showed pics of endorsers AOC and Rep. Nydia Velázquez, along with the logos of the DSA, the Working Families Party, and DC 37, the large union of city government clerical workers. It concluded with poll site info and a photo of a smiling Zohran. That is a lot of campaign info to pack into a single piece of campaign lit, but the presentation made it quite visually appealing.

The reverse side of the same piece was in Spanish, with a new top photo showing Zohran with Avilés and fellow DSA lawmaker Marcela Mitaynes as well as Brooklyn Borough President Antonio Reynoso. Sunset Park's diverse Spanish-speaking population includes many Puerto Ricans (e.g. Avilés) and Dominicans (who may identify with Reynoso). Until 2022, Velázquez represented the area in Congress.

Stylish and fluent, Zohran's campaign lit reinforced the candidate's upbeat message. It was also produced and paid for by the insurgent's own team, via public funding amassed overwhelmingly with small donations from teachers, health care workers, and sundry creative professionals. Cuomo's big-money backers got much less bang for their bucks.

*

After he entered the race in March, Cuomo quickly amassed $4 million, spurred by hundreds of maximum donations ($2,100) from people who clearly are not educators or health care staffers. By the end of the primary, the frontrunner received over $4 million in matching funds. About half of the $5.5 million Cuomo's campaign doled out was for TV ads.

Dark money did most of the talking on Cuomo's behalf. Although New York City has a quite progressive matching funds program, outside spending for candidates cannot be restricted (because of *Citizens United*). The city's Campaign Finance Board tracks the money flow from PACs.

Fix the City, the lead PAC supporting Cuomo, hauled in just over $25 million by June 30, almost entirely from

1% donors or major corporations. Michael Bloomberg blazed the money trail, dumping $8.3 million into the PAC's coffers. DoorDash, angry about pro-delivery worker measures recently passed by the City Council, made a down payment of a million bucks on Cuomo. Three people connected to the Estée Lauder cosmetics empire also delivered a combined $1 million.

Billionaire financiers Bill Ackman and Daniel Loeb, both leading Israel hawks, kicked in $500,000 and $350,000, respectively, with Loeb also spearheading Cuomo's campaign fundraising. Oil baron John B. Hess ponied up $500,000 to Fix the City and entertainment mogul Barry Diller dropped $250,000.

Over fifteen high-rollers matched Diller's ante. Several leading real estate developers joined that list, including those responsible for Manhattan "supertall" skyscrapers and large luxury condo projects on the Brooklyn waterfront.[68] By the time polls opened on June 24, Fix the City had spent over $20.5 million[69] on everything from taxi-cab billboards to text messages. Mailboxes across the five boroughs overflowed with pro-Cuomo campaign literature. So many different candidates distribute mailers during election season that the impact of any single glossy piece seems minimal, especially the generic material produced on Cuomo's behalf.

---

68 Alice Walton, the Walmart heiress, was the most recognizable name among the 35 or so donors giving between $100-$250,000.
69 By the end of the primary, the PAC spent roughly $22.4 million, presumably keeping $2.7 million to spend on the general election. A handful of other groups spent over a combined $4 million more.

Meet Mayor Mamdani

Despite its deep reservoir of funds, Fix the City did not invest in an even minimally creative ad creation team. Team Cuomo's marketing output was cartoonishly retrograde, which was especially surprising given that Bloomberg, the Lauders, and Barry Diller surely know a few inventive folks on Madison Avenue.

The gist of Fix the City's output was stridently anti-Mamdani. Because of his criticisms of Israel, his past support for defunding the NYPD, and his socialist worldview, Zohran needed to be stopped. The PAC's arguments regarding why voters should support their candidate were far less affirmative. "For a safe and more affordable NYC, vote Cuomo," urged Fix the City in one of its countless mailers. The handbill's front side further included the PAC's preferred photo of the veteran Democrat, in which the wincing former governor sports a furrowed brow and stern expression. The flip-side of the same glossy mailer warns "YOU MUST VOTE TO STOP ZOHRAN MAMDANI'S RADICAL PLANS." No policy details accompanied the generic rally cries.

In smaller font, "We Demand Defund the NYPD" is superimposed over a photo of a young Zohran wearing a non-Western shirt. In a second, more recent picture, the less-exoticized insurgent candidate holds a microphone. A deceptive *New York Post* quote placed between the two shots of the candidate declares that "Mamdani wants to take 'police out of high-crime areas.'"[70]

---

[70] The quote is taken from an interview in which a Muslim female host asks a younger Zohran about the aggressive actions of police in "high-crime areas." Mamdani responds by discussing the need

The PAC's attacks never invoked *All in the Family*'s Archie Bunker, but the specter of the archetypal Queens working-class bigot of the 1970s hovered. Legally, the Cuomo campaign could not coordinate with Fix the City, although candidates can denounce slurs made on their behalf, which Mario's son never did.

Yet in presenting their guy from Queens as a sneering modern-day Archie, Fix the City may have unwittingly built support for a halal version of "Meathead," Bunker's lefty son-in-law.

*

Fix the City spent roughly $6.5 million running TV and internet ads from early March through mid-May. They were more polished and contemporary than the PAC's other productions. Two initial 30-second TV spots featured Cuomo interacting with older, mainly Black folks and touted his record.

Starting in early June, the Fix team started to focus almost entirely on attacking Cuomo's fast-ascending rival, spending over $7 million on a new round of TV and internet placements (and another $7 million or so on mailers, etc.). Mamdani, the ads reiterated, was a "radical" and "a risk we can't afford" who continued to support defunding the police.

As primary day neared, Team Cuomo's TV spots also played up the *New York Times* editorial board's denunciations of

---

for more community intervention teams but does not actually say that cops should play no role.

the newcomer. The same crew of mixed-race purported Cuomo fans who appeared in the initial ads cropped up again in the later round. The former governor spent such a minimal amount of time interacting with voters that there was little other footage to use.

It's hard to grab someone's attention with a mass text message, no matter how exciting the candidate might be. Zohran for NYC's blasts also lacked punch, primarily because an automated statement is an impersonal form of contact. Fix the City's spam was nonetheless revealing.

After a lengthy paragraph touting the former governor's "experience," one of the PAC's text missives read, "In these uncertain times, we must STOP Zohran Mamdani." The alert offered no explanation as to why Zohran posed such a dire threat. One potential, unintended effect of such a statement might have been to spur an unfamiliar voter to seek out more details about the charismatic new contender.

Although "robo-texts" may be ignored or viewed simply as a nuisance by recipients, they're very cheap, enabling campaigns or outside spenders to send two million messages for well under $100,000. They also can target specific subsets of voters. Like their preferred candidate, Fix the City's communiques on election day were a throwback to New York City's tribal politics of yesteryear.

In a message aimed at the "NYT audience,"[71] a robot identifying as "Beth" started by declaring that the "*New*

---

71 The city's Campaign Finance Board website includes copies of the materials distributed by outside spending groups.

York Times, *Daily News* and *New York Post* all agree: DO NOT RANK MAMDANI." In the late twentieth century, such unanimity likely would have knocked out an upstart candidate. But unlike the primary just four years before, pronouncements by the *Times* and *Post* carried no weight in June 2025.

Fix the City's election-day missives provided a theater of the absurd. In reaching out to "working-class voters" (presumably white ethnics), "Harry" claimed that his wife is terribly afraid of Mamdani. Jewish voters, meanwhile, heard from "Rachel, for one last time, I promise!" A purportedly Black texter named "Dave" began his message by telling recipients that "I couldn't stay away!"

The various PAC attacks sought to deflate Zohran's momentum, but it is tricky to gauge the impact of the multi-pronged effort. Amid the deluge of smears, polls showed steadily increasing support for Mamdani. Cuomo gained no ground from the many millions of dollars spent on his behalf.

*

Fix the City's egregious sleaze spawned a viral backlash against the mix of anti-Muslim bigotry and bullying funded by the city elite. On June 11, the day before the second televised debate, Jacob Kornbluh, senior political reporter for the *Forward*, posted what appeared to be a new Fix the City mailer. The content—which asserted that Mamdani "rejects" Israel and "Jewish rights" (as well the NYPD and capitalism)—was incendiary, but a clumsily photoshopped thickening and darkening of Mamdani's beard caused the story to blow up.

Mamdani seized the opportunity to connect Cuomo's elite donors to an obvious Islamophobic hit job. Just before noon on June 12, the insurgent's team released a statement in which Zohran declared that "Andrew Cuomo's SuperPAC—funded by the same billionaires that elected Donald Trump—is trying to buy this election through fear-mongering and ignorance."

A Fix the City spokeswoman insisted that the mailer with the distorted beard was a rejected mock-up that never circulated. Regardless, Team Cuomo's slimy tactics ended up benefiting Mamdani, who pointedly invoked the distorted mailer in that night's debate.

On the weekend before the primary, with the trendlines during early voting clearly favoring Zohran, the flailing Cuomo crew solicited headline-making endorsements from two members of the Democratic Party's old guard. First up was Jim Clyburn, the seventeen-term House member from South Carolina who helped snuff out Bernie Sanders' 2020 presidential bid. Next was Mario Cuomo's pal Bill Clinton, who had made Andrew a member of his Cabinet.

Favorable legacy media coverage notwithstanding, neither Democratic pillar's backing suggested that Cuomo might be the candidate of the future. But what is most notable is how the high-profile plugs reached voters. Team Cuomo touted the fact that Clyburn and Clinton had recorded robocalls, which harkened back to the pre-cellphone era.

Clyburn's Southern drawl may have appealed to some older Black voters; and although his voice sounds a bit shaky these days, there is no mistaking Bill Clinton's familiar inflections. But how many voters picked up the phone, listened to the entire call—and felt inspired to vote for Cuomo—is an open question.

When Cuomo visited Brooklyn's large Christian Cultural Center on the Sunday before the primary, the congregation responded enthusiastically to mention of Clinton's support. Reverend A.R. Bernard, a powerful off-stage player in city politics, told a *New York Times* reporter that Cuomo spoke "brilliantly" for five minutes, during which he slammed the DSA. But instead of interacting with the congregation after his remarks, the former governor exited. In general, Cuomo "was not on the streets, where the people are," observed Rev. Bernard. "Maybe we have to be careful when we assume that we've got enough reputation, history, and gravitas to float."[72]

As Bernard acidly noted, even when he showed up to a friendly room, Mario's son seemed temperamentally unwilling to engage with voters. After his humiliating primary defeat, Cuomo appeared to realize that he needed to interact with people more. He hit the streets in casual clothes and shook a lot of hands. Cuomo's new approach to the general election initially yielded mixed results. As CNN's Gloria Pazmino reported in late July, when the candidate visited a public housing site in East Harlem, a man "pulled Cuomo in for a handshake, took

---

72 As quoted by Nicholas Fandos on X (6-27-2025).

out his phone for a selfie, and as the former three-term governor of New York smiled for the camera, told him, 'I can't wait to watch you lose again.'"

*

Like the veteran Democrat himself, Cuomo's campaign team and Fix the City projected a downbeat, dreary vision of the future. Mamdani and his millennial crew were the polar opposite. Team Zohran projected future vs. past, optimism vs. cynicism, vitality vs. fatigue.

On the weekend before the primary, Cuomo talked up his handling of Superstorm Sandy, which happened thirteen years earlier. "This is not the time for on-the-job training," he insisted. It was his umpteenth attempt to call attention to Mamdani's lack of executive experience. In truth, Cuomo's handling of Sandy had sparked much criticism.[73] As his campaign showed, disaster management is not Cuomo's strong suit.

---

73 As Zephyr Teachout reminded her X followers (6-24-2025), during Sandy residents of Long Island experienced extended power outages, sparking criticism of Cuomo and other state officials for their poor communication regarding when area electricity would be restored.

CHAPTER 11
Buckle Up

"Mamdani passes on condemning the Holocaust," read the alarming email subject line of an influential morning newsletter from *Politico*'s New York Playbook on Friday, May 16. Thus began a whirlwind ride for Zohran, which did not stop until his victory party forty nights later. The journey saw Mamdani's stance on Israel move to the center of the race for mayor of New York City.

One night earlier, the insurgent candidate had appeared at a mayoral forum at the Public Theater near Astor Place hosted by the left-leaning publications *Hell Gate* and *New York Focus*. When Mamdani exited the stage prior to the other two candidates (chipper Brad Lander and very droll Scott Stringer),[74] those of us in attendance wondered where the DSA's man headed off to.

---

74 Asked to name their favorite New York City films, Mamdani answered *Do the Right Thing*, Lander said *Anora*, and Stringer (b.

Meet Mayor Mamdani

The next morning, as seen on his campaign socials, Zohran had zipped from the East Village to Xanadu, a roller rink in Bushwick. There, he took a panoramic selfie video that showed hundreds of wildly enthusiastic supporters in the house. It must have been dizzying for Mamdani to wake up to *Politico*'s Holocaust sucker punch. Yet while Zohran's Zionist critics turned up the heat, some of the insurgent candidate's pro-Palestine allies accused him of watering down his stance towards Israel.

Politico's buzzy Holocaust headline was not paired with a coherent story, but the *New York Post* and its social media devotees eagerly helped amplify it. Each year, the New York legislature approves scores of resolutions on subjects ranging from important historical events to current controversies including the use of A.I. The statements are passed via voice vote. Zohran, in fact, affirmed his support for this year's Holocaust resolution, as he had done previously. But unlike in past years, Mamdani was not a co-sponsor of the 2025 resolution.

As Zohran explained in a video statement recorded later on May 16, he decided at the outset of this year not to co-sponsor any resolutions because he and his fellow legislators are inundated with them. Although *Politico*'s coverage of Mamdani had not been favorable up to this point, it was now adopting the Murdoch organ's smear tactics.

"I am not a supporter of Zohran Mamdani but the notion that his non-sponsorship of the Holocaust resolution means

---

1960) said *Taxi Driver*, prehaps forgetting that Travis Bickle (Robert DeNiro) tries to assassinate a political candidate.

anything is disconnected from what goes on in Albany," Assemblyman Micah Lasher posted on X two days after the story went viral. A Jewish Democrat representing the Upper West Side, Lasher noted that he and his colleagues get "dozens of emails every day" about proclamations of all kinds, and that he finds the "resolution business to be rather silly."

The mundane facts mattered little to *Politico*, the *Post*, or kindred forces. Since 2021, *Politico* has been owned by German publisher Axel Springer, a stridently pro-Israel media powerhouse.[75] In a May 19 editorial, *AMNY*, a free morning paper owned by a longtime Cuomo ally, inanely (and inaccurately) declared that Zohran's unwillingness to condemn "the horrors of the Holocaust in writing and with a vote on the floor" disqualified him.

New York City was experiencing a twenty-first-century outbreak of what Dickens famously called "an age of foolishness."

*

Andrew Epstein, Zohran's communications director during the primary, vividly recalls his own reaction to *Politico*'s Holocaust smear. "I said, 'Wtf?' and started firing off texts and emails," explained Andrew, who is in his late thirties and lives near Zohran in Astoria. Along with Mamdani's then-political director Julian Gerson and the campaign's media strategist Morris Katz, Andrew is Jewish.

---

75 See Ari Paul, "Politico Staff Must Toe New Owner's Line—Including Endorsing Israel," *FAIR* (11-25-2021).

The same *Politico* hit job called attention to a second pro-Israel resolution in the assembly that Zohran did not support. Later that Friday morning, Zohran held a presser aimed at spotlighting his less-sensational plans to help small businesses in the city. After Mamdani opened the floor (actually, the sidewalk) to questions, reporters asked, "Do you support Israel's right to exist?"

"Yes, I do support Israel's right to exist as a state," Zohran replied. On social media, numerous millennial Mamdani backers began to ridicule the media's relentless focus on Israel. Even when he stated his positions clearly, Zohran was portrayed as somehow evasive.

Along with Epstein and campaign videographer Donald Borenstein, Zohran spent that Friday afternoon filming the insurgent's response video. That night, Andrew and Donald went out to dinner.

When Andrew returned home to Astoria around 10:30 p.m., he got a call from Zohran. The tireless contender wanted his comms guy to join him outside Madison Square Garden, where the Knicks had just finished off their arch-rival Celtics and fans were celebrating like they'd won the NBA title.

Earlier that week, Zohran posted a clip of himself wearing a Knicks cap backwards at a watch party outside of the Garden. A middle-aged white guy in a sleeveless shirt had his right arm around the candidate, while his left index finger pointed to the multi-colored Knicks basketball spinning rapidly on the candidate's head. "Here we are," Zohran said playfully. "We're spinning a ball." It was a memorable moment that did well across platforms. Spontaneity yields results.

Andrew journeyed back from Astoria and met up with campaign aide Spencer Goldberg and Zohran, the only person outside the Garden sporting a suit and tie. The upbeat mayoral hopeful used his lapel mic to interview an assortment of young male fans. Nearly everyone at such gatherings is a social media maven, and many are aspiring performers. "I'm feeling impeccable," said a large, likely Eastern European guy in his twenties. A 21-year-old Latino jumped in to say he would be voting for Zohran. A rotund Black guy, clad in a matching Knicks jersey and beanie, launched into a comedy routine. To the Pacers (the Knicks' next-round opponent), the twenty-something offered fake advance condolences: "I'm so sorry. I'm so sorry...for absolutely nothing!" he yelled at the camera, with his pals roaring behind him and Zohran laughing along.

Andrew returned home, edited the footage and posted clips on the campaign's platforms at 3:15 a.m. A day that began with the Holocaust attack ended on a boisterous note. Amid the madness, Zohran did not stop having fun, suggesting that hate sometimes can be counteracted by ignoring it.

While the insurgent candidate was out on the streets with Knicks fans, his name, face, and message reached people watching at home or in bars. According to Elle Bisgaard-Church, Zohran for NYC's campaign manager during the primary, "We made a massive investment in visibility during the Knicks playoff run, understanding that a victory would be dependent on a feeling of joy and possibility."[76]

Starting in late April, Zohran's campaign was the first to hit the airwaves, with its initial ad debuting during a Knicks early playoff game. Produced by Fight Agency, run by Democratic consultant Rebecca Katz,[77] the initial 30-second spot was a state-of-the-craft mix of campaign messaging and criticism of Cuomo, Adams, and their billionaire funders. Another ad that aired later in the Knicks run showed Zohran walking up to tenants and informing them about his rent freeze plan. With New York City apartment buildings providing the stage, the spot evoked *West Side Story*. Here, Zohran was straightforward, not playful. Rather than sing and dance, Mr. Cardamom played it straight.

The Knicks' playoff run eventually flamed out, but Zohran's quest for the title continued. With polls showing the insurgent gaining increasing strength, Mamdani soon faced new foes.

*

At the same time as the Israel controversies blew up, Zohran gained increasing support from city residents. Taken in the first week of May, a Marist College survey of nearly 3,400 likely Democratic voters showed Cuomo leading the second-place Mamdani by 37-18%, with the

---

[76] After the primary, Bisgaard-Church became Mamdani's senior advisor.

[77] Katz is no relation to Mamdani's media strategist Morris Katz, although the latter also works for Fight Agency.

frontrunner not reaching the necessary 50% until the fifth round of ranked-choice tabulations.

Between May 14 and 18, Workbench Strategy, a progressive research firm retained by the Mamdani campaign, conducted an internal poll that showed Cuomo up 41-28% in round one and not prevailing until round seven. Because they are commissioned by specific candidates, internal polls should be taken with a grain of salt. The Workbench sample size was also only 500 likely voters. The mid-May findings nonetheless started to make an upset win for Zohran seem realistic. His momentum was growing fast.

A few nights after *Politico*'s hit piece, Zohran spoke in Brooklyn's Gowanus at an issue launch party for *Acacia*, a progressive Muslim magazine that debuted in 2024. After the candidate's remarks received a friendly reception, a Palestinian American activist named Anas Saleh angrily confronted Mamdani.

Saleh pointedly accused the candidate of "being hypocritical" when calling for "Free Palestine while saying Israel has a right to exist." The activist said that he had family in Palestine who were under attack, insisting that "Israel does not have the right to exist." The candidate heard him out, but Saleh exited before Mamdani could reply.

Palestinian American Muslim leader Nerdeen Kiswani, the Bay Ridge-based founder of Within Our Lifetime, promoted Saleh's statements on social media. In Kiswani's view, Zohran "never should have" affirmed support for the colonizer's statehood. Mamdani, Kiswani argued, was "trying to appease genocidal maniacs."

As I explained in *Drop Site News*, Zohran responded by addressing concerns about his position directly. The night after the Saleh confrontation, Zohran attended a trans community town hall hosted by Park Slope-based Ceyenne Doroshow, a leading Black activist. Many attendees had participated in Palestine solidarity protests.

Prior to detailing his plans to defend trans rights as mayor, Zohran told the gathering that he wanted "to address something I know is on many of your minds." The candidate assured the group that his position on "Palestinian human rights, liberation, and Gaza" had not changed.

"I will not walk away from my principles or my track record," Zohran continued. "And I don't believe any of us can look away while Israeli war crimes continue to escalate, and thousands of children are being slaughtered." He then reaffirmed his support for BDS and spoke about his "Not on Our Dime" legislation that strips tax-exempt status from New York nonprofits that aid Israel's war crimes.

Andrew Epstein, meanwhile, issued a statement stressing that "Zohran has been consistent in his belief that Israel has the right to exist [with] a responsibility to adhere to international law, and that he supports non-violent movements to ensure compliance with that law."

Rather than modify his support for Palestinian rights, or try to mollify his anti-Israel critics, the DSA candidate remained steadfast. This meant that he was now incurring fire from two different directions, although one side's arsenal contained far heavier artillery.

*

As June opened, Zohran was clearly ascending. But it still remained hard to project victory. I checked in with New York City's next-gen vote wiz Michael Lange, who served as an adviser to Mamdani's campaign.

Eric Adams received 290,000 first-place votes in the 2021 primary, so I asked Lange whether he thought 250,000 was attainable for Zohran. "Yes, I think he can," Michael said, "but turnout would need to exceed one million." The insurgent had been polling well in Brooklyn and stood to collect plenty of votes in Northwest Queens. But as Lange noted, Mamdani couldn't win without racking up large totals in Manhattan.

Late on Monday night, June 2, a far-right city councilwoman from Queens took aim at Zohran. Vickie Paladino (b. 1954), one of six Republican members on the 51-seat body, is a hard-core Trumper who represents a northern Queens neighborhood called Whitestone, the population of which happens to be quite white.

That evening, Paladino's team[78] appeared to have conducted a very deep dive into Mamdani's tweets from 2019. Lo and behold, they found something "damning." The councilwoman shared it with her 33,000 followers on X.

As the 2020 presidential race took shape, Zohran had tweeted three photos of himself from Bernie Sanders' 2016 campaign, including one in which he and Nina Turner

---

78 When the Proud Boys-aligned Paladino first ran for state senate in 2018, her son Thomas Paladino, Jr., then 41, told *Gothamist* (10-17-2018) that he handled his mom's social media accounts.

jointly held a small Bernie sign. Above the pics, the tweet from the aspiring assemblymember read:

> *I couldn't vote for @BernieSanders in 2016 because I wasn't a citizen yet, but I can't wait for my first presidential vote to be for him in 2020.*
> *And I'm even more excited to share a ballot with him and help build the political revolution from Albany to Washington.*

Although Mamdani, who became a dual U.S.-Ugandan citizen in 2018, expressed pride in exercising his right to vote, Paladino seized the opportunity to stoke Birtherist hate. At least one guy from Queens surely approved when Paladino declared:

> *Let's just talk about how insane it is to elect someone to any major office who hasn't even been a US citizen for ten years—much less a radical leftist who actually hates everything about the country and is here specifically to undermine everything we've ever been about.*
> *Deport.*

The one-word second paragraph furnished Paladino's crystal-clear message.

In New York City's not-distant past, any comparable display of nativist bigotry toward immigrants by a prominent figure would have been roundly condemned. Editorial boards would call foul, religious and civic leaders would demand an apology, and there would be a loud chorus of calls for the hatemonger to resign.

"Everyone should denounce this," veteran civil rights attorney Norman Siegel (b. 1943) told me at the time. Although Mamdani and his fellow Democratic candidates blasted Paladino, good government groups, faith leaders, and editorial boards mostly remained silent.

The *New York Times* ran a story that foregrounded Zohran's steadfast response: "Death threats. Islamophobic bigotry. Now a sitting councilmember calling for my deportation. Enough. This is what Trump and his sycophants have wrought." Brad Lander offered similar criticism, as did Adrienne Adams, Andrew Cuomo and a few other contenders. But that was about it.

At its midway point, the *Times* report took a curious detour: "Mr. Cuomo is a staunch supporter of Israel; Mr. Mamdani uses the term 'genocide' to describe Israel's actions against Gaza." For good measure, the "paper of record" then tossed Zohran's support for BDS into the mix.

Although Paladino did not mention the Middle East conflict when slamming Zohran, the *Times* made sure to inform readers that the councilwoman is a "strong supporter of Israel." Moreover, the story matter-of-factly noted that, in May 2024, the Whitestone warrior had called pro-Palestine campus protesters "monsters" who need to be "slayed."

"This incident illustrates perfectly the need for President Trump's mass deportation policy," Paladino said in defense of her Mamdani attack. The salty demagogue sought to remove "future Zohrans" from the U.S. "before they have a chance to take root in America."

With all due respect, ma'am, that ship has sailed. Zohran scored massive support from young voters, who are not full of yesterday's bigotry.

Not long ago, the *Times* editorial board paid close attention to goings-on in New York City. But these days it doesn't even matter to this esteemed body if the NYPD fires a weapon into a college campus office. More surprising than the *Times* board's silence regarding Paladino's incendiary statements is that the *Post* ignored them.

Paladino typically does not need to do much to get coverage in the Murdoch rag. In mid-May, her social media diatribe about the city's composting plan—in which she argued that the small kitchen buckets used in the program worked better as "beer coolers"—earned her a *Post* puff piece. It's not clear why the tabloid ignored her crusade against Zohran, but it's hard to believe that Murdoch's crew disagreed with it.

At City Hall, Mayor Adams appeared to be troubled by the denounce Paladino/support Mamdani binary, so he sought a third option. The mayor, who famously declared that the migrant crisis will "destroy New York City," and claimed that he faced federal corruption charges because he criticized the Biden White House on the issue, did not want to sound too pro-immigration or in any way anti-Trump.

"We should all tone down our rhetoric," Adams said, limply advising New Yorkers to avoid "meanspirited, hateful language." News flash: Nobody listened.

CHAPTER 12

It's Getting Hot

In late May, it was easy to see why Zohran's foes were getting nervous.

An Emerson College Poll, co-sponsored by New York City local news station PIX11 and the Beltway publication *The Hill*, now showed Cuomo not winning until the tenth ranked-choice round. "Could Andrew Cuomo Lose NYC Mayoral Primary to Democratic Socialist Zohran Mamdani?" asked the *Forbes* Breaking News Channel on YouTube.

On Monday morning, June 2, Zohran's campaign rolled out a big endorsement. State Senator John Liu, New York's first Asian American citywide elected official (as comptroller, in office from 2010-2013). Born in Taiwan (in 1967), Liu and his family came to the U.S. when he was a young child. Liu represents the heavily Asian Queens neighborhoods of Flushing and Bayside, just south of

Paladino's council district.[79] The former comptroller—who clashed with Mayor Bloomberg and ran for mayor as a left populist in 2013—is also a widely respected figure in various ethnic enclaves across the city.

"As a fellow immigrant to this city at a young age, [and] an Asian American," Liu said at the endorsement presser outside City Hall, he and Zohran could identify with "the struggles that our communities go through and the need for a focus on education and economic empowerment." Liu further noted that the insurgent's small-donation fundraising showed that Mamdani was not "beholden to monied interests" and "doesn't owe anybody anything."

Liu nonetheless stressed that while he fully backed his fellow Queens lawmaker's bid for mayor, the two have a "big disagreement" about Israel-Palestine. Somewhat paradoxically, Liu's not-exactly progressive pro-Israel position opened up new terrain of support for Zohran, informing older voters with concerns about Mamdani's pro-Palestine stance that they could still support the newcomer.

Outlets seeking to keep Israel at the center of the mayoral campaign treated Liu's endorsement in a different light, however. "Pro-Israel pol backs Zohran, with reservations," read the headline on *Politico*'s New York Playbook.

Mamdani's campaign, meanwhile, created its own stylish coverage of Liu's announcement, starting with the two

---

79 In the aforementioned 2018 race for state senate, Liu trounced Paladino.

figures walking up the subway steps at City Hall. The video gained strong traction on TikTok and Instagram.

Two weeks later, Zohran posted a dazzling clip of city councilman Chi Ossé (who was born in 1998 and raised in a Haitian-American household in Brooklyn) and Liu explaining their support for Mamdani in Mandarin. Social media is made to be shared, and it can span generations. "My 89-year-old mother loved it!" activist and book editor Andy Hsiao told me regarding the Ossé-Liu exchange.

Zohran's manifest ability to control his own narrative maximized his gain from Liu's endorsement. The same event was thus viewed quite differently by mainstream media audiences versus those seeing it through the candidate's own channels.

From a campaign's perspective, such command is a quite potent weapon. In Journalism 101, we instruct students that, in theory, political media should inform readers, not serve powerful interests. Amid Mamdani's rise, several outlets appeared to be aiding Israel's attempt to muzzle all of its critics. But the effort seems to have backfired. A very large number of Democratic voters shared the DSA candidate's pro-Palestine views—and countless others did not view support for Israel as a major concern.

Given the endless barrage of smear pieces against Zohran, who can fault him for telling his own story?

*

On the same Monday in which Liu endorsed Zohran and Paladino called for the insurgent's deportation, a third, less-noticed event illustrated the new terrain of New York City politics. That evening, two of the city's most venerable civil rights organizations, the NYCLU and the NAACP (New York chapter), sponsored a well-attended forum for mayoral candidates.

Presidential candidate Abraham Lincoln, abolitionist figurehead Frederick Douglass, and President Barack Obama have all taken the stage at the Great Hall at Cooper Union. In 1993, Governor Mario Cuomo introduced President Bill Clinton at an event there. On June 2, 2025, Mario's son evidently needed to be somewhere else.

Zohran and seven fellow candidates opted to join the conversation. No-show Cuomo may not have many enthusiasts among the NYCLU crowd, but he was counting on the NAACP's older Black members to help put him in City Hall. Only the longstanding Harlem-based *Amsterdam News* covered the event. The article's mention of Cuomo's unexplained absence likely raised at least a few eyebrows.

The lack of widespread media coverage—or criticism—of the frontrunner's slight again showed that the old rules of city politics no longer applied. Cuomo cynically but correctly calculated that since he had already blown off most candidate forums, the media would not pay attention to yet another non-appearance. And civic organizations meant very little to him.

Because of his participation in the city's campaign finance program, Cuomo was required to attend the two televised debates, the first of which was slated for Wednesday,

June 4. Whether in first or second place, or very far behind, in the polls, candidates started laying the groundwork for the first showdown.

One of the longest shots, hedge-fund billionaire and Mike Bloomberg wannabe Whitney Tilson (b. 1966), sought to make his name by outflanking Cuomo to the right. Tilson, who looks like Steve Martin's classic character in *The Jerk*, was a first-time candidate best known for helping found Teach for America, an anti-union initiative. Strangely, when he and Cuomo started attacking Mamdanis for his lack of experience, nobody asked the deep-pocketed novice pol why he was qualified to run City Hall.

In the run-up to the Wednesday debate, Tilson's campaign released a scattershot attack on Zohran. Inflammatorily titled "Socialists at the Gate," a fifteen-second spot posted on YouTube and other platforms showed a montage of clips of the DSA insurgent, including when Zohran angrily confronted MAGA border czar Tom Homan. Many Democrats familiar with Mamdani's show of force no doubt supported the direct action.

Like Cuomo, Tilson is not Jewish (although his wife is), but the New England WASP is also incensed by Mamdani's criticisms of Israel. With "antisemitism" written across the screen, the narrator of "Socialists at the Gate" warns that the leftists "demand consequences for genocidal Zionist imperialism." The assumption here is that viewers would be alarmed by such a position—but the phrasing simply reinforced the pro-Palestine contention that Israel is, in fact, committing genocide.

Tilson's hit piece further assumes that Zohran and company's call to "abolish capitalism" would shock audiences and thus required no explanation. In this respect, Whitney shares the blinders of Bloomberg, Bill Ackman and their ilk. Capitalism obviously has been very good to the 1%. Why on earth would anyone oppose it?

*

Zohran rolled up to the Wednesday night debate at 30 Rock in high style. A marching band played a Mardi Gras Dixieland rendition of Woody Guthrie's anthem, "This Land Is Your Land," a staple at Bernie's presidential campaign events. A rag-tag group of cheerful volunteers held posters reading "Freeze the Rent," "Childcare for All," and the familiar "Zohran for NYC." The upbeat candidate seemed relaxed but ready.

When the debate kicked off, it was instantly clear that Zohran's run had fundamentally changed the focus of the election. Rather than Israel-Palestine, WNBC-TV politics reporter Melissa Russo explained, "We're going to begin tonight with the issue that polls show is number one for New Yorkers: affordability." After a brief rundown of how city residents feel "squeezed," Russo then asked candidates to present their "one big idea" that could help address the crisis "now."

What ensued was mind-boggling. Although Zohran's turn at the plate came seventh (among the nine candidates in the studio), the first six batters whiffed. Despite several decades of combined experience on debate stages, and two reminders from Russo that the question asked for an immediate cost-of-living remedy, each of the first five contenders launched into an opening statement focused mainly on their bios and long-range goals.

Before batter number six, Whitney Tilson, took his turn, Telemundo New York moderator Rosarina Bretón again stressed that the question is what candidates would do "NOW" about affordability.

"'Now' may take another two years," declared the cartoonish billionaire. Rather the "freeze the rent," the hedge-funder claimed he would "drop rents by 20% by unleashing the private sector" to produce two million units of new housing (a process that would take much longer than two years). Incredibly, none of the first six candidates coherently responded to a simple question.

The energetic "rookie" stepped to the plate, thanked the hosts, then stated the following:

> *We are live here [at 30 Rock] in the most expensive city in the United States of America. One in four New Yorkers are living in poverty. And I am running to be your next mayor to make this city affordable. I will do so by freezing the rent for more than two million rent-stabilized tenants; by making the slowest buses in the country fast and free; and by delivering universal childcare. And I will pay for this by taxing the 1%—the billionaires and profitable corporations that Mr. Cuomo cares about more than working-class New Yorkers. I will ask them to pay their share, so that we can have a city that everyone can afford.*

Zohran capped off the second part of his final sentence with a smile. It would be hard to script a more cogent response or surpass his polished delivery. From the jump, Mamdani told debate viewers the same thing that his thousands of canvassers did when they knocked at voters' doors. New Yorkers could now see for themselves that the up-and-comer believed in his own message.

Moreover, while presenting himself as an advocate for the 99%, Zohran also put Cuomo in a bind: How could the governor supported by Bloomberg and DoorDash deny that the 1% owned him?

It would be an exaggeration to claim that Zohran "won" the debate based on his first response, but it is easy to see how voters of all ages and backgrounds might embrace the likable young contender. New York has always had plenty of bullies, including one currently in the White House and a fellow Baby Boomer who grimaced on stage while a millennial insurgent stuck it to him.

Zohran was by no means the only candidate who ripped into Cuomo during the debate. Longshot Michael Blake, a former assemblyman from the Bronx, made headlines by calling the accused sexual harasser the "greatest threat to public safety." City Council speaker Adrienne Adams charged Cuomo with "slow-walking" Covid safety protections to minority communities during the pandemic. Brad Lander accused the frontrunner of lying.

The TV ratings showed a large upswing from four years earlier. Over 725,000 viewers tuned in. Regardless of whether that was to see the rising star or a familiar face, the numbers favored Zohran. He needed more voters to turn out, whereas Cuomo sought less.

*

Perhaps more important than the back-and-forth in the debate itself is how various media outlets presented the highlights. It's quite likely that a large majority of viewers did not hang in for the full two hours (with the first half televised before it switched over to the internet). Whether or not they caught it live, prospective voters digested news clips the next day that helped shape their views of the race.

Even rival campaigns surely would be forced to admit that Zohran fared surprisingly well in local TV news reports. The audiences for such programs are generally older, and the few reporters Cuomo trusts are fixtures on city television stations. Intentionally or not, many of those same newscasts ended up giving lots of positive coverage to Mamdani. When a candidate is the center of controversy, news teams pay close attention.

On Thursday morning, June 4, NY1's popular morning host Pat Kiernan played a set of clips that started with Zohran questioning Cuomo's funding from billionaires.[80] On WABC TV, which has the largest local viewership, the highlights began with the Queens assemblyman declaring that his "biggest mistake" was "trusting Cuomo," who cut Medicaid funding during the pandemic. FOX5's sequence

---

[80] Segments are also looped repeatedly on the cable network.

opened with the frontrunner incurring fire from Mamdani, Blake, Adrienne Adams, and Lander.

Most of the news segments included a Cuomo jibe against Mamdani. In one of his viral statements that night, Zohran insisted that he was "Trump's worst nightmare—a progressive Muslim immigrant who actually fights for the things that I believe in." Cuomo shot back that "Donald Trump would go through Mr. Mamdami [sic] like a hot knife through butter." Prior to Cuomo's usage, the metaphor had recently appeared twice in *Forbes*.

Even when he scored points, Mario's son seemed like he was living in a different era, griping about Zohran's use of "Twitter." More unexpected was that after leaving office amid two scandals nearly four years earlier, Cuomo's responses to any questions about nursing homes during the pandemic or the harassment allegations lacked punch.

Given the firestorm of criticism Zohran faced over the preceding three weeks regarding Israel-Palestine, it seemed certain that the issue would come up sooner than the tail end of the second hour. But the exchanges still provided plenty of tabloid fodder. Unlike Cuomo, Tilson, Adrienne Adams, and Scott Stringer, Mamdani said that his first trip as mayor would not be to Israel. Instead, he would stay home and "confront antisemitism directly."

Next asked whether Israel has the "right to exist," Zohran replied "Yes, as a state with equal rights for anyone." Cuomo and Tilson got pretty worked up about Mamdani's position.

In the eyes of the Baby Boomers standing to his right, Zohran's twin declarations were nothing short of political heresy. Tilson declared that in the unlikely event that he got elected mayor, he'd make his "fourth trip" to Israel, followed his "fifth trip to Ukraine."[81]

One month before the Fourth of July, the fireworks were already getting started.

---

81 Despite its importance to many Eastern European voters in the city, the Russia-Ukraine war rarely surfaced in the primary campaign.

CHAPTER 13
Five-Alarm Fire!

Immediately after the debate at 30 Rock, Zohran's team released major news: An endorsement from Alexandria Ocasio-Cortez. The congresswoman's backing for her fellow millennial DSA member representing northwest Queens[82] helped Mamdani move into the national spotlight.

After the *New York Times* first announced AOC's support, Zohran was all over the mainstream media. Leading national Democrats now paid close attention. On the night after the debate, MSNBC host Jen Psaki called Mamdani's campaign a "litmus test" for the party. The always on-message newcomer talked up his November 2024 outreach to Trump voters.

---

82 AOC's district spans from Astoria across the East River to the southeast Bronx (thus including Rikers Island). Zohran's assembly district covers Astoria and Long Island City.

AOC's plug for Zohran caused one of the candidates on stage at the Wednesday debate to humiliate herself. State Senator Jessica Ramos, who never gained traction in the race, had long feuded with AOC. Ramos' senate district, which covers Jackson Heights, Corona, and East Elmhurst, is also the Congresswoman's turf.

After AOC came out for Zohran, Ramos tried to shank her rival but in the process became a laughingstock. The state senator suddenly opted to join the dozens of elected officials who had righteously called for Gov. Cuomo to resign in 2021 but now endorsed his 2025 bid for mayor because they thought he would win. Multiple platforms blew up with ridicule for Ramos.[83]

On Friday morning, the ever-so gracious Cuomo advised a very large throng of reporters at the Carpenters Union Hall that Ramos "is endorsing me. I am not endorsing her." AOC weighed in by posting "lol. lmao" above Cuomo's remark, a double-diss that seemed far more appropriate than repetitive.

Why there was so much coverage of the Ramos-Cuomo presser merits attention. As I noted on X at the time, this gossipy "story" was totally irrelevant. A candidate with miniscule poll numbers now backed the frontrunner out

---

83 While in the state senate since 2018, Ramos, a former union activist, had allied with the left. Shortly after Trump was elected, Ramos insisted that she had "always been to the right of the left," a craven move (and the opposite of Zohran's response to the Dems' defeat).

of spite. How could this possibly affect the outcome of the primary?

Alas, in-fighting and backbiting can yield clicks.

*

Someone else was hungry for attention that Friday morning in Downtown Manhattan. Last seen menacing Zohran and company five days earlier in Sunset Park, RR now showed up at a Mamdani campaign stop in the financial district. He was soon taken away in handcuffs.

As PIX11's website matter-of-factly explained, "The suspect confronted Mamdani at the event, accusing him of being insufficiently supportive of Israel and Jewish people, and allegedly bit [a] volunteer when she intervened."

It's not clear whether RR, who is 55 and often wears a Puerto Rican flag, is Jewish. But like Cuomo, Whitney Tilson, and many of the key figures at the *New York Post*, he fashions himself as a ferocious opponent of antisemitism. Or perhaps he just really disdains Muslim candidates. RR's rage against Zohran caused him to chomp on the forearm of a young female housing activist, which led the Manhattan DA's office to charge him with misdemeanor assault. Media coverage of the sickening incident was scant, presumably because most local reporters were attending Jessica Ramos' major announcement.

Throughout June 6, Zohran sported an aqua blue kurta in honor of Eid-al-Adha, one of the two most important Islamic holidays. Since 2015, local public schools have closed for two Eid celebrations, illustrating the growing presence of Muslims in New York City. On Friday evening, Mamdani landed at a different faith's house of worship.

"This is the first Eid I've spent in a church," quipped Lina Khan, the antimonopoly activist. Zephyr Teachout, Cuomo's 2014 Democratic challenger who is closely allied with Khan, also sat on the panel held at the Church of the Village on W. 13th Street.

As the three figures began discussing bans on junk fees and ending noncompete agreements, a pro-Palestine activist stood up and raised the "Israel's right to exist" question. "May all normalizers burn in hell!" shouted the female protester as she was escorted out. The panelists then offered criticisms of billionaires, monopolies, and Cuomo.

As captured on video by *Semafor*'s Dave Weigel, a second female demonstrator, clad in a hijab, soon jumped up and angrily repeated the criticism of the first activist, but also questioned whether Mamdani's recognition of Israel betrayed his faith. After reiterating his position on the obligations of international law, Zohran added, "the question of whether I'm a good Muslim is a step too far." It was a memorable Eid for both Mamdani and Khan.

Although the attacks on Zohran's position on Israel-Palestine overwhelmingly came from the political establishment, the DSA insurgent continued to incur fire from the radical left. In the not-distant future, the activist-turned-pol surely will square off with his former comrades, as well as the next generation of protest leaders that he is currently inspiring. It will be interesting to watch.

*

Theodore Hamm

On the same Friday morning, Zohran went on HOT 97's *Ebro in the Morning*, a popular FM-radio show that streams across multiple platforms. The program appeals to fans of hip-hop culture, providing the former Mr. Cardamom with a chance to explain his ideas to a cross-section of Black and Latino listeners.

Ebro Darden (b. 1975 and raised in the Bay Area, where he attended Hebrew school) began the extended conversation by asking Zohran how he would pay for the key items on his agenda. Previewing a post-primary dust-up, the socialist candidate explained that rapper 50 Cent "is not going to be happy" about Mamdani's plan to tax the rich. Ebro seemed on-board, however.

The host allowed the fast-rising pol to thoroughly refute the "higher taxes will make rich people leave the city" line thrown around by the 1% and their minions. As the guest explained, the numbers show the opposite: it is working-class people who are leaving the increasingly unaffordable city. Ebro summed up his guest's position as "rich people are full of shit." "You said it," Zohran laughingly replied, "but that's the accurate conclusion."

The show's Latina co-host Laura Stylez then opened the door for Zohran to discuss his plan to open city-run grocery stores in "food deserts," with the candidate explaining the problems faced by residents of Queensbridge Houses, the massive public housing complex in Mamdani's assembly district. And after Zohran explained what he referred to as his "universalist" position on Palestinian equal rights, co-host Peter Rosenberg averred that "I'm sure you have a lot of support from the progressive Jewish community."

In the aftermath of the first debate, mainstream news outlets continued to attack Mamdani regarding Israel as well as the cost of his policy proposals. The short format of most contemporary political news stories typically allows for only a brief comment or two from a candidate explaining an issue. And hit pieces are not intended to foster discussion.

Ebro and company thus gave Zohran the chance to inform listeners about the actual details of his positions. Three weeks later, *Documented NY* reporter Prajwal Bhat mentioned that a Turkish immigrant named Erhan Tuncel was listening attentively to the interview while driving a taxi. It's hard to directly calculate the impact of any single interview on voter turnout—but HOT 97's hip-hop crowd clearly showed up for Mamdani.

Ebro was neither the first nor the biggest urban media figurehead to take interest in Zohran. Dominican American Kid Mero (b. 1983)—who frequently partners with Jamaican American Desus Nice (b. 1981) as a comic duo best known as the Bodega Boys—hails from the Bronx (as does Nice). When Mero first sat down with Zohran in late April, the host began by calling Cuomo a "disgraced bozo," setting the table for the newcomer to win over the Kid's fans.

In the final ten days of the primary race, Mero would play a high-profile role in the campaign. But a low-key figure with a massive audience gave Zohran an even stronger push. South Carolina-raised Charlamagne Tha God (b. 1978) is the main co-host of *The Breakfast Club*, a nationally syndicated radio program with at least 4.5 million listeners. The show also has comparable numbers of enthusiasts on Instagram and TikTok.

Although Charlamagne over the past decade has been a frequent critic of the Democratic Party establishment, he has not supported Bernie, arguing that the senator's 2020 presidential agenda did not directly address the concerns of Black voters. However, on Wednesday morning, June 11, the host clearly was impressed by Zohran.

"I love that idea," Charlamagne responded after the newcomer explained his proposal to send teams of trained outreach workers to help people experiencing episodes of emotional distress on the subway and elsewhere. A leading proponent of mental health awareness, Charlamagne relayed the clip to his 4.5 million followers on Instagram. In the comments section, a post that "this guy may be making too much sense for a politician" got 200 likes in the first six hours.

Charlamagne further observed that "anybody who is going to be the future of the Democratic Party [must] throw that old regime under the bus." That means "Not just Cuomo, but Schumer" and company, the host continued. "Trust me, I hear you," Zohran replied. "Because I have been critical of the style of leadership that gave rise to Donald Trump."

When the primary results came in two weeks later, Zohran's numbers showed strong gains among all voters categorized as millennials, meaning ages 25 to 39. As leftist Substacker Josh Ettinger observed on X, along with South Asians, Black people in that bracket came out in droves. The *Breakfast Club* appearance was by no means the only reason why Zohran racked up large numbers of young PoC votes, but the show certainly helped boost the insurgent's momentum.

Charlamagne may not be an actual god, but Zohran's vote totals in Harlem and Central Brooklyn suggest that the hip-hop figurehead strongly influences mortals.

*

Zohran and his team found a slot in his packed daily schedule in early June for the candidate to return to Staten Island. This time it was to illustrate that his key platform proposal regarding free buses had a clear precedent: the no-cost ferry that brings residents back and forth from their island to the slightly more famous one.

By this point, everything Zohran posted garnered lots of attention on social media. Even though the ferry video lacked gimmicks, it got plenty of traction. Perhaps even more important was the favorable coverage the candidate's trip received in the *Staten Island Advance*, the borough's longstanding "hometown" outlet. Older residents of the oft-neglected borough no doubt appreciated a visit from the celebrity newcomer.

Cuomo and his sputtering campaign may not have won over many new voters, but Michael Bloomberg got on board. Zohran's momentum caused Bloomy (as the *New York Post* often called him) to make a last-ditch effort to boost the guy who had been so friendly to luxury condo developers as governor. Mere mention of the word socialism is deeply unsettling for the former mayor.

In the 2020 Democratic campaign, Bloomberg spent over $1.1 billion of his own money in order to help party leaders sink Bernie. The DNC even changed its own rules regarding the required number of donors so that Bloomy could participate in a debate (in which Elizabeth Warren memorably slammed him). The former New York City mayor won very few delegates but somehow prevailed in the American Samoa caucus.

While there was no "perfect choice" in the race, and Bloomberg acknowledged that Cuomo was a difficult figure to work with, the billionaire praised the former governor's work in renovating La Guardia Airport. Bloomy sounded a bit gloomy about his choice. Over the next week, he nonetheless pumped $8.5 million into Fix the City's grimy efforts against Zohran.

Bloomberg's endorsement allowed Zohran's campaign to amplify its recurring line of attack on the increasingly vulnerable frontrunner. "Billionaires are consolidating around Andrew Cuomo because they know he will preserve the broken status quo," declared Team Mamdani.

Elsewhere in Midtown, the *New York Times* tried to wield its influence, but the organization was still recovering from a self-inflicted gunshot wound. In the summer of 2024, the *Times* made an odd decision, opting to no longer endorse candidates in local elections. Few organizations voluntarily surrender their own power, but in the outlet's own coverage of the decision, opinion editor Kathleen Kingsbury offered no clear explanation for it.

Four years earlier, the *Times* editorial board strongly backed novice pol Kathryn Garcia, who almost defeated Eric Adams. The paper's endorsement was also a leading reason why Alvin Bragg prevailed over a very well-heeled opponent in the race for Manhattan district attorney that year.

As the 2025 primary took shape, there were rumors that Kingsbury and company were rethinking their decision. Word traveled that the *Times* was consulting the city's leading lights for guidance.

On the morning of June 12, the Gray Lady—as the *Times* was often called in the twentieth century, referring to the paper's somber, anti-sensational tone—rolled out what turned out be its first big editorial statement about the race. Seven of the fifteen "experts" consulted by the Lady had selected Brad Lander as the best candidate for mayor. Mamdani was tied for second, with two votes, the same number as Cuomo and Tilson (!).

Like the *Times* target readership, the panelists skewed from professional middle class to the city elite. Although roughly 20% of the city's workforce is unionized, only one member claimed a labor affiliation in their bio. The president of the far-right Manhattan Institute joined Mike Bloomberg's deputy in backing billionaire Tilson. The co-founder of Warby Parker eyewear saw good things in Cuomo, and restaurateur Danny Meyer hungered for a Lander administration.

Victor Ng, an Asian graphic designer and Brooklyn political activist, and longtime Bronx Black community organizer Mychal Johnson provided Zohran's two votes. Although the *Times* released the expert panel's findings in order to give Lander a boost at that night's debate, the roundabout plug was not the same as a full declaration of support from the influential outlet.

While the *New York Post* editorial board is always hyper-aggressive, ready to smash a beer glass on your head, the *Times* here was needlessly passive-aggressive, essentially saying "we're not thrilled with Lander but several people we respect like him."

Bloomy and the *Times* would soon link arms in their fight against Zohran, with unexpected results.

*

CUNY's John Jay College of Criminal Justice hosted the second and final televised debate on Thursday night, June 12. NY1 was the lead sponsor. *Inside City Hall*'s Errol Louis, WNYC's mainstay Brian Lehrer, and *The City*'s Katie Honan moderated.

This time the seven leading contenders (thus excluding Jessica Ramos and Michael Blake) on stage began with 60-second opening statements. Batting third, Tilson quickly segued from presenting his bio to attacking Zohran. With his fingers randomly pointing in different directions, the ultra-rich dude declared that "we need a mayor who is experienced, competent and can get things done—not a social media phenom with cute videos." Tilson was clearly on track to get more than 450,000 fewer 1st-place votes than Mamdani.

Up sixth, Zohran again started strong, energetically invoking affordability, taxing the rich, Trump, Cuomo's funding from right-wing billionaires, authoritarianism, his own immigrant experience, the need for "a new generation of leadership," and his grassroots momentum. He then cheerfully invited viewers to "join us—and let's win a New York you can afford." Cuomo followed with a downbeat emphasis on "management" and "experience."

All week, the unnerved frontrunner had been repetitively attacking Zohran's because the insurgent's resume listed no executive positions. Cuomo summoned his preferred local TV reporters, including WCBS shotcaller Marcia Kramer and WABC veteran N.J. Burkett, to an empty pocket park somewhere in Midtown East (the former governor's version of a "Rose Garden.") As he belittled his youthful rival, Cuomo called his big backer Bloomberg the "last great manager-mayor" of the city.

When Errol Louis raised the age question, he included a twist, pointing out that if elected, Zohran would be the youngest New York City mayor in over a century, but Cuomo would be the oldest. The 33-year-old came to the debate with a ready response. "Judge me by the campaign I am running," Zohran declared. "A campaign that we began with about two full-time employees, polling at one percent, [has] now grown to be one in which we manage over 36,000 volunteers that have knocked on nearly a million doors."

When Louis then asked Cuomo whether his advancing age might raise any concerns, the 67-year-old fired off a bunch of talking points about Mamdani's lack of accomplishments. While the non-answer did not make the frontrunner look good, it also opened the door for the insurgent—whose name the veteran Democrat again mispronounced—to fire back. Virality ensued.

In a clip seen worldwide, Zohran confidently stated:

> *To Mr. Cuomo: I have never had to resign in disgrace. I have never cut Medicaid.* [Loud cheers from debate audience.] *I have never stolen hundreds of millions of dollars from the MTA. I have never hounded the thirteen women who credibly accused me of sexual harassment. I have never sued for their gynecological records. And I have never done those things because I am not you, Mr. Cuomo. And furthermore, the name is Mamdani: M-A-M-D-A-N-I.* [Raucous cheers.] *You should learn how to say it, because we gotta get it right.*

As the young title contender pounded away for thirty seconds, the split-screen showed Goliath looking down the entire time, fuming. The bigoted bully responded by once more mispronouncing Mamdani, causing Zohran to correct him yet again.

Hasan Piker and the rest of the internet went nuts. The debate was effectively over, and in retrospect, so was the primary.

Meet Mayor Mamdani

"When we simulated the second debate a few days beforehand," noted Andrew Epstein, "I played Cuomo's part. I needled Zohran quite a bit, consistently botching his name." Andrew says that deputy communications director Lekha Sunder suggested the needling during the rehearsal, accurately predicting that it would inspire Zohran to fight back.

At John Jay that Thursday night in June, Mamdani summoned the spirit of Muhammad Ali, who famously demanded that a rival in the ring say his name.

*

Two nights later, the theater of action was just two blocks away from John Jay. Terminal 5, a 3,000-capacity concert venue, was a hot ticket that night. Once the "warm-up act to the warm-up act" in Kampala, Zohran was now a Manhattan headliner. AOC, a.k.a. Jessica Ramos' archrival, shared the bill.

Kid Mero hosted. Mamdani's campaign events coordinator Katie Riley handled logistics and Julian Gerson assembled an impressive undercard. There was John Samuelsen, the transit workers leader who had once been close allies with Cuomo, John Liu, and Maf Misbah Udin, the Bangladeshi president of the national Alliance of South Asian-American Labor. The DSA's Alexa Avilés and Claire Valdez also stepped up to the microphone.

After Mero warmed up the mostly twenty-something crowd, the fifty-something Samuelsen touted Zohran's plan for free buses in his distinctive Brooklyn accent.

Next came Avilés, a Boricua contemporary of Samuelsen who also speaks in an old-school way. "That's right, boo," the councilwoman said repeatedly, as the crowd joined her in deriding Mayor Adams, Cuomo, and their billionaire backers.

When Avilés declared that Israel hawks were targeting her because of her support for a "free Palestine," the polyglot entourage of Mamdani supporters on stage wildly cheered, and the next-gen audience went nuts. It was a beautiful sight to behold.

A city led by working people expressing global solidarity is not what Mike Bloomberg, the *New York Times* and the *New York Post* envision. But that's the way the cookie crumbled.

CHAPTER 14
The Spoils of Victory

"We need a 'big swing,'" Zohran advised his inner circle as primary day neared. Invoking a malleable term used in public policy circles, the candidate here referred to a spectacle that captured the essence of his campaign. Amid the topsy-turvy final week of the primary, Mamdani and his team brainstormed ideas.

Julian Gerson, then Zohran's political director (now speechwriter), proposed that the magnetic figure walk from the top of Manhattan to the bottom. As Julian explained to other members of the candidate's inner circle, a "march" would help Zohran invoke Mahmood Mamdani's participation in SNCC protests in the mid-1960s. Moreover, the younger Mamdani "radiates hope and joy in a joyless time—so getting him out there to interact with as many different people as possible seemed like the right move," Gerson later told me.

Meet Mayor Mamdani

After Zohran supported Julian's proposal, the planning began, with Elle Bisgaard-Church handling logistics like security and staffing, and deputy campaign manager Katie Riley plotting the route. The weather looked good for the evening of June 20, the first night of summer and the final Friday before the primary. And things worked out rather well. This big swing produced a home run *and* a sixer.

With Julian and top aide Spencer Goldberg at his side for the distance, Zohran—clad in a white business shirt with a black tie, black pants, and gray sneakers—got numerous dabs, shoulder bumps, thumbs ups, and peace signs from folks uptown. As the candidate-led entourage traversed down Broadway through the Upper West Side, young women hopped and clapped at the sight of Mamdani. Middle-aged men squealed.[84]

Under the bright lights at Times Square, a hip-hop workout entourage—mostly likely fans of Charlamagne, *Ebro in the Morning*, and/or Kid Mero and his sidekick Desus—took selfies with a beaming Zohran.[85] Young Black and brown dudes showing love for a socialist in the city's most iconic location wasn't exactly what Mike Bloomberg and his crowd wanted to see. Neither did the media powerhouse that gave rise to the name of Times Square.

---

84 As *Gothamist*'s Elizabeth Kim stated on X that night, "The democratic socialist candidate for mayor walking down Park Ave [i.e. Bloomberg's Upper East Side turf] would sure be a photo for the ages."

85 In mid-July, Jamaal Bowman brought Zohran to a Wu-Tang Clan show at Madison Square Garden. Mamdani then posted a video showing the candidate receiving a friendly reception from both fellow concertgoers and Wu-Tang figurehead RZA (b. 1969).

Theodore Hamm

As Zohran zigzagged through the East Village after midnight, twenty-somethings poured out of bars to catch a glimpse of a potential future mayor not much older than them. One burly lad who clearly appeared to enjoy his suds whooped deliriously after shaking the rock star's hand. The would-be mayor soon posed for a picture beside the statue of a clapping Fiorello La Guardia near NYU.

Within a month, the Mamdani campaign's three-minute sizzle reel of the event—with campaign videographer Donald Borenstein directing a crew and Olivia Becker editing copious footage—surpassed 15 million views on the Musk platform. A 19-second TikTok clip that showed Mira Nair hugging Zohran along the route, expressing concern that her son had been "eating unhealthy things," clocked over 2.3 million looks.

A walk from Inwood Hill Park at the northern end of Manhattan to Battery Park at the southern tip is 12.5 miles and typically takes nearly five hours. Detours add mileage. If you're shaking hands and taking countless selfies with fans, the clock extends. Zohran and company reached the Staten Island ferry terminal in Battery Park at 2:15 a.m., over eight hours after Mamdani's Manhattan waltz began.

Along with roughly three dozen youthful supporters, Mamdani posed for a cheerful group pic. According to *Hell Gate*'s Max Rivlin-Nadler, the candidate then chatted with his enthusiasts for about half an hour before departing.

"I'm exhausted but I'm living off the adrenaline of it," Zohran told Max the end of the night. "We're right where we want to be." Primary day was just over 72 hours away.

Rather than take a free ride on the 24-hour ferry to Staten Island, Zohran went home to Astoria. As noted by Rivlin-Nader, the candidate needed to get some rest before returning to Harlem in order to address Rev. Al Sharpton's Saturday morning meeting. There, after explaining why his middle name is Kwame, Zohran informed a receptive audience that Mahmood Mamdani "marched with SNCC." Although he did not mention his tour through Harlem the previous night, at least a few folks in the audience likely knew about it.

On Monday, GoodPoliticGuy (GPC), a DC-based socialist YouTube commentator, quote-tweeted Zohran's release of the Friday night walk video. Referring to a Mamdani victory the next day, GPC spoke for many on the left across the globe when he stated, "I know nothing good ever happens but please god can we have just this one."

*

"Friday is a blessed day," Brooklynite Asad Dandia tweeted on the morning of Zohran's Manhattan march. Noting that the candidate and his team had reached out to over 130 mosques,[86] Asad included a picture of himself embracing Zohran, then wrote, "I'm Sunni, you're Shia, so we've got our bases covered" with a laughing emoji.[87]

---

86 Mohamed Alharbi handled the campaign's outreach to Muslim and South Asian communities. Raised in a Yemeni household in the Bronx, Alharbi is in his mid-twenties.
87 At the June 12 debate, Errol Louis asked Cuomo if he had ever visited a mosque while a statewide elected official. "I believe I have," the veteran Democrat replied, without citing an example.

Born in 1992 at Coney Island Hospital, Asad grew up in a Sunni household in Brighton Beach with family roots in Pakistan. Like Bernie Sanders and Chuck Schumer, Asad graduated from James Madison High School in Midwood, Brooklyn. During Mayor Bloomberg's final year in office, Dandia was a lead plaintiff in *Raza v. City of New York*, a landmark ACLU case that helped curtail NYPD surveillance of Muslim communities.

Zohran and Asad, now a New York City historian and tour guide, became pals in August 2024, when the assemblyman reached out to the Brooklyn activist to discuss his potential run for mayor. When they first met in person at Café Reggio in the West Village, Asad wore a T-shirt featuring the familiar Greek NYC coffee cup accompanied by a bacon, egg, and cheese on a roll.

The shirt prompted Zohran to jokingly quiz his fellow Muslim about his diet. "Don't worry, it's turkey bacon," Asad assured him. The two became fast friends.

At the end of the fall 2021 hunger strike that Zohran had joined with taxi workers, the future mayoral candidate noted that he usually ended his ritual fasting by first eating a date. I asked Asad about the relationship between this Ramadan practice and Zohran's politics.

"We do so in the spirit of sacrifice," Asad explained. "We give up food and sex and resist other urges in the name of helping others." Like running marathons, fasting also requires incredible amounts of self-discipline.

Meet Mayor Mamdani

When I first interviewed Zohran in late March, he told me that he looked forward to Jummah, the early Friday afternoon prayer congregations at mosques that the aspiring city leader joined regularly during the primary. "It's a brief moment of respite from the world," Mamdani explained. "In the midst of a campaign stop, that moment of losing oneself into a larger collective provides beauty for just a few minutes." There would be plenty of noise late in the race, heightening the importance of any quietude the candidate could find.

As a distance runner and a practicing Muslim, Zohran can tap into a vast reservoir of self-regenerating energy. People who worked closely with him during the primary remain awestruck by his stamina.

Andrew Epstein said Zohran's daytime fuel is most frequently derived from peanut butter and banana smoothies. Mamdani drinks chai in the morning and iced coffee later in the day, albeit not regularly, and plenty of water. At night he consumes lots of different food, preferably Indian. One of the few positive stories in the *New York Times* about Zohran mentioned that Mira Nair once cooked biryani with chicken for her son and campaign staffers.

Shortly after Zohran's upset win, MAGA influencers on the Musk site including Laura Loomer, Charlie Kirk, and @endwokeness posted a clip of a 2023 interview in which Mamdani ate a halal platter of chicken and rice with his hands. The practice is common throughout South Asia, Africa and many parts of the world, but its "foreignness" was too much for the Trump crowd. "Civilized people in America don't eat like this," declared a next-gen far-right

Texas congressman, demanding that Zohran "adopt Western customs or go back to the Third World."

In the wake of Mamdani's primary victory, Rep. Marjorie Taylor Greene, the MAGA congresswoman from Georgia, circulated an image of the Statue of Liberty wearing a burqa. Tucker Carlson called Zohran a "foreign-born nitwit." MAGA strategist Steve Bannon, a far-right populist, sought to understand why a far-left populist succeeded in the June election. "This guy is a very skilled politician," Bannon told *Meet the Press* host Kristen Welker. "He's got radical ideas, but he presents them in a sunny upbeat way and people feel like he's fighting for them, particularly on an issue that Republicans haven't connected on yet: affordability."[88]

Meanwhile, Trump pushed through a deeply regressive tax cut that rewards the 1%.

*

Mamdani's homestretch run was full of highs, including a Working Families Party rally in Crown Heights on Sunday night, June 22. The event was hosted by Tish James and Chi Ossé, with appearances from Jabari Brisport, Justin Brannan, and a slew of mayoral candidates opposing Cuomo. "Zohran has sparked a level of enthusiasm that I have not seen since the days of 'change,'" James declared, referring to Obama's ground-breaking 2008 campaign.

---

88 MTG, Carlson, and Bannon were impressed by Mamdani's ability to succeed while criticizing Israel. It appeared that the MAGA figureheads sought to win over Democrats angry with their party's deference to Netanyahu.

But the last week also brought plenty of lows. On Tuesday, June 17, the insurgent did a streamed podcast with *The Bulwark*, a Never-Trump outlet. Near the end of the one-hour conversation, host Tim Miller (b. 1981), a former Jeb Bush operative, brought up Israel, Palestine, and antisemitism.

"'Globalize the intifada' is a very popular phrase at protests on the left," Miller asserted. "Maybe some people are saying that with good intent, but there are certainly some people who are saying that phrase with violent intent." The host did not offer specific examples of the phrase instigating violence against Jewish people. But Zohran's response provided his pro-Israel foes with a weapon they would deploy ceaselessly for the next several weeks.

Rather than offer the blistering denunciation that his critics demanded, Zohran committed what has become a thought crime in Trump's America. Rather than a kneejerk reaction, Mamdani offered context and nuance. The candidate first referred to the "horrific war crime of October 7," then provided anecdotes he had heard from Jewish city residents about the fear they felt in the aftermath.

Although Zohran further mentioned his campaign's proposal to greatly expand anti-hate crime programming, the host remained focused on activist slogans, prompting this exchange:

> Mamdani: *I am someone less comfortable with the idea of banning the use of certain words—and I think it is more evocative of a Trump-style approach to how to lead a country.*

Miller: *Sure, but does the phrase globalizing the intifada make you uncomfortable?*

Mamdani: *I know people for whom the phrase means very different things. And to me, ultimately, what I hear from so many people is a desperate desire for equality and equal rights in standing up for Palestinian human rights. And I think what's difficult also is that the very word has been used by the Holocaust Museum when translating the Warsaw ghetto uprising into Arabic because it's a word that means struggle. And as a Muslim man who grew up post-9/11, I'm all too familiar with the way in which Arabic words can be twisted, distorted, and used to justify any kind of meaning. And I think that's where it leaves me with a sense that what we need to do is focus on keeping Jewish New Yorkers safe.*[89]

Prominent voices on the left applauded Zohran's thoughtful response. Brooklyn College professor Corey Robin called it "a model of integrity—not sacrificing one's values or pandering to voters—while demonstrating sensitivity to those voters and their concerns." Nerdeen Kiswani, the founder of Within Our Lifetime who previously slammed the candidate's position on Israel's "right to exist," now praised Mamdani's resolve.

But thoughtful responses are a distinct exception in the era of soundbite discourse. Thunderous condemnation of

---

[89] Note: Edited for clarity. See https://podscripts.co/podcasts/the-bulwark-podcast/zohran-mamdani-fypod-crossover.

Meet Mayor Mamdani

Zohran's often-distorted comments reverberated well into July, egged on by Andrew Cuomo, Rep. Hakeem Jeffries, the CEO of Pfizer, and anyone seeking to burst the socialist candidate's bubble. After a torrential month-long downpour, the Democratic mayoral nominee told the Big Pharma guy and his crowd that he would "discourage others" from using a phrase that Mamdani had never stated.

From late October through the middle of June, Zohran and his team made almost no significant tactical mistakes. Opening the door to the Never-Trump crowd carried more risks than rewards, however. It's not clear how the old-guard Republican audience could yield votes in a New York City primary contest in which voters needed to be registered Democrats.

One day before *The Bulwark* conversation, Mamdani chatted with *The Meidas Touch*, an extremely popular podcast that is certainly "anti-Trump" but—unlike *The Bulwark*—not aligned with the Bush wing of the Republicans. *Meidas* host Ben Meiselas is Colin Kaepernick's lawyer and business partner. That conversation was friendly, whereas Tim Miller clearly laid a trap, one that could have been avoided.

As Corey Robin pointed out, many of Mamdani's loudest critics, including Miller and Hakeem Jeffries, "are not Jewish but nevertheless like to speak on behalf of us and our alleged fears." In mid-July, the former governor (raised Catholic) told upscale congregants at a synagogue in the Hamptons he would "wager that a majority of Jews" voted for Zohran. Even though Cuomo claimed "most Jews voted for Mamdani," Peter Beinart observed on X, he still insisted that "Mamdani must be defeated in order to keep Jewish New Yorkers safe. Makes perfect sense."

As Beinart stated in his initial post-primary analysis, Zohran's victory showed that very large numbers of young voters in New York City were now pro-Palestine. As even pro-Israel analysts surely would concur, that is a monumental shift in U.S. politics. Meanwhile, many liberal Jews over 35 likely shared the perspective of Brad Lander, the third-place finisher whose supporters overwhelmingly ranked Mamdani second. Lander told CNN's Jake Tapper in late June that he and fellow Jewish voters objected to being used as "pawns" by Bibi's backers.

Tapper and many of his peers in the national media downplayed the bread-and-butter issues integral to Zohran's rise, instead keeping Israel at the center of their coverage of Mamdani's victory. Waleed Shahid, a Democratic strategist who worked for both AOC and Cynthia Nixon, conducted a revealing study that reviewed the first week of broadcast coverage after June 24.

Whether from a liberal (MSNBC), centrist (CNN), or conservative (Fox News) outlet, over 60% of national TV reports about Zohran foregrounded his positions on Israel-Palestine. Fox, of course, led the pack in Mamdani mentions, churning out 154 segments (nearly double the amount by the other two networks). Shahid found that 64% of those reports explicitly referred to Israel or antisemitism. "You've got Hamas sympathizers winning in NYC, and the media's silent about it," declared one Fox commentator, seemingly unaware of his own bluster.

New York City's local TV outlets placed more emphasis on Zohran's cost-of-living agenda. According to Shahid, these stations, including the Fox affiliate, nonetheless brought up Israel-related controversies in just over 40% of the segments.

At the Hamptons synagogue on July 20, Cuomo highlighted his "family tradition." "Like my father before me," the defeated primary candidate said, "I was the most aggressive governor in the United States on behalf of Israel." Blind loyalty is quite a dangerous tradition. Meanwhile, one of Eric Adams' two fall ballot lines is called "EndAntiSemitism."[90]

While the Boomer Dems pander to Israel's murderous regime, the party's growing ranks of young pro-Palestine voters advocate both peace and equality.

*

Soon after the "globalize the intifada" controversy exploded, Mamdani called attention to the violence he had faced in recent weeks. At an East Harlem sidewalk presser highlighting his endorsement from Maya Wiley, the progressive third-place finisher in the 2021 Democratic primary, the rising star became emotional. "I get threats on my life and on the people that I love, and I try not to talk about it because the function of racism, as Toni Morrison

---

90 The other is "Safe&Affordable."

said, is distraction," Zohran said, fighting back tears. He then pivoted back to making the city affordable.[91]

While Mamdani walked the city streets, Cuomo preferred to sit at the wheel of his Dodge Charger. On Monday, June 16, *Daily News* reporter Josie Stratman posted a pic of the frontrunner's car parked in a left-turn lane in Midtown, a move known to further slow down already creeping traffic. The former governor had dropped by the hotel workers union headquarters to receive the group's backing, but his Charger antics got far more coverage than the 11th-hour endorsement.

Meanwhile, the escalating venom toward Zohran summoned darker sentiments shared by the city elite. Desperate for attention, Whitney Tilson—whose June polling numbers matched his 1% socioeconomic status—sought to whip up Islamophobic outrage. The billionaire donned a yarmulke and went to Brooklyn's Boro Park, home to many pro-Trump Orthodox Jews.

A 71-second video followed Tilson as he sought responses to the "globalize the intifada" controversy he helped stoke.[92] "I don't like what he said," an elderly man in a yarmulke said regarding Zohran's response to Tim Miller, adding that the insurgent candidate was a "danger." Things were starting to get pretty hot in that Boro Park bakery.

---

91 As MSNBC host Chris Hayes later noted, Zohran's ability to always stay on-message takes a page from the Bernie Sanders playbook.
92 The video included a clip of Tilson bringing up the phrase at the June 12 debate at John Jay College.

Meet Mayor Mamdani

A middle-aged white guy who is not identifiably Jewish then informed the yarmulke-sporting WASP that Mamdani "looks like a dangerous person." Pouring gas into the proverbial dumpster, Tilson suggested to him that "you have to be looking around a little more" when people like Mamdani are nearby. It was not clear whether Whitney meant Zohran or all young Muslim men.

Tilson's attack belonged somewhere beneath the gutter. Like Vickie Paladino's call to "deport" Zohran, it should have been roundly denounced—instead, over the next month, *Jewish Daily Forward* reporter Jacob Kornbluh's X post debuting Tilson's ad was viewed nearly 300,000 times. In the age of Trump and Musk, hate travels quickly.

An even more incendiary anti-Zohran statement went live only a few minutes before Kornbluh rolled out Tilson's attack piece.[93] Ever since the Holocaust smears started in the middle of May, it seemed only a matter of time before a Mamdani opponent played the Hitler card. With four days to go, Elisha Wiesel, son of the famous Holocaust survivor and author Elie Wiesel, finally dealt it.

In a one-minute statement set to an ominous soundtrack, Elisha, a former chief information officer at Goldman Sachs, solemnly warns about where the election of a Muslim, pro-Palestine mayor would lead. Narrating while clips show Hitler at a microphone followed by Nazi flags, gunfire, and mass roundups, Elisha states that "rhetoric turned to violence—it metastasized into genocide."

---

93 Tilson posted the video on X three hours after Kornbluh.

When Wiesel refers to "new attacks on Jews," he first presents snippets of the October 7 Hamas kidnappings and incidents of antisemitic terror in U.S. cities—before adding footage of nonviolent pro-Palestine campus protests in New York City. A one-word banner reading "Intifada" drives home Elisha's far-right message: Any criticism of Israel is antisemitic.

Zohran first surfaces at the 20-second mark, with a clip of the mayoral candidate telling activists that he had co-founded Bowdoin College's chapter of Students for Justice in Palestine. Viewers next glimpse a news report stating that the group's New York State branches have "endorsed the use of violence and attacks against civilians." Wiesel does not bother to clarify that Bowdoin is in Maine.

The statement ends at Auschwitz, with a cameo from Oprah standing next to Elie Wiesel. "Talk to your friends, Jewish and non-Jewish," implores Elisha, "and ask them not to rank Zohran Mamdani—and to keep antisemitism off the ballot." Paid for by the Wiesel family, the hit piece ended with "#DoNotRankMamdani" across the screen. Over the next month, it garnered over 1.5 million views on X.

Two days after Tilson and Weisel stoked the fire, a small plane carrying a similar message circled Lower Manhattan, making it visible from Sunset Park. "Save NYC from Global Intifada. Reject Mamdani," the sky banner advised. Cuomo's irascible longtime spokesman helped call attention to it on the Musk platform.

Meet Mayor Mamdani

This time the support came from a different set of ultra-nationalists. An outside spending group called Indian Americans for Cuomo paid $3,600 for the aerial statement. At the Public Theater forum in May, Zohran criticized India Prime Minister Narendra Modi, a Hindu nationalist. Akash Mehta, publisher of event co-sponsor *New York Focus*, asked candidates about India's ruler. Mamdani explained that his father's family hails from Gujarat, a large state northwest of Mumbai where Modi rose to power in the early 2000s.

At the candidate forum, Zohran told the audience that India's current prime minister "helped to orchestrate the mass slaughter of Gujurati Muslims." As a result, Mamdani stated, "We should view him in same manner as we do Benjamin Netanyahu—as a war criminal."

While his support for Netanyahu was quite evident, Cuomo had not said anything about Modi. The "Global Intifada" sky banner, meanwhile, only mentioned one candidate's name: Mamdani. Anyone from the "no publicity is bad publicity" school (from which Trump holds an honorary doctorate) can explain why the aerial attack did not hurt the insurgent.

*

Zohran's triumph on June 24 prompted a wave of death threats. According to a Council of American Islamic Relations-affiliated entity, there were over 125 hate-related reports involving the candidate or his campaign in just the first three days. At least 6,200 statements online during that same span contained an Islamophobic slur. Pro-Israel zealot Bill Ackman would soon play the 9/11 card, painting Zohran as pro-Al Qaeda because in 2004 Mahmood Mamdani argued that suicide bombers should be placed in the "category of soldier."

Mayor Adams responded to Cuomo's defeat by cozying up to Ackman and Daniel Loeb, who quickly cut ties to the primary's big loser. Ackman, who prefers not to play his cards close to the vest, wrote screeds on X detailing his search for a volunteer write-in candidate, which went nowhere. Ackman and Loeb thus settled on Adams, whom Loeb and other Israel hawks had pressured to bust up the pro-Palestine protests at Columbia the spring of 2024. The always-transactional mayor landed donations from the Bibi-loving billionaires.[94]

Adams invited Ackman and Loeb to choose key staff for his reelection bid. For campaign manager, the duo selected Eugene Noh, known in local politics for his no-holds-barred style. During the primary, Noh handled Whitney Tilson's field operation, which helped the bomb-throwing billionaire collect 8,500 votes, not a particularly good ROI for a campaign that spent over $3 million. Loeb and Ackman clearly know talent when they see it.

"We value their judgment very much, Dan and Bill," Adams' fixer Frank Carone told the *New York Times*. "These guys, they could be doing anything they want, but they're in the

---

[94] As reported by the *Washington Post* (5-16-2024), shortly before the NYPD's violent raid on the Columbia campus, Adams participated in a Zoom call with Loeb, NYC developers Len Blavatnik and Joe Sitt, and Daniel Lubetzky, founder of Kind snack company.

trenches here worrying about the state of New York and understanding affordability is a big issue."

Fixers say the damnedest things. So, too, do the city's leading news outlets.

*

Just prior to the start of early voting on June 14, Hasan Piker, Medhi Hasan, and countless other influential commentators helped the "M-A-M-D-A-N-I" takedown of Cuomo at the June 12 debate blow up. Meanwhile, the *New York Times* brass was shook. One might even say that the handwriting was all over the internet. As they scrambled together a response over the weekend, the *Times* editorial team watched Zohran, AOC, and company rally their excited ranks. Populism of any variety unnerves the Gray Lady.

On Monday, June 16, the *Times* editorial board issued a statement for the ages. The mannerly title, "Our Advice to Voters in a Vexing Race for New York Mayor," evoked the first Gilded Age, before Manhattan became the power center of a five-borough city. The actual "advice" suited the second Gilded Age, when billionaires in Midtown skyscrapers control the unruly metropolis.

There is no doubt about which billionaire the *Times* most reveres. His cops may have visited terror on minority teenage males, and planted spies in mosques, but Mike Bloomberg understood the need for "effective management," or so the editorial team declared. This bunch clearly cherishes the e-word, using it five times in a not-long statement, including an evidence-free assertion that Whitney Tilson was "effectively running as Bloomberg's heir."[95]

Despite his very successful universal pre-K rollout, Bill de Blasio, according to the *Times*' finest minds, "set back the city's K-12 school system." The pro-Bloomberg set then declared that de Blasio's "main legacy is to have contributed to the city's recent decline." The insult would have been stinging if it rang true.

After grudging flattery about Zohran's "charisma" and "fresh political style," the *Times* team moved in for the kill. "Unfortunately, Mr. Mamdani is running on an agenda uniquely unsuited to the city's challenges," the board huffed. "He is a democratic socialist who too often ignores the unavoidable trade-offs of governance." The city surely did not need anything Zohran's platform offered. "We do not believe that Mr. Mamdani deserves a spot on New Yorkers' ballots," maintained the Gray Lady, a suggestion widely ignored.

It was quite disturbing, the *Times* said, that the 33-year-old candidate, who came-of-age during the Bloomberg era of stop and frisk and Muslim surveillance, had the nerve to call de Blasio the "best New York mayor of his lifetime." Even though they called for Cuomo's resignation in 2021, the editorial team now concluded that Mario's obnoxious

---

95 Bloomberg's longtime operative Howard Wolfson was on the panel of fifteen "experts" and provided one of two first-place votes for Tilson. It's not clear if he was directly consulted for this statement, but his influence seems present.

kid really was the only option, citing Bloomberg's plug for the disgraced former governor as the main reason why.

In 21st-century parlance, the *Times* essentially said, "Cuomo sucks, but anything is better than Mamdani." Because the outlet's brass had voluntarily surrendered its endorsement power, the statement only "advised" voters to back the former governor. It did not mention Zohran's stance on Palestine—but, given the paper's clear bias for Israel, it's hard to ignore that as a leading reason for the *Times*' animus.[96]

The bombast backfired, producing yet another self-inflicted wound for the *Times*. A tsunami of derision flooded multiple platforms. Will Zohran's legions of young readers ever subscribe to a publication that hates what they stand for? The eleventh-hour plea for Cuomo was a "wimpy, disingenuous" move by the Gray Lady, de Blasio told *New York*'s Nia Prater. The former mayor added that if the attack on progressive politics "had come from the *New York Post*, I wouldn't have been surprised."

Rather than soften its stance towards the Democratic nominee, the *Times*' hostility towards Zohran after the primary mirrored the *Post*'s. First there was the aforementioned pseudo-scandal about Mamdani's Columbia application. At the end of July, the paper of record again stirred the pot.

---

[96] See Adam Johnson's analysis of the *Times*' coverage of Gaza in *The Intercept* (1-9-2024).

In the wake of a mass shooting in Midtown Manhattan, the *Times* joined the *Post* and Andrew Cuomo in spotlighting the fact that Zohran was in Uganda at the time. "Mr. Mamdani's absence could hardly have been more poorly timed," asserted a story in the outlet's local section, thus suggesting that the candidate's ten-day trip to Uganda to celebrate his recent wedding was somehow a failure in leadership. When the Democratic nominee returned to town 36 hours after the incident, he was quickly embraced by family members of two of the Midtown murder victims.

Because the *Post* had spent the ten days beforehand cheering on Israel's strikes against Iran,[97] Mamdani did not return to the tabloid's cover until primary day. "Say It Ain't Zo!" warned the front page on June 24. A large sub-headline then brazenly stated, "The *POST* says: NYers must reject radical, antisemitic socialist in today's primary."

A full-page cover photo showed Zohran speaking at a 2021 rally, at which a female activist wearing a hijab stands next to him holding a Within Our Lifetime poster reading "There is only one solution: Intifada, Revolution." Beneath that young woman, a small box of text calls attention to the poster and falsely claims that Mamdani "still defends" use of the phrase "globalize the intifada." For the fast-dwindling number of *Post* fans who read the tabloid's print edition, the anti-Mamdani message was loud and clear.

That same morning, I chatted with Queens-based Ali Najmi, Zohran's election lawyer and a trailblazer in the

---

97   From June 13 through June 23, seven *Post* covers focused on Israel-Iran.

political advancement of New York City Muslims. We discussed the possibility of a defamation lawsuit against the *Post*. "Zohran has never said anything antisemitic," Ali said. But among other obstacles, the Murdoch machine has powerhouse lawyers who can make a legal battle very costly.[98]

The following day saw the "NYC SOS" cover, after which Zohran appeared frequently on the tabloid's front page, including four times during the first week after his victory. On July 5, a *Post* cover read "Uganda Be Joking," a weak pun that referred to the *New York Times*-hyped "scandal" regarding Mamdani's college application. The *Post* was happy to amplify a hit piece that seemed more suited for the Murdoch rag.

Two weeks later, when Zohran and his wife, graphic artist Rama Duwaji (b. 1998), traveled to Uganda for their wedding party, the candidate took a memorable swipe at the *Post*. In a short clip set to a generic contemporary African beat, Zohran stated that "since you will undoubtedly read about this trip in the *New York Post*"—adding "*Inshallah*, on the front page"—the candidate prepared some potential bad pun covers. Mock-ups showed lead headlines such as "M.I.A.? Mamdani In Africa," "Uganda Miss Me," and "He Afri-Can't Be Serious."

---

98 Even when a defamation plaintiff can establish that the defendant knowingly lied, establishing "harm" is often difficult. As Ali and I agreed on primary day, it looked like Zohran was en route to victory, so the *Post*'s smears would have no damaging impact.

Andrew Epstein, who in July changed his role in the campaign to become creative director, told me that he and Zohran scripted the much-shared video, with Andrew writing the spoof headlines. Graphic designer Debbie Saslaw, whose team at Melted Solids worked frequently with Zohran for NYC during the primary, composed the fake *Post* covers, which looked quite real. Donald Borenstein handled the shoot.

Rather than a lengthy defamation lawsuit, Mamdani and company fought back against the *Post* with clever ridicule. The tabloid responded by writing a story about Zohran's spoof. Amid its zealous pursuit of clicks, Murdoch's crew seemed punchdrunk.

*

In the middle of May, the DSA contender was consistently polling second, but still trailing Cuomo by 20 points. Even so, on May 15, *Indypendent* publisher and editor John Tarleton's story "Zohran Mamdani's Path to Victory" went live on its website. Six weeks later, John seemed like a modern-day Nostradamus.

In order for Zohran to win, Tarleton argued that three things were essential: a "youth quake" in voter turnout, a vast mobilization of South Asian and Muslim communities,[99] and a strong show of support from rent-stabilized tenants. While the city's matching funds gave Mamdani sufficient resources, Zohran's DSA-led field operation provided a

---

99 As the *New York Times* reported after the primary, there are approximately one million Muslims currently living in New York City.

volunteer army. As Tarleton forecasted, endorsements by AOC and the Working Families Party would help, and the two televised debates in June would give Zohran a chance to shine.

One major twist that no one could predict at the time was how Israel-Palestine would play out. *Politico*'s dubious Holocaust attack on Zohran, which went live the morning after the prescient *Indy* story came out, triggered a chain reaction. Although they were not enemies at the time, Brad Lander and Mamdani became much closer allies over the next month, bonding against the Israel hawks' weaponization of antisemitism in order to stoke Islamophobia.

On Friday, June 13, Zohran and Brad announced that they would cross-endorse each other. They did so in a lighthearted video shot in Central Park, with each candidate holding a Greek NYC coffee cup. On the night before the primary, the duo sat for an extended, not very scintillating interview on *Late Night with Stephen Colbert*.[100]

In the month after Tarleton's roadmap came out, Zohran received particularly helpful endorsements from ex-Rep. Jamaal Bowman, Public Advocate Jumaane Williams, the Working Families Party, AOC, and then the latter's mentor, Rep. Nydia Velázquez, who touted Mamdani's readiness to fight ICE deportations. As the early voting returns started rolling in on Saturday, June 14, things immediately looked good for Zohran. The large numbers of first-time

---

100 The host made Israel the primary focus of the discussion, leading *Defector*'s Samer Kalaf to observe that "Colbert grilled [Mamdani] harder than he did Donald Rumsfeld."

voters strongly suggested that those under thirty, along with many new South Asian and Muslim participants in the political process, were indeed casting ballots.

Harlem and Washington Heights, which have very sizable numbers of rent-stabilized tenants, produced extremely strong margins for Zohran, who benefited from hip-hop media influencer support. During the homestretch, Kid Mero cut a clip showing that younger folks uptown were very excited to meet the candidate they already knew so much about.

Progressive Black state senator Robert Jackson, a native son of Harlem, endorsed Zohran on June 18, with the pair walking the streets and riding the subway together. "Brought my brother-in-the-struggle uptown," the energetic 70-something Jackson told his Instagram followers.

An early endorsement from State Senator Gustavo Rivera (b. 1975) helped put Zohran on the map in the former's district that straddles Fordham Road in the central Bronx. Amid early voting, Michael Blake (b. 1982) and Mamdani cross-endorsed a few neighborhoods south of Rivera's, producing a quick video on Blake's home turf. As the former Bronx assemblyman later told me, after he and Cuomo's leading opponent cut the video, they walked around Morrisania. "The positive energy on the street was palpable," Blake said. "Zohran's momentum was real." Even though Cuomo captured more votes in the area, Mamdani still racked up numbers.

Mamdani scored big returns in Bed-Stuy, which, like Harlem, is experiencing rapid gentrification but still retains significant numbers of Black voters. Zohran's totals in both neighborhoods undermines the frequent claim made by the DSA's critics that only newcomers support socialist candidates. Overall, Cuomo still carried the city's mostly Black areas by sixteen points over Mamdani, but Mario's son had anticipated that his former base would produce much larger margins.

As housing activist Charlie Dulik detailed in *New York Focus*, renters came out in force for Zohran. In the city's 52 assembly districts in which tenants are the majority, Zohran defeated Cuomo by 12 points. Cuomo, by contrast, won 11 of the 13 homeowner-led districts. Of the 2.4 million city residents who live in rent-stabilized units, over 40% are immigrants, and roughly 75% are people of color.

"Many older Black voters in Crown Heights are rent stabilized and Zohran's rent freeze message really resonated with them," explained Phara Souffrant Forrest, the DSA assemblymember representing the district. Here, again, Cuomo's name recognition and longstanding ties to local leaders enabled him to win the area, but Zohran still gained ground.

Cuomo's inability to grasp why tenants embraced Zohran was on full display when he chatted with Errol Louis in mid-July, as the failed primary candidate started his general election campaign. As they walked around Cuomo's childhood neighborhood of Holliswood, Queens, an area with lots of large single-family houses, the NY1 host teed up a softball question about the importance of homeownership. The failed primary candidate struck out.

Homeowners, Cuomo told Louis, share a "culture of vest[ment] to their community." The longtime suburbanite contrasted those he viewed as neighborhood pillars to renters who come and go. He advised Louis that tenants, like hotel guests, are most concerned about "how many towels they use." In a studio interview with Errol a few nights later, Zohran called out Cuomo for denigrating the millions of city residents who do not own their homes.

*

During the hectic last week of the primary, Zohran carved out time to speak with Geo News, a Pakistan-based outlet. Speaking mostly in Urdu, liberal nightly TV host Shahzeb Khanzada asked Mamdani about how Jewish voters in New York City viewed what Khanzada called the genocide in Gaza. Answering mainly in English, the surging mayoral candidate explained that he was gaining increasing support from Jewish voters angry about Israel's war crimes.

Pakistani American voters in the city came out in force for Zohran. Brooklyn's "Little Pakistan," which runs along Coney Island Avenue in and around Kensington, produced plenty of Mamdani votes. After the victory, Gyro King, an area Pakistani restaurant, enticed the candidate's fans to a celebration in Prospect Park by offering over 500 free meals.

During the last few weeks of the race, Palestinian American leaders including Ruwa Romman, Georgia's pioneering Muslim elected official who was not allowed to take the stage at the 2024 Democratic National Convention, knocked on doors in Bay Ridge, Astoria, and the Bronx for Zohran. Across the five boroughs, neighborhoods with substantial numbers of South Asian and/or Muslim residents produced very strong returns for Mamdani.

Just before primary day, Egyptian American comedian Kareem Rahma's multi-platform series "SubwayTakes"—which has many Muslim fans—featured Zohran. The two pals discussed the socialist's agenda while using their MetroCards as faux microphones. Instagram influencer Wear the Peace helped the episode go viral.

As Democratic consultant Amit Singh Bagga documented on X, by the end of June 24, Yemenis in the East Bronx joined Bangladeshis in Kensington and a wide range of South Asians in Jackson Heights and central Queens in support of a candidate who looked like them. In many such areas, Zohran's first-round tallies more than doubled Eric Adams' totals from four years earlier.

Documented NY reported that Jagpreet Singh and DRUM Beats had "deployed volunteers speaking Urdu, Bengali, Punjabi, Nepali, Tibetan, and Guyanese Creole to conduct door-to-door outreach in immigrant neighborhoods across the city." Bagga's analysis showed that the efforts paid off. "When you talk to people in the languages that they speak, literally and proverbially, about issues that they care about, they respond," Amit stated. "And when you don't, they don't."

On the Saturday before the primary, NY Communities for Change (NYCC) joined the NYC-DSA, CAAAV, and DRUM for a spirited rally in Jackson Heights. As young speakers wearing hijabs denounced Trump's immigration crackdown, veteran Black and brown NYCC organizers held a banner bashing billionaires, while CAAAV activists hoisted a "Freeze the Rent" poster featuring a red dragon. Zohran showed up, tapped rhythmically on a tassa drum, then raced off to more campaign stops.

The following day, more than 100 volunteers came out to canvas for Zohran and Alexa Avilés in Sunset Park. On this Sunday afternoon, the surging mayoral candidate and the vicious antagonist who shouted about "antisemitism" were elsewhere. Jewish Voice for Peace, along with CAAAV and UAW Local 9A, brought out many members, with the DSA's trained canvass leaders furnishing instructions to door-knocking teams.

Mamdani volunteer John Whitlow, a CUNY Law professor, told me he saw "no organic expressions of support" for Cuomo while speaking to Sunset Park voters that afternoon. In the Chinatown section of the Brooklyn neighborhood, Zohran signs appeared in the windows of coffee shops frequented by younger East Asians. Unlike adjacent Boro Park, a Trump stronghold that overwhelmingly supported Cuomo, Sunset Park solidly backed the democratic socialist.

At the pre-canvas rally, Avilés showcased many of the hit mailers that Ackman, Loeb, and fellow Israel hawks had funded against her, with the councilwoman laughing at the absurd smears. DSA assemblymember Marcela Mitaynes (who joined Zohran's Friday night Manhattan march) told me that she and Alexa were confident that Avilés would win the primary, but now wanted to "run up the score."

Like progressive Shahana Hanif in the neighboring district, Avilés indeed crushed the Israel hawks' candidate.

In late July, the Board of Elections released full details regarding the ranked-choice voting process. After round one, Zohran's 470,000 votes outnumbered Cuomo by over 80,000. Due mainly to the fact that 75% of Lander supporters ranked him second, Mamdani's final tally surpassed the former frontrunner by 130,000. As the DSA's Aaron Narraph explained on X, in terms of total ballot mentions (or 1-5 rankings), Cuomo finished a distant fourth, trailing Mamdani, Lander, and Adrienne Adams. Along Sutton Place, the socialist even collected a few hundred votes.

Zohran's primary win is "one of the greatest accomplishments by the left and the socialist movement in the last century," NYC-DSA co-chair Gustavo Gordillo told *The Dig*'s Daniel Denvir during a two-hour-long podcast interview about the campaign. "We built a working-class coalition that expanded the electorate in a way that no one thought was possible anymore." While the socialists and fellow travelers did so without much support from organized labor, most of the city's leading unions quickly got on-board for Mamdani's general election run.

In late July, Amit Singh Bagga's research firm announced the findings of a recent extensive survey that showed Zohran receiving very strong support from nearly every demographic, from Asian voters to men of color, reform Jews to LGBTQ+ voters, and from women of color to public transportation riders.

Put differently, the historical record shows that during the 2025 primary, Zohran and company opened up two cans of whoop-ass.

*

"He's a 100% Communist Lunatic (CL)," Trump posted the day after the primary on Truth Social, the president's in-house platform. One week later, the petty tyrant declared that the CL "will destroy New York," questioned Zohran's citizenship status, and threatened to arrest Mamdani if he blocked ICE deportations. Trump's VP then blasted the socialist for not showing sufficient "gratitude" on the Fourth of July.[101]

In mid-July, the MAGA figurehead praised Cuomo, thus deflating the hopes Zohran's other main challengers, Mayor Eric Adams and Republican candidate Curtis Sliwa, who vied for DJT's blessing. In sync with Cuomo, White House Press Secretary Karoline Leavitt told reporters that the president "does not want to see *Zem-donny* elected."

Leading New York Democrats including Gov. Kathy Hochul (b. 1958) and Rep. Hakeem Jeffries (b. 1970) sharply criticized Trump's threats against Zohran, but as of the end of July, both party figureheads declined to endorse a mayoral candidate overwhelmingly selected by the Democrats' own voters. Sen. Chuck Schumer also withheld his support. So did Sen. Kirsten Gillibrand (b. 1966),

---

101 On July 4, Zohran tweeted: "America is beautiful, contradictory, unfinished. I am proud of our country, even as we constantly strive to make it better."

who slandered Mamdani by falsely telling WNYC's Brian Lehrer that Zohran had made "references to global jihad."

Gillibrand was forced to apologize. But she and the other top New York Dems faced minimal mainstream media pressure to support the party's candidate. While Zohran sought to make his cost-of-living agenda a centerpiece of the Democrats' national platform, the Schumer-led brass looked the other way.

Starting in the early 2000s, Schumer (b. 1950) has helped his party focus on issues faced by the middle class, and the Dems' loss of working-class support does not seem troubling to him. What really irks him is any criticism of a certain U.S. ally. "My job," as the senate minority leader recently explained to the *Times* right-wing columnist Bret Stephens, "is to keep the left pro-Israel."

Coming from someone who usually says nothing insightful, that is a very revealing statement. Given the direction of the left on Israel in recent years, Chuck clearly has not performed his self-assigned "job" successfully. But it is not hard to see why he disdains Zohran, whose pro-Palestine statements at rallies at Grand Army Plaza may still ring in the senior senator's ears.

Why Jeffries did not quickly follow the lead of Rep. Jerrold Nadler (b. 1947), the Upper West Side-based chair of the Congressional Jewish Caucus who immediately endorsed Mamdani after the primary, was not fully clear. The Democrats' top figure in the House cited his grave concerns regarding the "globalize the intifada" issue. In addition to his outspoken disdain for socialism, Hakeem has long been an ardent Israel supporter.

Jeffries is not an ally of Eric Adams,[102] so Cuomo appeared to be his only other option. Meanwhile, the results of the primary posed a problem for the aspiring House majority leader. Zohran won Hakeem's district by twelve points—and Jabari Brisport, the local DSA state senator, is waiting in the wings.[103]

When she first ran for governor in 2022, Hochul assured the city's billionaire crowd that she would not support any effort by the state legislature to raise income taxes. Bipartisan deference to the 1% is a signature feature of the second Gilded Age. Hardly a minute passes in the national conversation without mention of a robber baron's name. As left-wing journalist Ken Klippenstein noted on X, CNN transitioned from a post-primary conversation with Zohran—during which the candidate stated that he "doesn't like capitalism"—to fluffy coverage of Jeff Bezos' $50 million wedding in Venice.

"I don't think we should have billionaires," Zohran told *Meet the Press* host Kristen Welker a few days after the primary, creating a stir. Faiz Shakir, Bernie Sanders' Pakistani American senior adviser, told an MSNBC panel that Mamdani should adopt FDR's notorious response to

---

102 In the 2021 primary, Jeffries backed Maya Wiley, marking one of the few times that he aligned with AOC in local races.
103 Although Brisport opted to run for reelection to the state senate, his ally Chi Ossé proposed a primary challenge to Jeffries, which Mamdani helped thwart soon after his November victory.

hostility from his foes among the economic elite. "Welcome their hatred," Shakir counseled.

As the Baby Boomer-Gen X ultra-rich count their money, tomorrow's leaders seek a more egalitarian future. A recent You.Gov survey found that 62% of US residents between the ages 18-29 view socialism favorably. In mid-July, *Drop Site*'s X account showed a clip of a podcast in which Andrew Schulz, a popular comedian, observed that Zohran's democratic socialist agenda is "what the base wants—what the people are into." "Honestly, that's what America wants," replied Charlamagne.

Many other stars circled Zohran's orbit in June. Comedians including pro-Palestine Saagar Shaikh and Asif Ali (stars of the *Deli Boys*) and Astoria-based lefty Stavros Halkias (*Tires*) joined West Village resident and pop icon Lorde in plugging the socialist.[104] On primary day, filmmaker Ava DuVernay chatted with Zohran on Instagram. That morning, supermodel Emily Ratajkowski, a longtime Bernie supporter, lit up the same platform by posting a clip in which she interacts with the socialist while sporting a Hot Girls for Zohran T-shirt. The fashionista group lent cheeky support throughout the campaign, most notably by hosting a Mamdani lookalike contest in mid-June.[105]

---

104 Bill de Blasio's November 2013 victory party at Brooklyn's Bell House featured New Zealand-raised Lorde's "Royals," a neo-Leveller anthem.

105 *Saturday Night Live* stars Bowen Yang and Sarah Sherman also plugged Zohran, with Sherman posting a much-viewed TikTok chat with the candidate.

It is easy for both naysayers and hardcore activists to dismiss celebrity backing as mere attention-seeking by people who love to be in the public eye. But the Old Left's "cultural front" of the 1930s reeled in artistic support from Langston Hughes, Paul Robeson, Woody Guthrie, Dorothea Lange, and countless other legends. Three decades later, New Left and Black freedom struggle sentiments reverberated throughout rock and roll, Motown, and funk. The revolution requires hard work, but it can and should encourage creative expressions of every kind. Note to self: insert Kid Rock joke here.

How Zohran would handle the New York city's frightened, hyper-sensitive billionaires became an immediate concern because attention must be paid to this neglected lot. At a mid-July summit with the 1%, the socialist candidate reportedly did not recognize James Tisch, a right-wing entertainment mogul and leading figure in Israel support networks who sat in the first row. The high rollers wanted to know if Mamdani would retain Jim's daughter Jessica Tisch, a dour technocrat currently serving as Eric Adams' fourth NYPD commissioner in the former cop's current four-year term. Zohran reserved his decision.

On the first Saturday night after the primary, the triumphant candidate thanked his many supporters across the city. At the Barclays Center in Brooklyn, Zohran assured a roaring Haitian crowd that "we will stand up for Haiti because you taught the world about freedom." Across town at the Beacon Theatre, comedian Ramy Youssef invited Mamdani to the stage with the recently freed Mahmoud Khalil, thrilling the packed house. As Muslim poet Hanif

Abdurraqib wrote in the *New Yorker*, "It was a delight to catch a glimpse of [Mahmoud and Zohran] laughing."[106]

Mamdani and his next-generation voters share a fundamentally different set of values from New York City's power elite. They are pro-Palestine and unafraid to be painted red. In describing Zohran's bases of support, voter turnout guru Michael Lange (b. 1999), an adviser to the campaign, coined the term "Commie Corridor" to describe the East River waterfront neighborhoods from Astoria south through Williamsburg that put up large numbers for the socialist. While many older voters view "commie" as a term of derision, twenty-somethings laugh at it.

*

"We are approaching the dawn of a new era in New York City," Zohran told reporters at a 5:30 a.m. presser in Astoria. Thus began a long day's journey into a night that saw the candidate hop about town before delivering his victory speech in Long Island City, then exchange hugs on the street with AOC.

After Cuomo's concession, the election-night celebrants chanted "A-li! A-li!" when Zohran's consigliere appeared on the big screen, in an interview broadcast live on NY1. The X feed of the Muslim Democratic Club, a group Najmi cofounded with Palestinian activist Linda Sarsour and

---

[106] Both Zohran and Mahmoud met with Bernie Sanders during separate July visits to DC, with Sanders posting smiling pics of himself with his arm around each figure.

others in 2013, called Ali "Zohran's brother and forever the People's Champ."

The next morning, Queens activist Jaslin Kaur posted a photo of herself with a middle-aged South Asian male fellow party attendee, with both showing their pearly white teeth to the camera while Lina Khan mingled in the background. "Last night," Kaur happily reported, "i stood next to the same taxi drivers and union members i went on hunger strike with as we watched our friend declare victory for mayor."

Kaur's lower-case "i" illustrates that no individual, including the candidate himself, can claim credit for Zohran's victory. But it was mostly certainly a triumph for the city's growing South Asian and/or Muslim communities, the DSA and kindred left-wing activists, Palestine supporters, hip-hop legions, and youth across the five boroughs. It was a resounding defeat for Mike Bloomberg and his friends at the *New York Times*, the *New York Post*, Bill Ackman, and Mario's son.

And let's not forget Whitney Tilson. Or perhaps we should.

"We all love this city, and yet it doesn't mean much if we can't afford to stay here," Zohran told the *Guardian*'s Erum Salam back in October. When the dust finally started to settle a few weeks after the primary, Donald Borenstein, Zohran for NYC's videographer, reflected on the campaign's efforts. The "most essential ingredient to our video style," Donald posted, was "a genuine love for the city and all of its people." Amid the torrent of hate he faced in the last six weeks of the campaign, Zohran frequently invoked his advocacy for "the city we love," often in sync with the June sunshine.

As we open the book on the politics of the future, let's close this chronicle with a blast from the past. At the *Hell Gate-New York Focus* mayoral forum at the Public Theater in mid-May, Zohran said that his favorite film about New York City is Spike Lee's[107] *Do the Right Thing*, which premiered during the racially charged 1989 Democratic primary contest pitting David Dinkins versus three-term incumbent Ed Koch.

In a standout monologue, the film's pivotal character Radio Raheem (Bill Nunn) tells Mookie (Spike Lee) why he's wearing two sets of gold brass knuckles, with his right hand reading love and his left spelling out hate. "One hand is always fighting the other," Raheem says while shadowboxing on a Bed-Stuy block.

In the imaginary fight Raheem presents to the camera, hate first puts love "on the ropes," but love then makes a dramatic comeback, knocking out hate with repeated right-hand blows. "I love you," Raheem tells Mookie. The plot then spirals in the opposite direction.

Unlike in Lee's 1989 classic work, in New York City's 2025 Democratic primary, love triumphed.

—August 3, 2025
Sunset Park, Brooklyn

---

[107] During the general election, Spike became an outspoken Zohran supporter.

Part Two

MEET MAYOR MAMDANI

THE SPECTACULAR VICTORY OF A DEMOCRATIC SOCIALIST IN NEW YORK CITY

Note: In the following chapters, *RZR* refers to *Run Zohran Run!*

CHAPTER 15

Group Therapy

A disgraced former governor, an embattled mayor, and a wannabe sheriff walk into a bar. Therein, the three Baby Boomers encounter a Gen X lawyer challenging a millennial socialist to a fight. Fists waving, the pol and mayor rush to the plaintiff's side. The Guardian Angel breaks it up. The leftist emerges unscathed.

Thus went the second half of summer along New York City's 2025 mayoral campaign trail. While Zohran Mamdani endured round after round of flailing attacks from oh-so familiar politicians in their twilight, an attention-hungry novice challenger desperately tried to enter the ring. At times, the Democratic nominee appeared to be deploying Muhammad Ali's infamous "rope-a-dope" strategy, allowing his opponents to pound away at him with harmless blows. But the vigorous Boomers showed no signs of fatigue.

Meet Mayor Mamdani

"Andrew has nothing else to do, you know?" Mario Cuomo's former senior adviser Michael Del Giudice told *New York Times* mainstay Adam Nagourney, whose bio noted that he first covered Cuomo family politicking during Mario's 1982 run for governor.[1] The toppled 2025 primary frontrunner now running as an independent in the November general election appeared to have few other late career options. Although Mario's son had pledged his legal skills to Benjamin Netanyahu, few other clients—whether facing international war crimes or more quotidian charges—seemed to be lining up at his door.

One of the few savvy moves that Cuomo's campaign made during the primary was collecting enough petition signatures from city voters in order to run as an independent candidate in November. Any such figure creates a party name listed under their name on the ballot. In sync with his style and emphasis on his track record, Cuomo opted for "Fight and Deliver" (F&D).

During the primary, the veteran pol repeatedly told older voters that he was defending the Democratic Party from the insurgency led by the NYC-DSA. After losing the nomination to the socialist candidate, Cuomo now tried to enlist the party's traditional base in his battle against the newcomers. If successful, the F&D contender would have created total chaos for New York City Democrats. But

---

[1] Pop culture enthusiasts may recall a famous similar line from a Hollywood film that premiered amid the 1982 race. "I got nowhere else to go!" aspiring officer (Richard Gere) cries out to the hard-ass sergeant (Louis Gossett, Jr.) trying to weed him out of the Navy in *An Officer and a Gentleman*.

given his grudges against the innumerable party leaders who helped spur his resignation as governor in 2021—a list that included AOC, Zohran and fellow DSA elected officials—Cuomo appeared eager to enact revenge. As suggested by his bespoke ballot identifier, Mario's boy would not go down quietly.

To add nobility to his scorched-earth campaign, Andrew summoned his father's ghost. "Remember," the candidate advised his followers in a homestretch pinned post on X, "while I am a lifelong Democrat just like my father Mario Cuomo before me, this year I am running on the Fight & Deliver independent ballot line." The statement provided no lofty rationale for the shift. Unlike his old man, the younger Cuomo is not known for his eloquence.

Although he was by no means the only challenger to Mamdani, Cuomo was by far the noisiest. Like another dude raised in postwar Queens, the former governor viscerally understood that angry pols who say mean things get plenty of media attention. Amid the dog days of August, Andrew barked loudly.

*

In the wake of his humiliating late June loss, Cuomo conducted precious little soul-searching. In addition to reaffirming his uncritical loyalty to Israel before a pro-Netanyahu synagogue in the Hamptons in mid-July, the former frontrunner insisted that the leftist defeated him because he "wasn't aggressive enough—which is really ironic because all my life I'm 'too aggressive' or 'too tough.'" Cuomo was amped to sling even more mud toward Mamdani in the fall election.

Throughout much of August, Cuomo literally tried to hit the Democratic nominee where Zohran lived, namely in a rent-controlled apartment in Astoria. As we shall see, after that blaze sputtered out, the F&D challenger continued to swing above and below the belt—and when his blows did not land, he seemed ready to resort to the belt. Along with longshot lawyer Jim Walden, the city's muscular mayor also lobbed grenades.

Now running on a ballot line he titled "Safe&Affordable/EndAntiSemitism," Mayor Eric Adams registered record-low numbers for an incumbent in the polls, struggling to reach double digits. Meanwhile, his inner circle managed to spark even more controversies in August for the scandal-scarred pol. Longtime adviser Winnie Greco made national headlines for trying to bribe a local reporter.

Greco was no stranger to controversy. Amid Adams' 2024 federal corruption case, her two Bronx homes were raided by the FBI. At an August 20 campaign event in Harlem, Greco handed *The City*'s Katie Honan a small bag of Herr's Sour Cream & Onion potato chips containing a red envelope full of cash. After Honan refused the enticing offer, Greco—Adams' liaison to the city's Chinese business leaders—absurdly claimed that her gift was "a cultural thing."

One day after Chipgate, Manhattan D.A. Alvin Bragg indicted the mayor's closest adviser Ingrid Lewis-Martin on four counts of bribery, which doubled the total of state criminal corruption charges that Adams' right-hand woman now faced. Prosecutors alleged that in exchange for a cameo appearance in Hulu's series *The Godfather of Harlem*, Lewis-Martin helped block a proposed Greenpoint street safety project opposed by the show's production company based nearby. The new round of scandals meant that the mayor, who had famously boasted about his "swagger" upon entering City Hall, now appeared to be staggering toward the exit.

While his peer contenders became seriously cartoonish, the formerly cartoonish Curtis Sliwa turned distinctly serious. No longer habitually sporting his signature red beret, the Republican nominee now frequently wore a suit instead of his trademark Guardian Angels gear. For over four decades—as leader of his volunteer safety patrol organization and a right-wing media personality—Curtis had been a household name in the city. Rather unexpectedly, Sliwa was also the only mayoral candidate who pronounced Mamdani's name correctly and generally treated the next-gen leader with respect.

At the outset of the 2025 mayoral race, few would have bet that a millennial socialist would be the Democratic nominee. The odds were even worse that a shock jock like Sliwa would campaign with far more dignity than his fellow Boomers. For the Hamptons elite, Zohran's ascent produced a summer of profound discontent—it was the hour of "group therapy," declared the *New York Times*. For theater enthusiasts in the city, the summer campaign provided no shortage of screwball comedy.

*

With Zohran as the new front-runner, the dynamics of the race flipped. In the primary, Cuomo led the pack, causing Mamdani and fellow contenders to set their sights on the former governor. With the DSA figurehead now topping the general election polls, Zohran's bickering rivals agreed on only one thing: A socialist must not control City Hall.

That line of attack was amplified by the septuagenarian New York City real estate developer holding down the White House. "I don't [want] to see a communist become mayor," stated the president—who is not known to be a political theorist—during a meeting with Bibi Netanyahu. The outsized bully from Queens soon dubbed Mamdani the "Little Communist."

Although Adams and Sliwa vied for Trump's blessing, throughout the month of August Donald talked up Mario's son. Andrew and Fred's boy went back a few years. "Let's put it this way: I knew the president very well," the former Democratic frontrunner told a mid-August 2025 shindig hosted by right-wing media mogul Jimmy Finkelstein at his Southampton estate. While Cuomo made several summer fundraising visits to the Hamptons, this one was notable for its MAGA connections.[2]

Starting in the 1980s, the city's best-known real estate mogul filled Mario Cuomo's campaign coffers. "I believe there's a big piece of [Trump] that actually wants redemption in New York," Andrew now claimed, referring to Donald's three lopsided local rejections in his presidential runs. Although most observers would say that *revenge*

---

2   *Politico* New York obtained a recording of Cuomo's remarks.

animates the president, Cuomo—no doubt aware that Finkelstein's wife (Pamela Gross) had close ties to Melania Trump—added a more noble gloss.

The career Democrat craved MAGA support. His fellow Queens dude received the backing of 30% of New York City voters in 2024, which Cuomo hoped to supplement with conservative Democrats. The former governor assured the Hamptons set that the president would help clear the field so that the general election would pit only Andrew versus Zohran. "I feel good about that," he advised the high rollers. After *Politico* reported Cuomo's remarks, his longtime attack dog Rich Azzopardi loopily insisted that the campaign was "not asking for or expecting help from anyone."

If nothing else, the Fight and Deliver challenger seemed ready to deliver a fight. Outside of the former governor's inner circle, it is not clear who advised him that "not enough saber-rattling" explained his flop in the primary. But whether on his team or not, everyone—including Cuomo—agreed that his social media operation needed an upgrade.

As seen in *RZR*, back in June the longtime frontrunner claimed to have "*intellectually* but not *practically* mastered" 21st-century communications. After a crash course, Cuomo went to work. Gone was the figure who launched his 2025 campaign with a video monologue in which he spoke directly to the camera for 17.5 minutes. In came memes, jump cuts, and countless quick shots of the candidate chatting up regular folks.

Cuomo outlined his revised social media game plan for the general election in an early August discussion with Bloomberg Surveillance (BS), a longstanding finance talk show carried on the eponymous network owned by the media titan turned mayor. As detailed by *Hell Gate*'s Adlan Jackson, BS host Tom Keene (b. 1952)—rocking a bow tie on a hot summer day and fretting about the wayward youth that supported Zohran—asked Andrew how he planned to do things differently over the next three months.

"It is all about social media, especially for the under 30, and that is something that I'm now focusing on very heavily," Cuomo assured Keene via webcam. The aging pol nonetheless vowed to inform next gen voters that Zohran's affordability proposals are "not real solutions." At the same time, he merely paid lip service to bread-and-butter concerns. As Jackson observed, Cuomo seemed to think that he just needed "to 'rizz' Zoomers up with just a few more things about affordability." The cynical Boomer thus appeared to believe that tomorrow's leaders can be easily duped.

After his upset defeat in June, Cuomo also dispensed with the Rose Garden approach that failed him in the primary. He was now out and about, often in summery business casual attire. The veteran pol popped up on Midtown streets and hopped aboard the Staten Island Ferry, although unlike Zohran, he did not call attention to the fact that it's free. The campaign's revamped comms team posted lots of endearing stuff on Instagram. Followers saw a fuzzy mutt sporting a Cuomo bandana. Outside the Hollis, Queens house where he first grew up, Mario's eldest son told syrupy anecdotes about family history to Mariah Kennedy-Cuomo, one of his three millennial daughters.

In late August, the suddenly outgoing 67-year-old pol visited All-n-All, an auto body shop in his old neighborhood, an area visually indistinguishable from the nearby Long Island suburbs. Mario's son waxed nostalgically about fixing fenders as a teenager while working at an outfit called Cross Island Collision. As the muscle-car candidate and white, middle-aged body shop guy agreed, various unspecified "regulations" made it tough for small businesses to thrive in today's New York City. Cuomo vowed to cut the red tape.

Amid his five-borough outreach, the fallen star still seemed to ignore an essential reason why Zohran's campaign captured the votes of well over a half-million New Yorkers in the primary. Mamdani's three-pronged message—freeze the rent, make buses fast and free, provide universal child care—appealed to sizable swaths of the city electorate. By contrast, Mario's son doggedly insisted that voters most valued a candidate's track record, a sales pitch that is intrinsically more focused on yesterday than tomorrow.

*

Long before Zohran entered the race for mayor in late October 2024, "Freeze the Rent" had been a rallying cry for the NYC-DSA. Despite Cuomo's evidence-free claims to the contrary, Mamdani repeatedly clarified on the campaign trail that his staple pledge only applied to the roughly one million apartments units overseen by New York City's longstanding rent protection program.

For example, in January 2025 blues poet and songstress Aja Monet welcomed Zohran to the stage at the NYC Winter Jazzfest. In briefly introducing himself to a large nightclub audience, the DSA candidate talked up affordability and his desire to restore the "New York City dream." "I will freeze the rent for every single rent-stabilized tenant in this city," Mamdani declared.

Although over 1.3 million additional apartments in the vast metropolis are unregulated, a rent freeze nonetheless would benefit nearly 2.5 million New York City residents, who saw a 12% total increase during the landlord-friendly Adams administration.

Taking a cue from Republican strategist Karl Rove during the George W. Bush era, Cuomo decided that in the wake of Mamdani's primary triumph, he would attack Zohran's main source of strength[3]: the DSA candidate's support from rent-stabilized tenants, a category that includes nearly every demographic in the city.

Such a move was politically perilous, given the reality that many people vote with their pocketbooks—and it's not only lower-income New Yorkers that enjoy the benefits of rent protection. The program enables middle-income tenants to accrue familial wealth. Cuomo and his crew nonetheless seemed eager to slam Zohran over the issue,

---

3   In the 2004 presidential campaign, which took place amid the Iraq War, Rove famously orchestrated the Republican attack on Democratic nominee John Kerry's reputation as a "war hero" in Viet Nam.

mainly because it enabled them to hurl bitter insults at the socialist who upset their apple cart.

On Friday, August 8, Cuomo tossed a virtual Molotov cocktail. "Somewhere last night in New York City," the former governor bellowed, "a single mother and her children slept at a homeless shelter because you, Assemblyman Mamdani, are occupying her rent-controlled apartment." After a bunch of details about Zohran's family income, including the legislator's $142,000 salary, Cuomo's lengthy X missive added lightning to its thunder, stating: "Leaders must show moral clarity. It's time to move out."

Most unsurprisingly, Cuomo's eviction notice caught fire on Elon Musk's bot-ridden platform, with the initial post capturing 35 million views by mid-September (and related statements garnering millions more eyeballs). In the Age of Trump, fiery incoherence flies. For the hordes encouraged by billionaires to hate socialists, the blistering assault furnished a double shot of dopamine.

But upon close inspection, the Fight and Deliver dude's carefully scripted attack amounted to little more than sandbox-level taunting. As governor, Cuomo cared infinitely more about Manhattan real estate developers than homeless families. And the claim that people currently living in shelters could even afford $2,300 in monthly rent was pure hogwash. Indeed, the guy who pays nearly $100,000 per year for a Manhattan luxury rental reinforced Zohran's frequent critique that the longtime suburbanite was out of touch with everyday New Yorkers.

Meet Mayor Mamdani

Cuomo's scattershot assault was nonetheless very much on brand. Like the F&D candidate, the statement was nasty, brutish, and mean—or some combination thereof. The father of three daughters even blasted Zohran's intercontinental wedding celebrations, thereby insulting the Democratic nominee's family heritage. One month later, Cuomo smeared Zohran's mother, echoing *New York Post* insinuations that Qatari investor funding for Mira Nair's films somehow linked her to Islamic extremism.[4]

In his desperate bid to score points, the veteran pol weaponized his own family tree. On the same day as the rent attack, the flailing challenger issued a high-testosterone warning:

In case you forgot, I'm Andrew Cuomo, son of Mario, grandson of Andrea.

Welcome to the heavyweight bout, @ZohranKMamdani.

This is a two-man race. You look tired already. It's just the second round.

Rather than Sylvester Stallone's "Rocky," Cuomo sounded more like Jerry Quarry, the "Great White Hope" contender that Muhammad Ali famously pummeled in three rounds.

"I live rent-free in his head," Zohran quipped in response to Cuomo's ginned-up outrage. *Gothamist* reporters Brigid Bergin and Elizabeth Kim soon paid a mid-August visit to

---

4   "My mother was a teacher. His mother took him to Cannes where he walked the red carpet, funded by Qatari money," the always-classy former governor tweeted on September 9.

Mamdani's Astoria apartment building. One resident told them that the place is "comfortable, but nothing special." None of Mamdani's neighbors told Bergin or Kim that the assemblymember's salary qualified as exorbitant.

Along with tenant advocates across the city, the DSA candidate's Astoria neighbors denounced "Zohran's Law," a headline-friendly proposal by Cuomo that would require rent-stabilized tenants to pay at least 30% of their yearly income to landlords or leave the program. Instead of bolstering the economic security of renters, the initiative promised a windfall for building owners, many of which are Wall Street private equity firms. Cuomo's faux-populist outrage against Mamdani caused him to advance deeply unpopular plans, a rather problematic strategy for a struggling contender.

*

Mamdani deftly responded to Cuomo's relentless onslaught with stinging ridicule. On the Tuesday afternoon following the rent hubbub, Zohran posted a video underneath a simple statement: "#ReleaseTheCuomoList." The hashtag spun off from the roiling Jeffrey Epstein scandal.

In just under 90 seconds, Mamdani presented a sequence of clips that began with news coverage of the former governor's sexual harassment and pandemic controversies. As Zohran stated, "Less well known is what Cuomo spent the last four years doing—besides getting trounced in the Democratic primary." For added emphasis, an insert box placed aside Mamdani featured a nightly news clip showing the smiling victor collecting 56% of the vote and the scowling runner-up at 44%. The left hook landed.

Standing with his right hand palming a lamp pole, the Democratic nominee then narrated a montage of headlines referring to the mystery clients that retained Cuomo's consulting firm over the previous few years. As Zohran pointedly noted, although the former Albany shot-caller "raked in" more than a half-million dollars in 2024, he "refuses to say who paid for his services." Citing a *New York Times* report documenting Cuomo's longstanding ties to investor Andrew Farkas, Mamdani then highlighted Farkas' close association with Jeffrey Epstein. "*Habibi*, release your client list," the Muslim candidate closed out with a smile.

Although the presentation offered no direct link between Cuomo and Epstein, the viral statement showed that Zohran was ready to throw mud back at his spiteful rival. It also illustrated that the Democratic nominee would wrap his counterattacks around the second-place challenger's scandal-ridden track record. "Andrew Cuomo is someone who doesn't understand that no means no," the nominee advised reporters that week regarding why the toppled frontrunner stayed in the general election race. Zohran thus painted his opponent as both a predator and a sore loser, with Cuomo himself providing daily reinforcement of the latter point.

As seen by his sagging poll numbers, Mario's son's "limousine socialist" slams against Zohran made no measurable impact. The volleys might have carried more weight if the career pol had pulled himself up by the bootstraps. But like that other guy from Queens, the former governor inherited his status, thus making his attacks on Mamdani's privileged background sound foolish.

Meanwhile, in addition to snappy clips, Zohran peppered his posts with biting quips. Calling attention to news that Cuomo was again headed to the Hamptons, Mamdani stated, "He got homesick." On social media, three words pack far more punch than multi-paragraph screeds.

*

While Team Cuomo disseminated standard issue campaign content, the Zohran for NYC crew continued to create cutting-edge stuff. In one post that spawned national headlines, Mamdani never even appeared. Leftist actor Morgan Spector, who plays railroad magnate George Russell in HBO's *The Gilded Age*, carried the video segment. Cuomo was not its primary target.

Instead, the early September post lampooned a recent *New York Times* story that hyperbolically documented the anti-Mamdani sentiments shared by the Hamptons ultra-elite. Written by Style reporter Jacob Bernstein, the article's faux-inquisitive title "How Are the Very Rich Feeling About New York's Next Mayor?" raised precious little doubt about the answer.

Spector stays in character as robber baron George Russell, attired in evening wear and slowly delivering a slew of overblown lines from the story, which the actor holds in a Gilded Age-era large leather folio. The reading takes place in a stately home library, with generic classical music running throughout the 91-second clip. Spector calls special attention to the reporter's use of "freakout" and "group therapy" to describe the collective Hamptons reaction to the democratic socialist's rise. The thespian also adds mock nobility to the fallen frontrunner by pronouncing his name as "Andrew M. *Cue-oh-mo.*"

Prior to becoming a lead actor in *The Gilded Age*, Spector, a Reed College graduate, produced a documentary titled *The Big Scary 'S' Word* (2020), which featured Bernie, AOC, Cornel West, Naomi Klein and many other prominent leftists extolling the socialist tradition. "I think Zohran Mamdani is a fantastic candidate," Spector told *Rolling Stone* in June.

Zohran for NYC creative director Andrew Epstein told me that when he first read the *Times* piece, he found it "completely absurd" and ripe for parody. Andrew wanted Zohran to perform the reading, but campaign senior advisor Zara Rahim suggested that because of his *Gilded Age* role and political commitments, Spector would be perfect. They did the shoot at the Brooklyn Heights home of a Mamdani supporter. "I've been told that it made the rounds internally at the *Times*," Andrew noted ten days after the much-touted post went up.

Most politicians avoid antagonizing the New York City establishment. As seen quite dramatically during the 2025 primary, the 1% regularly bankroll challengers against their critics. Prominent figures in the arts also generally prefer to stay in good standing with the *Times*, an outlet that helps steer the national conversation. But Mamdani and Spector showed that they were unafraid to fight back against the bullies—and do so via winning satire.

CHAPTER 16
Heavy Lifts

During the primary, Zohran ran a grassroots campaign, frequently giving pep talks to pre-canvass rallies. After his victory, his style of outreach changed, with the front-runner now making far fewer public appearances at large outdoor events. Rather than choice, safety considerations explained the shift.

As noted in *RZR*, when Zohran visited Coney Island for the annual festivities on New Year's Day of 2025, he traveled only with Andrew Epstein, then the campaign's communications director. *Indypendent* publisher John Tarleton recalls chatting with the duo on the boardwalk before Zohran memorably joined the plunge into the cold bay. As Epstein explained to me shortly after the primary, the winner no longer went anywhere without an NYPD security detail. "It's really weird," Andrew said in early July. "Everyone is still adjusting, especially Zohran."

Meet Mayor Mamdani

Gone were the days of spontaneous outings and impromptu chats with reporters.[5] When *Inside City Hall* host Errol Louis interviewed Mamdani in September, an NYPD SUV trailed the duo as they walked around Astoria. There was no question that the now internationally prominent figure needed protection. Death threats against him persisted.

After MAGA influencer Charlie Kirk was assassinated on September 10, many fellow Zohran supporters and I feared that something comparable might occur to the leftist Muslim candidate, especially given the proximity to 9/11. After attending the tightly secured annual morning memorial event at Ground Zero, Mamdani stayed out of the public eye that day. One week later, the Queens district attorney indicted Jeremy Fistel on 22 counts for threats made against the ascending city leader in June. Raised in an Orthodox Jewish household in the Boston suburbs, Fistel now calls north Texas home. Prosecutors alleged that the 44-year-old left voice messages threatening the Muslim mayoral candidate with a car bomb and invoking the IDF.

Mayor Adams—then lagging far behind Mamdani and Andrew Cuomo (while also trailing Curtis Sliwa)— seized the moment to criticize the Democratic nominee. It was

---

5   After a mid-August *Time* cover story (penned by Mark Chiusano) reported that Zohran—because of security concerns—liked to take walks in city cemeteries, Curtis Sliwa, along with Cuomo's hatchet man and the *New York Post*, ridiculed the new habit. The phony scandal served as a reminder that even in the "city that never sleeps," August is the slow season in the news cycle.

"ironic," declared the former precinct captain, that the frontrunner who once criticized the NYPD now benefitted from the police investigation that led to Fistel's capture. The fourth-place figure struggled to stay relevant.

*

As Labor Day neared, the race for mayor became a traveling theater of the absurd. On Saturday, August 23, Zohran traveled to Crown Heights for a street fair hosted by 500 Men, a Black empowerment group. The annual event featured youth-friendly activities including a circus and Double Dutch lessons. Mamdani's visit to the outdoor gym quickly captured global attention.

Egged on by 20-something Black bodybuilders who enthusiastically called him the "next mayor," Zohran took off his sport jacket and agreed to bench press 135 pounds, roughly his own bodyweight. He needed the help of a spotter to complete the task. MAGA influencer @Libsof TikTok quickly posted a clip of the action that started with an extended "lol." The *Post* pounced. A rather muscular podcaster in Austin who chats endlessly with his guests shared the clip with his 1.7 million-member Reddit group. "'Weak Little Man,'" the pro-Narendra Modi *Hindustan Times* told its vast readership, pulling the quote from an unidentified X account.

To nobody's surprise, Eric Adams and Andrew Cuomo got really worked up. Above a clip of himself pumping iron, the mayor stated on X: "64 vs. 33. A lifetime of hard work vs. a silver spoon. The weight of the job is too heavy for 'Mamscrawny.'" Cuomo's take was slightly less juvenile but still freighted with testosterone. "This guy can't bench his own body weight, let alone carry the weight of leading the most important city in the world," he declared.

Neither Adams nor Cuomo saw any need to explain the relationship between bench pressing and leading New York City. The alpha males also did not think through the implications of their stance. "Imagine if female candidates were forced to partake in competitive Pilates," the NYC-DSA's Susan Kang told *Inside City Hall* host Errol Louis regarding "Dumbbell Gate."

Not far from the Crown Heights street fair, Zohran exhibited different athletic skills. The former high school soccer captain took off his boots and kicked a ball at a massive inflatable dartboard set up near the Brooklyn Museum. Even Zohran's arch-nemesis the *New York Post* acknowledged that he "expertly" and "vigorously" scored points. Two weeks later, the socialist again showcased his love for the beautiful game, this time matching it with his passion for affordability.

On September 9, Zohran posted a video in which he attacked FIFA price gouging for 2026 World Cup tickets while playing soccer in business attire. Mamdani's declaration came as seats went on sale for the major global event hosted by the U.S., Mexico and Canada, with the final taking place at New Jersey's Meadowlands, near New York City. By mid-October the cheapest ticket for the ultimate match checked in at $2,800, with FIFA using dynamic pricing.

As was the case in the primary, Zohran's statement mixed pleasure with business. After playfully speaking in a high British accent, Mamdani—showcasing his ball-handling skills—plainly laid out the details of FIFA's pricing scheme. The candidate then asked supporters to sign a Zohran for NYC website petition calling on FIFA to curb the scams and set aside 15% of tickets for local residents. Mamdani closed the statement by issuing a red card to the hyper-capitalist global organization with "GREED" written across it.[6]

While Mamdani showed off his footwork, back at the late August fair in Crown Heights, a different alpha male candidate in the race came out fists first—and paid the price.

Longshot Jim Walden (b. 1966) unwisely opted to box a few rounds with an NYPD sparring partner. A lawyer who once worked with Chuck Schumer's wife Iris Weinshall in trying to stop the creation of bike lanes along Prospect Park West, Gentleman Jim now ended up hospitalized with a concussion. The veteran litigator posted a pic of himself on Instagram with an IV drip in his arm and his index finger pointing to his head. If nothing else, the first-time candidate's actions gave new meaning to throwing one's hat into the ring.

Amid his neurological recovery, Walden—polling below one percent—began to see things clearly. The would-be Rocky soon announced that he would end his doomed

---

[6] In mid-September, anti-monopoly crusader Lina Khan joined her ally Mamdani for an interview with Pablo Torre, a left-leaning sports podcaster. Both guests denounced FIFA's rapacity, with Khan explaining that for today's global elite, "rules don't matter."

mayoral campaign, a move that received unmerited headlines. Before heading back to his law firm, the pugilist issued Whitney Tilson-style jabs at Zohran, accusing the Democratic nominee of "extreme bigotry toward the police, authentic commitment to communism, and antisemitic obsessions."

Meanwhile, like countless pro-Mamdani commenters on the Musk platform, I instantly received blistering replies to my statements about the race from a bot called CityDeskNYC. Perhaps uniquely, I challenged the spam machine to a fight.

In response to a late August promotional video that my pals and I put together—which played up my statement in the conclusion of *RZR* that Zohran "opened up two cans of whoop ass" in the primary—CityDesk came out swinging. "Hamm's book isn't hope—it's DSA fan fic," the bot insisted, larding the tweet with slams against "taxpayer-funded grocery stores" and "globalize the intifada."

With my honor on the line, I shot back. "Those are fighting words, Robot. Meet me outside the Barclays Center at 9 p.m. tonight so we can settle this." Quite predictably, the tough talker was a no-show.

The anti-Mamdani fervor became so bonkers that innumerable sentient humans could be found among CityDesk's 2,600 followers. Even though the account clearly stated that it was A.I.-generated material from a company called Rhetor—and every post carried the X label of "automated"—many fire-breathing Zohran haters, including at least one familiar figure in NYC social media circles, chose to add the robot's relentless stream of repetitious attacks on the leftist pol to their feeds.

In addition to MAGA faithful, as of mid-September the roster of CityDesk followers included Maria Danzilo, a 60-something white registered attorney who regularly attacked Mamdani in her own X postings; Tommy Torres, a 40-ish Latino school administrator who identified himself as a "special assistant to Mayor Eric Adams;" and a cross-section of people whose bios mentioned their college degrees. Memo to Penn State: no disrespect.

CityDesk itself followed only three accounts, a privilege typically reserved for mega-celebrities. One was Rhetor's creator, Saihajpreet Singh, a 20-something guy who lives in Canada and dons a Sikh turban.[7] "Many people hate me," the Carleton University-trained software engineer acknowledged after CityDesk's post-primary debut. As he explained to the *Ottawa Citizen*, a longstanding conservative outlet in Singh's current hometown, the spam creator initially faced derision after creating DOGEai, a MAGA bot on X dutifully amplified by Trump and his buddy Musk.

Singh's monotonous anti-Mamdani account briefly became amusing when Jim Walden ended his doomed bid for mayor. On the morning after Gentleman Jim threw in the towel, I posted campaign finance records on X that showed a curious string of maximum donations that Walden's extreme longshot campaign received from a clan of riverboat gamblers all the way down in Shreveport,

---

7   In early September, the account followed Singh. Later in the month, it no longer did so—a 21st-century *Frankenstein* tale.

Louisiana. ("WTF?" Justin Brannan told me in response to the info.) "The Dicksons backing Walden? Smart money against corruption," asserted CityDesk, which apparently didn't get the dropout memo from Jim.

*

While Walden jumped ship shortly after Labor Day,[8] Mamdani's three better-known foes formed a circular firing squad. The only thing that the hardheaded trio could agree on was that two of them should drop out so that one would have a better shot at beating the socialist frontrunner.

Although Adams, Cuomo, Sliwa are not literary men, their maneuvering was downright Shakespearean. Rumors spread that the Trump administration would give Adams a position at HUD in exchange for the mayor dropping out of the race—an implausible notion given the mayor's unslakable thirst for the spotlight.

Adams, in turn, attacked Cuomo. The former governor's backstage scheming drew the mayor's ire. Adams opened a September press conference by declaring that "Andrew Cuomo is a snake and a liar." The mayor made his angry declaration while standing outside of Gracie Mansion

---

8   After dropping out, Walden unsuccessfully sued the Board of Elections, seeking to remove his name from the November ballot. In late Sept., Jim's bio on X stressed that he was a "FORMER" mayoral contender, pleading "don't vote for me—I remain on the ballot against my will." If nothing else, the hostage crisis seemed unique.

in front of a very lush garden, which is fine habitat for a garter snake.

Sliwa, the Republican nominee polling around 15% in early September,[9] shot down any suggestion that he would take a job in Trump's DC. In addition to making the veteran Guardian Angel a fish out of water, such a move would have been a gift to Cuomo, a longtime foe of local Republicans. A victory by an independent candidate posed a major threat to New York City's two-party status quo.

The mercurial president soon shanked the GOP nominee by telling *Fox & Friends* that Curtis was "not exactly prime time." Trump also belittled Sliwa's animal rescue work, stating that "he wants cats to be in Gracie Mansion—we don't need thousands of cats." King Donald's blasts hit hard, but the Republican mayoral hopeful soldiered on.[10]

On Friday, September 5, a quadruple-bylined *Times* story reported that Steve Witkoff, Trump's Special Envoy to the Middle East and a fellow billionaire real estate developer, had been urging the president to nominate Adams for U.S. ambassador to Saudi Arabia, a low-profile post typically

---

9   Republican candidates in the city typically garner around 30% of the vote in large races (with Sliwa tallying 28% in his 2021 loss to Adams). An early September poll showed that Adams and Cuomo—both of whom, like Sliwa, sought Trump's backing—were siphoning off Republican support.

10 Despite their kindred spirits, the two veteran showmen had not been allies in recent years. In 2017, Sliwa called Trump "a crack" and "a screwball," telling *Newsmax* that he didn't support the MAGA candidate's first presidential campaign.

held by veteran foreign service officers, not exiled New York City mayors. For a brief moment, it appeared that Adams, a former police captain, might follow in the footsteps of the last cop turned mayor. Amid an NYPD corruption scandal, Democrat William O'Dwyer (in office from 1946-1950) left City Hall to become U.S. ambassador to Mexico.[11]

"No, I wouldn't do that," Trump told reporters regarding the proposed Riyadh deal for Adams. "There's nothing wrong with doing that," the president added. The mayor, however, bristled at the suggestion that he would depart his beloved hometown. In the run-up to a late Friday afternoon (September 5) presser outside Gracie Mansion, many observers predicted that Adams would announce that he was dropping his reelection bid. Instead, the son of a very different area of Queens than Trump and Cuomo came out swinging. As the *Times* team noted, when Adams denounced Mario's boy as a snake and liar, he "practically spit out the words."

At the Gracie event, the trash-talking mayor also called both Cuomo and Mamdani "spoiled brats." A *New York Times*-Siena University poll taken the same week showed that the self-styled "blue-collar mayor" was the favorite candidate of only nine percent of New York City voters. The incumbent now trailed Mamdani in every borough and with every group.

---

[11] As I explained in *The Indypendent* (9-30-24), O'Dwyer's ouster was orchestrated by Brooklyn's Democratic Party brass.

Although the battered mayor took swipes at his challengers' integrity, Adams deployed his own bag of tricks. On Thursday, September 4, his campaign team summoned two dozen or so imams and female Muslim leaders to City Hall for a purported celebration of the Prophet Muhammad's 1,500th birthday. Upon arrival, the delegation found out that Adams and his team now treated the event as *both* a tribute to the prophet's legacy *and* an endorsement of the mayor's reelection bid.

An imam named Mouhamed Mountakhka Sakho told a *Post* reporter that the flyer he received for the event stated that it would be an anniversary celebration, with no mention of Adams' campaign. "Politicians are politicians," Sakho noted. "Wherever they go, they show their true colors."

The *Times* broke the Saudi Arabia ambassadorship story the following morning. The gathering of Muslims at City Hall now seemed like it had been staged for an audience in Riyadh. Although the mayor's campaign denied that the community leaders had been deceived about the dual intent of the event, a key question lingered: Was Eric Adams so cynical that he might use religious figures as stage props in order to boost his fast-sagging political career? Short answer: yes.

*

As his stature grew, Zohran made it clear that he was not letting his celebrity status get to his head. He showed plenty of gratitude to the voters that propelled his upset victory in the primary.

Meet Mayor Mamdani

On a rainy Sunday afternoon in mid-August, he attended a Pakistan Day celebration held in Midwood, Brooklyn. The candidate joined the crowded street *mela* (festival), appearing in a photo surrounded by attendees. A pic showed two smiling middle-aged women in hijabs standing beside a beaming Mamdani, with his security detail staying out of the camera's eye.

The frontrunner also spotlighted the grassroots groups that worked in tandem with the NYC-DSA to propel his primary win. In late August, Mamdani hosted a victory celebration at historic Judson Memorial Church on Washington Square with members of CAAAV Voice, which mobilized East Asian and Bangladeshi tenants, and DRUM Beats (DB), which brought out South Asian and Indo-Caribbean voters. En route to his event with Bernie Sanders at Brooklyn College on the first Saturday evening of September, Mamdani joined DB folks at a rainy picnic in Prospect Park.

Soon thereafter, the Democratic nominee attended a large party hosted by Jews for Racial and Economic Justice (JFREJ) honoring the campaigns of both Mamdani and Brad Lander. On the second Sunday of September, Zohran for NYC partnered with JFREJ's sister organization Jewish Voice for Peace—which had backed Zohran since day one of his primary run—in waging a massive door-knocking effort. Canvassers fanned out from Brooklyn's Grand Army Plaza, which sits across the street from Chuck Schumer's pad.

Mamdani, meanwhile, forcefully reiterated his pledge to carry out the International Criminal Court arrest warrant for

Benjamin Netanyahu. In a September 11 sit-down interview with the *New York Times*, the prospective mayor stressed that he plans to "fulfill" his promise by ordering the NYPD to arrest Bibi upon the prime minister's initial 2026 visit to the city. As the *Times* explained, because the U.S. did not recognize the ICC, it was not clear whether any official in New York City or elsewhere in the nation possessed the authority to enforce the warrant.

Zohran, however, called attention to September 2024 military orders given by Netanyahu while in Manhattan. Shortly after he delivered a war-mongering speech to the U.N., Bibi's forces levelled several blocks of apartment buildings in Lebanon, thus committing yet another war crime by targeting civilians. A mid-September poll found that 57% of city Democrats expressed support for the Palestinian side amid the current massacre, with only 18% favoring Israel.

Despite his well-established support for Netanyahu—evidenced most prominently by his joining Bibi's Alan Dershowitz-led ICC defense team—Andrew Cuomo now became a "critic" of Israel. Suddenly, the second-place contender told the *Times*' Nicholas Fandos (on September 15) that the situation in Gaza was "horrific." In assuming his new stance, Cuomo proceeded cautiously. As Fandos noted, the career Israel hawk only "gently distanced himself" from Netanyahu and was "careful not to criticize the [IDF]."

Rarely had a politician's change of heart seemed less heartfelt. Pressed by Fandos to explain whether Bibi and company had been committing war crimes, Netanyahu's counsel reserved judgment, absurdly stating, "That would require a legal analysis that I haven't done."

Indeed, it was not evident that Cuomo had conducted any type of analysis at all. The sagging career pol now enabled his nemesis to take a victory lap regarding the hot-button issue in the race. Highlighting Cuomo's quote in the *Times* interview that "I never stood with Bibi," Zohran's team posted a widely shared short clip of Andrew's announcement that he would join the accused war criminal's legal team.

Immediately after the October 7 Hamas attacks against Israel, Zohran, along with Jewish Voice for Peace activists and many of his fellow local DSA elected officials, warned of an "impending genocide." Two years of mass slaughter had sadly proven Mamdani and company to be prescient. Cuomo's new position on the conflict, by contrast, was just plain sad.

True to form, the flailing challenger quickly revealed his insincerity. One day after his *Times* interview, the former governor told reporters that rather than Bibi, it was Zohran who "should be arrested" for wrongful enforcement of international law.

Perhaps Cuomo meant that as a joke, but war crimes are no laughing matter.

CHAPTER 17
Police and Thieves

Although Zohran had explicitly and frequently stated throughout the primary campaign that he no longer supported "defunding" the NYPD, his three main challengers loudly and repeatedly invoked the frontrunner's past support for the slogan.

Amid the George Floyd protests of 2020, calls for defunding the police contained a mix of activist perspectives. Prison abolitionists indeed sought to eliminate public funding for cops. Other criminal justice advocates sought to reallocate money from police budgets towards mental health interventions and related programs. Zohran for NYC's platform fell squarely into the latter camp.

Ever since the Giuliani era (1994-2001), the NYPD—with strong backing from the city's business elite—has wielded enormous power in both city politics and local media. The *New York Post* and kindred Murdoch outlets routinely amplify the department's party line. In any election season, candidates seeking the law-and-order vote regularly perform backflips in order to impress the *Post,* a routine that served Eric Adams well in 2021. But when the frontrunner is a leftist who dares to criticize the NYPD, some pols will add cartwheels and somersaults to their floor show.

*

As explained in *RZR*, Mamdani's proposal to initiate a new Department of Community Safety (DCS) did not receive much scrutiny during the primary. Amid general election noise about defund, Zohran now fully presented his vision.

As the Democratic nominee mapped out, the DCS would implement a public health approach to disorder. Rather than police officers, teams of mental health professionals would address nonviolent incidents involving emotionally disturbed people—an initiative with recent success in many cities, including nearby Newark, New Jersey. In early September, Rodney Harrison, a former top-ranking NYPD officer, lent high-profile backing to Mamdani's plan, arguing that it will enable cops "to focus on violent crimes, weapons-related incidents, and robberies."

Zohran soon raised eyebrows among many criminal justice activists by telling the *Times* that he would apologize for calling the NYPD "racist" amid the George Floyd protests five years earlier. While expressing support for the DCS initiative, Harrison noted that "It's important that [Mamdani] says some things that show he supports the rank and file." Given the likelihood that he would take office in January, the prospective mayor appeared to be advising the NYPD's extremely diverse rank-and-file that he did not view them as racists. At the same time, Zohran stood firm regarding his proposed DCS.

After an early September conversation with Mamdani before an audience at Columbia Journalism School, Errol Louis also touted the initiative. As Louis explained in a *New York* column, the studious candidate "deserve[d] credit for educating himself about proven innovations" focused on mental health outreach in cities including Denver and Philadelphia. During the discussion, Mamdani rattled off specific statistics that showed corresponding reductions in crime rates. As Louis stated, the frontrunner's reform agenda placed him a "world away" from his challengers, who sought to impress the *New York Post* by calling for more cops.

While the leftist leader advanced new, less punitive approaches to disorder, two of his three center-right challengers stuck with Giuliani-era tactics. Although he would gain the former mayor's endorsement, Curtis Sliwa sounded less like Rudy than Andrew and Eric. Both the former governor and current mayor spotlighted the Queens assemblyman's support for the decriminalization of sex work.

Soon after joining the New York legislature in 2021, Zohran declared his "enthusiasm and pride" to support legislation that removed many harsh penalties for sex workers that had long existed in the state's criminal code, most notably "loitering for the purpose of prostitution." As the Astoria legislator noted at the time, advocates had pushed the reforms for several years, which proponents called the "walking while trans" act. After briefly detailing specific incidents of NYPD violence, Mamdani dedicated his vote to "every trans woman who has faced police harassment."

While the NYC-DSA's Julia Salazar and then left-leaning Jessica Ramos championed the legislation in the state senate, a leading sponsor in the assembly was liberal Democrat Dick Gottfried, who had been in office since 1971. The veteran pol's support showed that it was not only next-gen activists who backed the pro-trans measure. Another prominent older Dem who supported the decriminalization bill was...then-Governor Andrew Cuomo, who signed it into law.

In mid-August the former governor now claimed that he did not remember approving the 2021 legislation. As noted by *City & State*'s Holly Pretsky and Rebecca Lewis, "Cuomo may be forgiven for not remembering every law he has ever signed, but the repeal of the 'walking while trans' ban came after years of public advocacy and received widespread coverage, even in some national outlets." As NPR reported at the time, Cuomo's office issued a press release about the bill, with New York's top executive calling it "a critical step toward reforming our policing system."

Amnesia notwithstanding, the cape-less crusader now vowed to protect the dignity of Gotham City. At a Midtown press conference staged to recreate his pandemic-era daily ritual, Cuomo called attention to a 2025 Albany bill supported by Mamdani and his fellow DSA colleagues that further decriminalized sex work. The fiery moralist projected a quote in which his new antagonist, Zohran, stated that he would follow the scaled-back prostitution enforcement practices initiated by Cuomo's former arch-nemesis, Bill de Blasio. Mere mention of the gangly ex-mayor's name still made the former governor's blood boil.

The *Post*'s preferred candidate also fanned the flames. "I don't know what Quran he is reading," Mayor Adams declared regarding Mamdani's position on sex work. "It is not in my Bible." The holier-than-thou incumbent received support from one of the nation's foremost secular analysts. Pop psychologist Dr. Phil, an Adams backer, warned his vast older audience that Mamdani intended to impose a "morally corrupt agenda on the biggest city in America."[12]

Cuomo refused to cede the high ground to the current mayor. During the last week of August, sex work featured prominently in the disgraced former governor's blistering, 20-slide PowerPoint attack that yoked Mamdani's campaign to several proposals not found in Zohran for NYC's platform. With a large red brush, Mario's son smeared the leftist frontrunner by linking him to various radical positions held by the national DSA, many of which were not espoused by the group's local chapter.

In descending order, the Fight and Deliver candidate's slides listed ten "alarming" positions culled from the national organization's agenda, with minor additions. Number nine stated "Boycott, divestment, and sanctions of Israel—but not Uganda," enabling Bibi's lawyer to paint Zohran as an antisemitic hypocrite because he ignored the

---

12 In a late August podcast, the MAGA megaphone called Adams a "good mayor" who will "make a great mayor when he's reelected in the fall." One month later, Adams showed that Dr. Phil was no soothsayer.

harsh repression of homosexuality in his native country.[13] Next on the list was "Decriminalization of sex work and the drug trade." Cuomo's hardline stance on prostitution also factored heavily in "End all misdemeanor offenses" (number three) and, of course, number one: "Defund the police."

Cuomo's showers of outrage yielded little late summer fruit. As Errol Louis noted in his *New York* column, "voters appear to be warming up to Mamdani's approach" to public safety. A *New York Times*/Siena University Poll conducted in the first week of September found that slightly more voters said Mamdani (30%) would do a better job than Cuomo (29%) in handling crime. The former NYPD captain now manning City Hall checked in at a mere 15%.

It was too soon to declare that there had been a sea change in the way New York City residents viewed the role of policing. But Mamdani clearly had a growing reservoir of support for a new, less-punitive direction. Cuomo, meanwhile, once again seemed to be swimming against the tide.

*

After his upset victory in late June, Zohran immediately expanded his coalition by reeling in support from many

---

13 Throughout October, Cuomo repeatedly called attention to a July 2025 photo (first run in the *New York Post*) of Zohran and Mahmood Mamdani smiling beside Rebecca Kadaga, a leading proponent of Uganda's harsh treatment of homosexuals. In November, a CNN exit poll showed Mamdani capturing 81 percent support from LGBT voters.

local Democratic Party leaders who had backed Cuomo or other candidates in the primary. Many key figures—including Representatives Jerrold Nadler and Adriano Espaillat, as well as the bosses of the Democratic organizations of Brooklyn and Manhattan—quickly got on-board. But the party's most powerful figures held out.

There was no shortage of news stories over the summer questioning whether Sen. Chuck Schumer, Rep. Hakeem Jeffries, and Gov. Kathy Hochul would back the clear winner of the Democratic primary. That two former party powerhouses—Cuomo and Eric Adams—were bitterly trying to sink the Dems' mayoral nominee did not appear to bother the brass. Meanwhile, two right-wing House Dems from Long Island crusaded against the city's leftist frontrunner, with one asserting that "Mamdani didn't win because of socialism."

The source of Chuck Schumer's animus towards Zohran seemed obvious. "My job," the veteran senator famously explained to conservative *Times* columnist Bret Stephens earlier in the year, is "to keep the left pro-Israel." The minority leader of the Senate represented the fast-diminishing number of New Yorkers who believed that Israel should be allowed to commit genocide. And there seemed no way that Chuck would lend support to a pro-Palestine mayoral candidate who shortly after October 7 committed civil disobedience outside the senator's Park Slope residence. Given that Schumer is not up for reelection until 2028, he faced little immediate pressure to change course. Nor was the *New York Times* inclined to hold his feet to the fire.

Meet Mayor Mamdani

As noted in *RZR*, Jeffries' non-committal stance toward the party's mayoral nominee was far more perplexing. Zohran won Hakeem's district by 12% in June—and many NYC-DSA members were eager to support a primary challenge. Jeffries' calculations nonetheless had little to do with what was happening in his district, which extends from central Brooklyn through south Queens.

On the final Tuesday in August, Zohran and Hakeem held a high-level summit at Cornerstone Baptist Church in central Bed-Stuy. They were joined by Brooklyn Congresswoman Yvette Clarke, a Jeffries ally—and fellow Mamdani holdout—as well as 20 Black clergy leaders. Media were not invited, but NY1's Ayana Harry reported that Jeffries and Clarke "showed no signs of endorsing Mamdani."

That night on NY1, Errol Louis, a longtime Jeffries confidante, explained the thinking of the leading House Dems. According to Louis, the Brooklyn figureheads feared how voters "west of the Hudson" viewed the party's shift to the left. It was not altogether clear how a democratic socialist taking the reins in New York City would threaten support for Democrats in swing districts from New Jersey to California. But it was quite evident that a victory for the left was not something that the national party's donor class wanted. Meanwhile, both Jeffries and Clarke shared Schumer's deference to Israel.[14]

Hakeem's non-support for Zohran subjected Jeffries to relentless ridicule on social media, spurred by leftists including podcaster Briahna Joy Gray and Substacker

---

14 In mid-September, Clarke endorsed Mamdani.

Ken Klippenstein. Known for quoting edgy rap lyrics, Jeffries' own statements to the press often sounded more like evasive boilerplate. In mid-September, Maryland Democratic Senator Chris Van Hollen, a left-leaning critic of Israel, referred to the party leaders not backing Mamdani as "spineless politicians" beholden to wealthy donors. "Chris Van Who?" Hakeem's comms team clapped back. The opposition party was not exactly unified.

New York Governor Kathy Hochul, a centrist Democrat, remained in-sync with Schumer and Jeffries through Labor Day. In late August, Zohran's campaign lawyer Ali Najmi told me that Hochul—up for reelection in 2026—was "coming around," which soon proved to be correct. The governor had a close working relationship with Attorney General Tish James, who strongly plugged Mamdani on the weekend before the June primary. When the moderate governor announced her support for Zohran in mid-September, a *New York Post* cover ludicrously depicted her as "Comrade Hochul," complete with a black beret and a Communist red backdrop.

Hochul's embrace of Mamdani placed her at odds with Jay Jacobs, leader of the New York Democrats' state party organization and a close ally of the governor. Echoing his fellow right-wing Dems repping Long Island, Jacobs quickly criticized Hochul's move, denouncing the DSA and citing Mamdani's stance towards Israel.

Although he potentially stood to gain from the party rifts, Cuomo could not stay out of his own way. Asked by the *Times* to name "living Democrats" that he admired, Mario's son replied that "none comes to mind." Evidently, Schumer,

Jeffries and the Mamdani haters from Long Island were of no use to him.[15]

*

While Zohran's victory in June jolted the New York establishment, various leading national left-leaning figures championed the new mayoral nominee. After making her case for Mamdani on national talk shows in July, Senator Elizabeth Warren toured the city with the Democratic nominee at the outset of August. The senator declared that the newcomer threatened the city's billionaires because they expected him to "bend the knee." Warren touted the DSA candidate's plan to create universal childcare and insisted that "New York City is the place to start the conversation" for national Democrats on affordability.

Warren's show of support for Mamdani carried particularly strong weight not simply because of her popularity among New York City liberals. Since taking office in 2021, Boston's progressive mayor Michelle Wu—a Warren protégé— has made the creation of free buses a centerpiece of her administration. During a June televised debate, Zohran said that he "admired" Wu.

National Democratic leaders including Barack Obama also voiced support.[16] Although he has few fans on the left these days, the former president remains popular among Black Democrats. Support from Obama and his inner

---

15 Far less surprisingly, Cuomo named his father, JFK, and RFK as three non-living Dems that he held in high esteem.

16 In mid-August, *New York Times* columnist Mara Gay reported that Obama called Mamdani on the day after the primary.

circle helped bolster Zohran's standing among a powerful New York City voting bloc. A September poll found that 41 percent of Black voters now backed the left-wing Democrat, placing him ahead of Cuomo (34 percent) and Eric Adams, who checked in at a paltry 11 percent. Party figureheads in Chicago and Boston seemed to view the results of the New York City primary with clearer eyes than their counterparts in Brooklyn.

"Flatbush" native[17] Bernie Sanders soon brought his "Fighting Oligarchy" roadshow to the city on behalf of Zohran. On Saturday, September 6, Sanders and Mamdani first marched together in the annual Labor Day march in Manhattan, then joined AOC for a school backpack giveaway in the South Bronx. The three socialists next walked about Astoria. That evening, Bernie joined Zohran for a boisterous town hall at Brooklyn College.

Mamdani opened the program by criticizing the CUNY outpost's crackdown on pro-Palestine activism. After a campus protest last spring, the Brooklyn College administration did not renew the contracts of four adjunct faculty members who participated. "No faculty member should be disciplined for supporting Palestinian human rights," Zohran stated. Bernie, in turn, brought the crowd to its feet by declaring that it was "not radical" to cut off U.S. military funding for Netanyahu's slaughter.

Although separated by a half-century in age, the two leftists seemed quite in sync. While Sanders calls himself a

---

17   Sanders still calls the south Brooklyn neighborhood now known as Midwood by its mid-20th century name.

democratic socialist, he is not a card-carrying member of the DSA. At the Brooklyn College event, Mamdani explained that he first rolled out his state assembly campaign at a Bernie rally held in Long Island City in October 2019. When an audience member voiced concerns about childcare costs, Zohran urged her to visit the NYC-DSA table in the auditorium lobby.

Earlier that day, the two leaders chatted at an Afghan kabab house in Astoria about Bernie's experience as mayor of Burlington, Vermont (1981-89). Bernie noted that soon after he took office, neighbors began planting trees, thereby expanding civic pride and building support for Sanders' larger agenda. In mid-September, *The Nation* featured "Mayor to Mayor," an engaging 14.5-minute video presentation of the conversation directed by Andrew Epstein.

*

While his rivals seemed stuck in the mud—with two eager to sling it—Zohran projected optimism about the future. To varying degrees, Cuomo, Adams, and Sliwa clung to the past, particularly in their beliefs regarding New York City voters. A Fox News poll taken at the end of summer found that 41% of respondents now viewed socialism favorably, with only 48% championing capitalism. With Elon Musk set to become a trillionaire, the trendlines strongly favored the left.

Yet while Mamdani called for modest redistribution of the city's vast concentrated wealth, his rivals went to bat for capitalism. "New York City people are not socialists," Cuomo assured Fox host Maria Bartiromo in late August. Echoing Trump, Adams told reporters that "Mamdani is not a Democrat—he's a communist." Later in the race, Sliwa called "New York the epicenter of capitalism in the world," vowing to protect it.

Although he was by far the youngest candidate in the race, Zohran and his team paid far more attention to New York City's rich past than his opponents. The day after "Dumbbell Gate," while the leftist's alpha-male opponents tried to score more cheap points, over one thousand more cerebral New Yorkers turned out for a Sunday scavenger hunt organized by the Mamdani campaign. The candidate announced the history-themed event by posting a video in which he ate from a bag of Herr's Sour Cream and Onion potato chips, thus invoking Team Adams' "Chipgate" scandal.

The scavenger trail indeed foregrounded the city's rich history of political corruption, launching from the former headquarters of Tammany Hall on Union Square and including at a stop at a West Village park named after Jimmy Walker, the vaudeville star who allowed Tammany hacks to pocket relief funds during the Great Depression. Participants traveled to various locations via city buses, connecting the hunt to a core Mamdani campaign issue. Zohran and company paid respect to the city's last multi-ethnic mayor by ending the tour at the Little Flower, an Afghan-owned Astoria café that shares the nickname of Fiorello La Guardia.

Crossword puzzle maven Natan Last—who helped create the clues that Zohran sent out regarding the scavenger hunt destinations—was impressed that many people "you might imagine self-styling as 'too cool' enjoyed something so unabashedly earnest." The shared experience also fostered solidarity, explained Last, a 30-something Brooklyn native. "While walking across that pedestrian bridge to East River Park," Natan told me, participants "chatted with all the other passers-by about where to find the John Lindsay running track." From day one of Mamdani's mayoral run, the phrase *bringing people together* was not empty rhetoric.

As summer 2025 wound down, Zohran maintained a comfortable lead. "Mr. Mamdani," *New York Times* national correspondent Annie Karni observed on September 19, "appears to be on a glide path to Gracie Mansion." After Mayor Adams made no public appearances on the final weekend of summer, rumors circulated that he was "quiet quitting" the race. Soon he would loudly bow out, while Curtis Sliwa 2.0 defiantly remained on the trail.

Now staffed by members of right-wing Democratic figurehead Rahm Emanuel's crew, Andrew Cuomo's campaign still insisted that if *both* Sliwa and Adams dropped out, the Fight and Deliver candidate had a clear path. Although not many fresh faces joined Cuomo's crusade against the leftist next-gen leader, in mid-September Woody Allen advised *Free Press* figurehead Bari Weiss that he backed Mario's son.

Throughout the summer, Cuomo's nonstop, often-personal attacks—including against Mamdani's family—frequently appeared to get under the frontrunner's skin. But in at least one respect, Zohran benefited. As he told reporters in mid-August, "I don't need to do much to make the governor appear extremely dislikable."

CHAPTER 18

Autumn in New York

The first week of fall brought a menacing U.S. president and Israel's accused war criminal prime minister to New York City. The two elder anti-statesmen took turns taunting the U.N. General Assembly. Frontrunning mayoral candidate Zohran Mamdani forcefully denounced the two figures, with the leftist leader's supporters filling the streets of Midtown in opposition to the Gaza genocide.

Meanwhile, Mayor Eric Adams warmly welcomed Netanyahu, listening attentively to the outlaw's speech and ignoring the mass walkout by gathered diplomats. The city's embattled City Hall figurehead insisted that Bibi was "defending the western world and our way of life." Global opinion disagreed.

Two days later, Adams mercifully suspended his reelection campaign. The mayor's own video announcement had a distinctly funereal vibe. Adams—carrying a large picture of his late mother—descended a carpeted staircase at Gracie Mansion to the tune of Frank Sinatra's schmaltzy "My Way." Although only 65, Adams seemed ready for the final curtain. His swan song dragged on for nearly nine minutes.

It was an ignominious end to a vainglorious era. Few compared Adams' statement to LBJ's comparable declaration in 1968, when the early success of antiwar candidate Eugene McCarthy prompted the president to call off his bid for reelection in a televised announcement. Dogged by corruption scandals, the mayor polled at a mere 10% in his bid for a second stint at City Hall. Although Kathy Hochul, Hakeem Jeffries and various other Democratic leaders praised Adams, no parades were planned in his honor.

Since early September rumors had swirled about Adams' potential new gigs—whether inside the Beltway, in Riyadh, or at home in New York City—but none became a reality. Meanwhile, Gracie Mansion was also home to palace intrigue. Adams' shadowy fixer Frank Carone freely admitted that he had been helping Andrew Cuomo long before the incumbent's September exit from the race.

Reporters focused on various schemes that the lame duck and his crew might hatch before the next mayor took over on January 1. In early October, the mayor made an unexpected trip to Albania. It was not clear whether Adams angled to replace the current interim U.S. ambassador. But he did pose for a smiling photo beside Edi Rama, the prime minister of Albania and a longtime chair of the nation's Socialist Party. The longtime DSA foe voiced no ideological objections.

Although Cuomo stood to gain from Adams' withdrawal, the Fight and Deliver (F&D) candidate still faced an uphill climb. Even if all ten percent of voters backing Eric now switched over to Andrew, Mario's son would still trail by Mamdani by ten points. It was by no means certain that the F&D guy appealed to the mayor's loyalists. In early September, Adams himself hissed disdain toward Cuomo outside Gracie Mansion. As a lengthy *New York Post* clickbait headline asserted two days after the dropout announcement, "Eric Adams is so anti-Zohran Mamdani he's warming to Andrew Cuomo—a mayoral candidate he once called 'a snake and a liar.'" Eventually, the two slithery pols patched things up.

Meanwhile, the disgraced former governor dialed up his anti-Mamdani outrage. In an *al fresco* interview with Errol Louis on the day after Adams threw in the towel, Cuomo repeatedly called Mamdani an "existential threat." The F&D dude warned that the leftist-led city would become an open-air drug market crawling with sex traffic. That Cuomo had supported marijuana legalization when he ruled Albany mattered little.

Throughout the final six weeks of the race, Cuomo's pro-Israel rhetoric became so overheated that he started to make the *New York Post* sound tepid. After telling Louis that the Democratic nominee's position regarding the phrase "globalize the intifada" indicated that Mamdani "sympathizes with terrorists," a few days later Cuomo advised *Meet the Press* host Kristen Welker that the activist slogan assuredly meant "kill all Jews."

Amid the renewed shelling, Zohran stood firm. He advised *The View*'s sizable national daytime TV audience that while Hamas committed a "horrific war crime" on October 7, Israel's ongoing "genocide" on Gaza resulted in "a war crime being answered with war crimes. And what we see is, every single hour, the Israeli military killing a Palestinian child for close to two years." The studio audience cheered on Mamdani's invocation of the "universality of international law."

Some pro-Palestine critics soon chastised the leftist mayoral candidate for "pandering" to Israel by first invoking Hamas' war crimes in his October 7 anniversary posts on social media.[18] Neocon propagandist David Frum attacked from the other side, taking offense at Mamdani's "intense angry passion" regarding "Israel's self-defense."

Most unsurprisingly, Cuomo echoed Frum, issuing a statement that made no mention of Gaza and shamelessly vowing, "To the Jewish people—I stand with you." Rather than echo Pope Leo XIV's call for peace, the Catholic former governor was all in for Bibi. A late September *New York Times*/Siena University poll now found slight nationwide support for the Palestinian side of the battle, however. Forty percent of respondents agreed that Israel

---

18 On X, podcaster Anders J. Lee posted Mamdani's almost-identical statement from October 7, 2024, two weeks before Zohran announced his mayoral run. Lee thus refuted any claims that the candidate had "capitulated" during the campaign.

was intentionally killing civilians. The MAGA crowd seemed increasingly appalled, with the poll showing a double-digit drop in Republican support for Netanyahu's slaughter.

Zohran's rapid ascent to national prominence over the past six months corresponded directly with the "seismic reversal" in support for Israel identified by *Times* reporters in their poll coverage. As a social media phenom and the likely next mayor of New York City, Mamdani's statements regarding any issue at home or abroad now garnered widespread global attention. That the fast-ascending leftist used his platforms to advance international law was a major breakthrough for the peace movement.

*

Curtis Sliwa continued to be Cuomo's main roadblock. In late September, the Republican nominee told reporters that sundry unnamed high-rollers promised hefty paydays if he dropped out. "Seven different people [offered] a total of $10 million when you bifurcate it out over the years," the Guardian Angel stated. One of the *Post*'s trusted anonymous tipsters said that John Catsimatidis, Sliwa's boss at WABC Radio, faced pressure to put the squeeze on Sliwa.

The Republican nominee's headline-generating claims regarding de facto bribes received support from another candidate. "I can tell you that of Andrew Cuomo, Eric Adams, and Curtis Sliwa, I trust Curtis Sliwa's word the most," Mamdani told reporters, amusing several older Black health-care union members who had joined him for an unrelated announcement. Although he and the veteran Republican "do not agree on much," Mamdani assured his

Facebook followers, "we do agree on this: City Hall is not for sale."[19]

Although the 21st-century edition of the Odd Couple agreed in their assessment of Eric Adams, the two figures expressed their views a bit differently. When Adams bowed out of the race, Curtis called him "a crook," which seemed unlikely to win over Eric's fanbase. Zohran, by contrast, released an upbeat video statement that circled back to his criticisms of Adams at the outset of the race. Instead of fulfilling his 2021 campaign pledge to help "working-class New Yorkers," the frontrunner noted, the one-term mayor "raised their rents." Four years later, Mamdani vowed, "a new day is coming."

In the video, the frontrunner threw down the gauntlet at his main challenger. "You got your wish," Mamdani advised Cuomo. "You wanted Trump and your billionaire friends to help you clear the field. But don't forget, you wanted me as your primary opponent too. And we beat you by 13 points. Looking forward to doing it again on November 4. Hope you're well." The sign-off was somewhat less than warm.

In the wake of Adams' departure, Zohran peppered his main opponent with jabs. A *Times* story noted that while the mayor's exit spurred the Democratic and Republican nominees to hit the campaign trail, "Andrew Cuomo calls

---

19 Amid the chatter about deals for Adams and Sliwa over the preceding month, Mamdani frequently used variations of the phrase, thus invoking *City for Sale* (1988), an influential work about Ed Koch-era corruption penned by the legendary muckrakers Jack Newfield and Wayne Barrett.

donors." In an X post with a screen shot highlighting that line, the frontrunner opined: "Same as it ever was." On Tuesday morning, a feisty Mamdani told reporters that while he's "fighting for Eric Adams' voters, Andrew Cuomo is fighting for his donors."

The ex-governor's most prominent transaction came from Alex Adjmi, who spent 44 months in federal prison in the 1990s after pleading guilty to money laundering charges involving a Colombian drug cartel. On his way out of office in 2021, Trump pardoned Adjmi, now a real estate speculator who also invests in political campaigns. The former Eric Adams backer moved into Cuomo's corner.[20]

By early October, Polymarket—the Wall Street futures site that correctly predicted Mamdani's primary win in June—listed the socialist as an 88 percent-favorite to win. Smart money thus shied away from Cuomo. In *The City*, veteran business reporter Greg David explained that shot callers in the real estate and tech industries now sought to develop a working relationship with Zohran, viewing him as the likely winner.

Although Fix the City, the PAC that spent over $20 million attacking Mamdani in the primary, stayed on the warpath, two of the group's largest revenue streams in the spring, Michael Bloomberg and DoorDash, now turned

---

20 In 2022, Adjmi dropped $69,000 (then the max allowed in the race for governor) into the campaign coffers of Kathy Hochul, Cuomo's successor. The NY legislature has since reduced the top donation in a statewide race to $18,000 total, divided equally between the primary and general election.

off the spigot. As the *Times*' Mara Gay reported in an early October column, at the end of their mid-September summit, Bloomberg was so impressed by Mamdani that the former mayor showed the next-gen leader photos from his days at City Hall. Unlike DoorDash, Bloomy later resumed his financial support on behalf of Cuomo.

As shown in *RZR*, Fix the City's creative output during the primary was utterly unimaginative. During the general election the PAC's materials only marginally improved. In late September, the group spent $300,000 distributing a handbill headlined "New York City Mayor is not a starter job" that carried the same stern-browed photo of Cuomo used throughout the primary. The group's subsequent productions featured more upbeat shots of the former governor.

In a banner ad that cropped up frequently on the Musk site in early October, the F&D candidate's mug did not appear. Instead, behind a beaming red-letter pledge that Cuomo would "Secure the subway for all New Yorkers," viewers saw a Photoshopped depiction of a young white couple exiting the platform, where they encounter a vagrant clad in bright white clothes sprawled across the stairwell. Although the ad's scenario was bleak, at least it was colorful.

Fix the City could not be blamed for the downbeat messaging. The fault, dear Brutus, lay in the suburbanite candidate himself. From 1989 through February 2025, Mario's son dwelled outside of the five boroughs. As governor, it was newsworthy when Andrew even rode the subway. Now

Cuomo watched helplessly as the Zohran for NYC express train sped past his station.

*

On the sunny first Sunday of October, Mamdani and his challengers made the rounds. The stops chosen by the three City Hall aspirants—and the statements they distributed—illustrated the shifting terrain of New York City politics.

With his revamped comms team in tow, Cuomo started his morning by addressing the veteran Democrat's longstanding base: An older Black congregation at the First Central Baptist Church in Staten Island. A well-crafted 50-second video post combined Cuomo's liturgy with a soundtrack from the church organist and enthusiastic choir. The candidate's message, however, was not exactly cutting edge.

After reminding the gathering that his father was "a gentleman named Mario Cuomo," Andrew mentioned that he had been HUD secretary under President Bill Clinton before becoming New York's attorney general and governor. Although he referenced the "affordable housing [built] across the nation" while he helmed HUD in the 1990s—something Cuomo's critics sharply dispute[21]—the dynastic pol neither touted his more recent achievements as governor nor talked up any current agenda items. Instead, Cuomo simply assured churchgoers that his track record demonstrated that he knew "how to make [New York City] a better place, and I am excited to bring you to a place

---

21   See Tracy Rosenthal's 6-13-2025 rundown in *The Nation*.

higher than you've ever been before." That boilerplate was piping hot.

From Staten Island, Cuomo journeyed to even lower ground. At Murdoch headquarters in Midtown, the F&D prophet warned Fox News host Maria Bartiromo that a Mamdani administration would create nothing less than "anarchy in New York City." Crank up the Sex Pistols.

On the same morning in Brooklyn, the new face of the city's Democratic Party visited a different Black house of worship. Mamdani was given a very warm welcome at Cornerstone Baptist Church in Bed-Stuy, which had hosted the Hakeem Jeffries summit with the frontrunner at the end of August. Jeffries' fellow Cornerstone member Errol Louis posted a pic on X that showed Zohran receiving a hearty welcome. The candidate sat down for an on-stage conversation with Senior Pastor Lawrence E. Aker III that aired on the church's podcast. "I have to earn every vote, that's my job," Mamdani explained regarding his outreach to the city's older Black residents.

Later that day, Mamdani met with a group of Palestinian community leaders in Astoria. The candidate sent out a pic that showed at least eight men and two women in attendance. Zohran stated that he "listened to what they and their families have endured as the genocide in Gaza continues, funded by our government." The Muslim mayoral candidate's much-shared post showed that he was not running away from his principles.

The leftist leader also made stops in Harlem and the Bronx. There he teamed up with Black and Latina elected officials for somewhat off-beat campaign events. Many city residents want to dispose of old paperwork but fear that dumpster divers may steal their personal info. Mamdani's campaign thus provided free paper-shredding, making the events festive with ice cream, DJs, and dancing.

Over in Brooklyn's Chinatown, Cuomo attended a small parade hosted by controversial city councilwoman Susan Zhuang. At a 2024 community protest against the opening of a Bensonhurst homeless shelter, the right-wing Democrat bit the forearm of a high-ranking police officer. Hard-on crime Mayor Adams called the incident "unfortunate," then met with Zhuang.[22] Via Facebook, Cuomo showed off his support for the ferocious pol.

Republican challenger Curtis Sliwa was also out and about that Sunday. Sporting his signature Guardian Angels beret while wearing a suit and tie—thus combining his old and new identities—the candidate visited the Pulaski Day Parade, a Manhattan event celebrating the city's Polish heritage, which Curtis and his wife Nancy share.

Sliwa also stopped at a very large street festival on Brooklyn's Atlantic Avenue and at a more modest neighborhood fair in Woodhaven, Queens. At the latter event, the third-place contender took a group photo flanked by a handful of mostly young campaign volunteers of mixed

---

22 In April 2025, Brooklyn District Attorney Eric Gonzalez, who identifies as a progressive Democrat, dropped criminal charges against Zhuang. The D.A. also did not prosecute MAGA city councilwoman Inna Vernikov after she flashed a gun amid a pro-Palestine protest at Brooklyn College in October 2023. Gonzalez, who aspires to higher office, plays nice with fellow pols.

ethnicities. The Angel's ground troops seemed no match for Zohran's army.

New Yorkers watching the Yankees' playoff game at home or in bars that afternoon saw ads that vividly captured the gaps separating the leading two candidates. Earlier that week, the release of Cuomo's first general-election spot sparked much derision because it relied heavily on A.I., superimposing the candidate's head on machine-generated actors portraying New Yorkers at work.[23] In the ad, Cuomo pledged to hire 5,000 new cops and remove homeless people from city streets but said nothing about the city's skyrocketing cost of living. In trying hard to be clever and connect with voters, the former frontrunner looked clueless.

Zohran then torched Cuomo on X:

In a city of world-class artists and production crew hunting for the next gig, Andrew Cuomo made a TV ad the same way he wrote his housing policy: with AI.

Then again, maybe a fake Cuomo is better than the real one?

By circling back to one of the former frontrunner's most notorious gaffes during the primary,[24] Mamdani's state-

---

23 On X, Morris Katz—a communications strategist and member of Zohran's inner circle—observed, "This is one of the worst ads I've ever seen & it's so funny imagining the conversations that led to its conception."

24 As discussed in *RZR*, back in April, Cuomo released a housing agenda that made clear use of ChatGPT. It was a clear early warning sign that his campaign was not running smoothly.

ment cuttingly called out Cuomo and his campaign's lack of competence. Zohran, by contrast, re-upped a rent freeze spot that worked well for him in the primary. In a *West Side Story*-like setting, tenants enthusiastically welcomed Mamdani's leading campaign pledge. Given Cuomo's machine creations, it did not matter whether the tenants were actors—more importantly, they were actual human beings.

With four weeks to go, Zohran clearly appeared to be in the driver's seat. While his ads appeared on voters' TV screens, thousands of the DSA candidate's volunteers knocked on their doors. The already large coalition that propelled his victory in June now included increasing numbers of older voters of color. Upon entering the race, the former governor had banked on support from the traditional Democratic base. As the finish line neared, the party of Mario Cuomo ran on fumes.

CHAPTER 19
Turn Signals

Throughout October, many leading New York City-based media outlets focused less on whether Zohran would win than how he would govern. Although the relentless bombast from Cuomo's camp about Mamdani's inexperience made the question seem like a potential trap, the frontrunner never tried to dodge it. After all, what *any* prospective political leader might do once in office is a fair line of inquiry.

Yet in myriad ways, Zohran was far different than his modern predecessors. His age, 34 (as of October 18), made him the youngest mayoral frontrunner in New York City since the Progressive Era.[25] In addition to his Muslim

---

25 In 1913, John Purroy Mitchel (b. 1879)—running as a progressive Republican—defeated a Tammany Hall Democrat and became known as the "Boy Mayor." Prior to the 1898 creation of the five-borough city, New York (Manhattan) and Brooklyn each had mayors a few years younger than Mitchel.

faith, Mamdani's family lineage clearly distinguished him from any previous City Hall aspirant.[26] So did his critical stance towards Israel. And, of course, Zohran's identification as a democratic socialist set him apart, placing him to the left of leading city pol in recent memory.[27]

This chapter detours from the campaign trail in order to look at the road ahead for a democratic socialist mayoral administration in New York City. Because Zohran answered many questions from reporters about how he would govern, his blueprint received plenty of scrutiny in advance of November 4. Indeed, since he embodied both a generational and ideological shift, Mamdani and his bid for City Hall produced far more in-depth discussion of "the future" than any recent mayoral campaign.

In a mid-summer interview with *The Nation*'s Katrina vanden Heuvel and John Nichols, the leftist mayoral hopeful touted the "sewer socialism" found in Milwaukee during the first half of the 20th century. Spurred by Socialist Party figurehead Victor Berger and Mayor Daniel Hoan (in office from 1916-1940), Wisconsin's largest city saw major improvements in sanitation and public health. Leftist German immigrants—many belonging to American Federation of Labor craft unions—helped Hoan overcome

---

26 Previous New York City mayors who were immigrants all came from Europe. Abe Beame (1974-77) was born in London. William O'Dwyer (1946-50) hailed from Ireland. In the 19th century, a handful of New York mayors were also born in the Emerald Isle.

27 As Mamdani highlighted during the campaign, Mayor David Dinkins (1990-1993) belonged to the initial iteration of the DSA. Dinkins neither campaigned nor governed as a democratic socialist, however.

opposition from the local Democratic and Republican parties.[28]

"The example of sewer socialism is one that I think of often," the frontrunner earnestly assured vanden Heuvel and Nichols. Mamdani explained that in his view, the term "represents a belief that the worth of an ideology can only be judged by its delivery. That means improving the services and social goods that working people experience each and every day: the sewers, the clean drinking water, the parks." If elected, the mayoral hopeful noted, it was his task to deliver the affordability agenda that he—in sync with the NYC-DSA—promised.

*

"What Zohran pulled off was a fucking earthquake," City Councilwoman Justin Brannan told me in late September regarding Mamdani's upset win in the June primary. "But that may end up being the easy part. Governing is where you really need to prove that this stuff works." As a former top official in the Department of Education (DoE) who helped facilitate the successful rollout of universal pre-kindergarten (UPK) during Bill de Blasio's first year in office, the councilman speaks from experience.

A tattooed hardcore punk guitarist known for his earthy tongue, Brannan (b. 1978) grew up in Bay Ridge, the same southwest Brooklyn neighborhood he represented for two terms in the city council (2018-2025). Before entering

---

28 See Nicholas Howland's account in *Tapestries* (2022) and Chris Maisano's in *Jacobin* (2025).

politics, he worked in the financial sector. After winning office in 2017, Brannan's facility with numbers eventually led him to become chair of the council's influential finance committee, which oversees the massive city budget. During Eric Adams' tenure, the progressive Democrat was closely allied with Council Speaker Adrienne Adams.

Running as a de Blasio ally in 2017, Brannan defeated NYC-DSA candidate Khader El-Yateem, for whom Zohran was a dedicated volunteer. While in the council, JB (as he is known) maintained a good working relationship with many DSA elected officials at both the city and state levels. His council district includes Bay Ridge's "Little Palestine," and Brannan was an early proponent of a ceasefire. Brannan ran in the 2025 Democratic primary for comptroller and lost to Mark Levine, a stridently pro-Israel candidate.[29]

"My comptroller campaign," JB explained over breakfast in Bay Ridge, "was all about the fact that we have this colossal $116 billion budget, yet people are struggling to get by in this city. It shouldn't be so hard to survive in the richest city in the world. Where are we spending all this money?"

The $116 billion largely derives from the revenue the city rakes in from property, income and sales taxes. The city cannot run a deficit without state approval.[30] In JB's view,

---

[29] In addition to mayor and public advocate, comptroller is one of three citywide elected officials. The role is akin to a chief financial officer, overseeing city contracts and pension investments. Brad Lander, who opted to run for mayor rather than reelection, is the current officeholder.

[30] New York City also produces 50% of state tax revenue, thus supplying funding for municipalities across New York. The 2025-26 state budget is just under $240 billion.

the "mission" for Mamdani and his administration is to find "secure revenue streams" so that their new initiatives do not get placed on the chopping block in the event of an economic downturn.

"All the things Zohran is talking about are expensive," Brannan noted. "Free buses would cost around $800 million, but that's much less than universal childcare, which is around $7-$8 billion." Nonetheless, "it's been proven that programs that make life easier for working people leads to broad-based economic growth. I don't have kids—but I know that universal childcare would be a game changer."

During the rollout of UPK in 2014, Brannan served as the point person within the Department of Education. In terms of building public support, he says, "Our first targets were the families with young children who stood to benefit." After securing popular approval, "We then went to the business community and said, 'Look at how this policy will bring all kinds of people back into the workforce.' Many key players understood that."

"Childcare is a clear free market failure," Brannan continued. "The city government's current providers will tell you that they get paid peanuts. And the parents will say they can't afford it. That's the perfect time for the government to swoop in and fix things."

Starting in the early spring, Zohran proposed to fund his proposals for universal childcare and free buses mainly via tax hikes on the 1% and corporations. Such moves would require Albany legislation and support from centrist

Democratic governor Kathy Hochul, an ally of the business elite. (Amid the fall campaign, Hochul expressed support for childcare but not free buses.) During his general election run, Mamdani repeatedly stated that he would welcome other sources of revenue than new taxes, provided they did not constrain him from delivering on his key pledges.[31]

According to Brannan, there are numerous ways to reallocate the city's current $116 billion budget. In addition to redundant spending lines, he says there are many programs that receive continual funding without evaluation of their impact. The DoE—which has a whopping $41 billion line—is known for large administrator salaries and wasteful expenditures. "It's the first place to look for cuts," JB says.

The outgoing council finance chair also notes that the city loses out on $5-6 billion yearly because of tax breaks handed out to large corporations by prior mayoral administrations, in particular Rudy Giuliani (1994-2001). "These incentives were handed out 20-30 years ago," Brannan explains. "We need to take a look at whether they're still warranted."

In JB's view, skepticism toward Mamdani's new spending initiatives stems in part from how the current mayor approached the budget. "Over the past four years," the councilman observes, "Adams pushed false austerity

---

[31] A rent freeze, Mamdani's lead agenda item, does not require new revenue.

bullshit. Actually, we had all the fucking money we needed. The reason why we know that the cuts to libraries and after-school programs were unnecessary is because they were all rolled back by the mayor!"

"With Zohran," Brannan states, "we're dreaming big again, just like we did under de Blasio."

Throughout the fall campaign, the White House vowed to punish New York City if Mamdani captured City Hall.[32] In late September, Treasury Secretary Scott Bessent declared that if the socialist mayor were to seek bailout money from the federal government, the answer "will be the same thing that Gerald Ford said: 'Drop dead.'" Ford did not actually state that,[33] but Bessent's point was clear: MAGA didn't like Zohran.

Soon after Bessent's warning shot, the Manhattan Institute, an influential right-wing think tank, released a report titled "Socialism on the Hudson," which viewed a leftward lurch as inherently alarming. Among the key fears highlighted was Mamdani's intent to "reduce the extent to which private entities deliver government services." Such moves—which might include bringing utilities back under public control—would reverse the neoliberal direction seen in the city since the Ford era. Although Zohran

---

[32] About six percent of the city's $116 billion budget comes from federal funding. After Mamdani's visit to the White House in mid-November, cuts no longer seemed like an immediate threat.

[33] Amid the fiscal crisis of 1975, Ford indeed declared that the federal government would not bailout New York City. But it was headline writers for the *Daily News* that created the infamous declaration.

for NYC's platform did not emphasize utilities, which are state-regulated entities, the mayor could use his bully pulpit to support progressive measures in Albany.

Brannan added that while the new mayoral administration would need to prepare for havoc wrought by the White House as well as opposition from various business interests, there may be less high-profile impediments to Mamdani's initiatives. Resistance to change may emanate from the middle tier of the city's roughly 300,000-member workforce, which consists mainly of civil service employees with union protection.

JB refers to that numerically significant strata as "the barnacle" known for bureaucratic inertia, a problem he witnessed firsthand at the DoE. Reform-minded agency heads, he predicts, will be confronted by "Jerry on the third floor whose been there since 1972 and will jam things up."

While Brannan acknowledges that these city government veterans possess ample institutional knowledge, in his experience they often tend to be less interested in innovating than "protecting the institution." Jerry and his ilk, JB says, "leave work at 4:59 p.m. and don't give a fuck who the mayor is."

*

While Brannan speaks from a progressive Democrat standpoint, his council colleague Alexa Avilés—who represents neighboring Sunset Park as well as Red Hook—is an NYC-DSA stalwart. As seen in *RZR*, Alexa (as she is commonly called), forcefully repelled the pro-Israel forces that showered funds on her primary challenger, a staffer for Netanyahu apologist Rep. Dan Goldman.

In mid-October, I sat down with Alexa at a coffee shop in Sunset Park that displayed an Avilés campaign poster on its front window. Although she faced a Republican challenger in November, Alexa had already taken initial steps towards a 2026 primary challenge against Goldman, who maintains an office in the district but is rarely seen. After securing the endorsement of the NYC-DSA in mid-November, Avilés dropped her bid one month later when Brad Lander entered the race with Mamdani's backing.

Born in 1973 and raised in Brooklyn's East New York, Alexa and her husband brought up their two now-teenage daughters in Sunset Park. Like many area residents over 50, Avilés hails from Puerto Rico and celebrates her Boricua heritage. Prior to winning her city council seat in 2021, Alexa was a nonprofit executive, community organizer, and member of the NYC-DSA.

Whereas Brannan's work as the council's finance chair informs his perspective, Avilés' role as head of the immigration committee shapes her views. Brannan, who frequently meets with business leaders, told me that much of the elite panic surrounding Zohran's ascent stemmed from a concern among longtime power players that they would lose "access" to City Hall.

"Justin rocks with the city elite more than I do," Alexa says with a laugh. "But yes, it must be hard for people who are entitled and privileged and have access to everything to suddenly worry about not having that access. That 'fear' also could be a more polite way of saying Zohran is a brown, socialist man who stands for ideals they do not share."

Regardless, the councilwoman explains, "the mayor has to deal with everyone—and not give access to people based on their capital portfolio." Alexa adds that while the DSA certainly will play an important role in Mamdani's City Hall, we should "keep in mind that it's a giant administration, with a workforce larger than many cities' total population and budget bigger than many states and nations." The NYC-DSA thus serves as one important component of a very large coalition that includes large unions and countless advocacy organizations.

Avilés concurs with Brannan regarding the need to place the city's current spending under the microscope. "It all needs to be on table," states Alexa. "There is plenty of bloat and wasted investments—and habitual spending in things 'just because that's what we have been doing.'"

Over the last four years, the New York City left has frequently denounced "austerity" measures imposed by Mayor Adams. Significant cutbacks in spending by Mayor Mamdani could open the door to similar criticism. I asked Alexa to explain how the new administration might frame such moves.

"What Adams did—imposing cuts during a budget surplus—amounted to 'austerity for austerity's sake,'" Avilés observes. "There is a real distinction between doing that and cutting funding because we don't have the money coming in." Misdirecting resources is not something that the left champions. "Socialists argue about redistribution of money all the time," Alexa says. "Zohran will have no problem making the case that any wasteful spending is hurting us from delivering the services that people need."

Like Mamdani and Brannan, Avilés is sharply critical of Mayor Adams' inattention to crises faced by working-class residents across the city. "Right now, we should be working with the mayor in protecting our immigrant communities," she maintains. "But Adams is not interested in doing that."

On the same morning we met, Alexa's neighborhood office in Sunset Park hosted an outreach event for the area's large community of Mexican immigrants. Claudia Sheinbaum, Mexico's extremely popular leftist president, had been promoting a "Consulate on Wheels" initiative, which Avilés invited to her storefront office located just outside of the subway stop at 45th Street. Officials provided help with passports and birth certificates as well as outlined the process of initiating dual citizenship for US-born children.

Alexa explains that "Zohran can engage in robust partnerships" that promote similar initiatives, "so that children can help their parents if they get detained—or at least plan for that possibility." That would be just one meaningful way for Mamdani to follow through on his campaign vow to help protect immigrant communities from ICE terror. Moreover, such use of the bully pulpit does not require a significant budget.

*

Meet Mayor Mamdani

In his many extended conversations with leading national media outlets during October, Zohran added his own insights regarding the city's current spending patterns. When *New Yorker* editor David Remnick asked him about the Department of Education's massive budget, Mamdani spoke of the need for "internal reform," spotlighting the $10 billion the DoE allocates to contracts with private companies that provide things like curriculum development and classroom technology.

Contractors that were originally relied upon to save the city money, Zohran noted, were now inflating costs. "We're talking about a city that's still paying McKinsey millions of dollars to design a trash can," he said. Since the Bloomberg era, the high-end management consulting firm has received large contracts—including from the de Blasio administration[34]—to review everything from city schools to Rikers. The prospective mayor now warned that McKinsey's gravy train may no longer stop at City Hall.

Mamdani also promised that his administration would make better use of the city's vast existing resources. In a late October appearance on the *Daily Show*, Zohran told Jon Stewart that earlier in the day, he encountered a homeless person while riding the subway with a reporter. The prospective mayor then explained that the city possessed

---

34 After serving as First Deputy Mayor in de Blasio's first term, veteran city government insider Tony Shorris became a partner at McKinsey. As *ProPublica* reported (in December 2019), while at City Hall Shorris helped McKinsey win a $27.5 million contract to study management at Rikers. The firm had no experience in corrections and offered numerous dubious suggestions.

4,300 units of supportive housing units that currently stood vacant, which roughly matched the number of homeless people living on the subways and streets. The next-gen candidate thus directed national attention to one of the city's most vexing and enduring problems.

As several European journalists as well as attendees at discussions of *RZR* told me, many of Mamdani's top agenda items are not at all controversial in France, Denmark and elsewhere on the continent. Although the far right in Europe objects to immigrant groups receiving social provisions like childcare, conservatives generally agree that it is a necessity. Yet even in the city that spawned the New Deal, many liberal politicians do not promote expansive social programs.

"We have a city government that is complacent with the fact that one in four New Yorkers are living in poverty in the wealthiest city in the country," Zohran advised the *Daily Show's* large audience.[35] The extent to which Mayor Mamdani will be able to rectify New York City's massive inequalities remains far from certain. But there seems little doubt that he will try.

---

35 In the first 36 hours after it went up, Mamdani's interview with Jon Stewart was viewed more than 2.2 million times on YouTube.

CHAPTER 20
Balls Out

As the race entered its final laps, Zohran resisted complacency, frequently stating that he did not want to repeat Cuomo's June flameout. Rather than try to simply ride his tidal wave of fame into City Hall, Mamdani and his campaign continued to apply the same grassroots outreach methods that scored their upset victory in the primary.

On Saturday, October 11, Zohran honored National Coming Out Day with a video tribute commemorating the life of Stonewall veteran and pioneering West Village trans activist Sylvia Rivera. The multi-platform post was the fourth installment of Mamdani's "Until It's Done" series linking influential figures from New York City's past to the candidate's current agenda.[36] As in other episodes, Zohran sat

---

36 Launched in mid-September, previous installments of the series (scripted by Zohran for NYC writing director Julian Gerson) featured legendary Gilded Age journalist Nellie Bly, lesser-known Progressive Era Brownsville birth control advocate Fania

at a desk at a relevant location, in this case Christopher Street Pier, where Rivera, 46, was found dead in July 1992. The NYPD quickly deemed her death a suicide, but many of Rivera's peers believed she was murdered.

In his widely shared two-minute statement, the would-be mayor blasted Donald Trump's "scorched-earth campaign against trans people" and pledged to create an office of LGBTQIA+ affairs that would oversee supportive housing and gender-affirming care. Rather than dismiss trans issues as "identity politics," Mamdani foregrounded them, declaring that on his watch, "New York will not sit idly by while trans people are attacked." His larger affordability agenda thus incorporated rather than erased specific group concerns.

The next day, Zohran participated in the 2025 Brooklyn Gaza 5K at Prospect Park. As the candidate noted on social media, this marked the third time he joined the event, which raised funds for UNRWA. A photo showed Mamdani wearing a white official 5K t-shirt and black running gear. Zohran declared that he was doing this year's event in conjunction with Harlem Run, a fitness group with over 20,000 followers on Instagram.

Zohran's posts about the event received both praise and outrage. "Dude, you do everything," Witchy Wisdom CEO Shawn Engel stated in her very popular Instagram

---

Mindell, and 1960s' Harlem basketball wizard Earl Manigault. The short profiles opened the door for Zohran to discuss his plans to address the city's mental health crisis, inequalities in reproductive care, and need for substance abuse programs.

response. "I've never seen a politician be this embedded in culture. It's almost like high school president in the best way." Meanwhile, Rep. Elise Stefanik got mighty steamed up. Previewing the MAGA crusade against Zohran that would soon light up the Musk platform, the pro-Israel firebrand responded to Mamdani's pro-Gaza action by invoking Hamas, October 7th, hostages, antisemitism and communism while denouncing both the Democratic nominee and UNRWA.

Although Mamdani stayed upbeat and on message, his campaign communications briefly fell flat. On Monday night, October 13, Zohran for NYC hosted a rally titled "Our Time Has Come" at the 3,000-seat United Palace in Washington Heights. While the on-stage visuals were striking—with the yellow and orange campaign logo vibrantly set against a black backdrop—the name for Mamdani's first major general election event was conspicuously out of sync. Featured on signage everywhere at the event, "Our Time Has Come" seemed an ill-suited rallying cry for a youthful candidate representing a sprawling new coalition.

"Not our best slogan!" Zohran for NYC creative director Andrew Epstein acknowledged via a text message to me at the time. It was "meant to signify that the election is finally arriving," he explained. The four-month gap between the primary and the general election no doubt created weariness within Mamdani's inner circle. On YouTube, the campaign's video of the speech was titled "Our Time is Now," the frontrunner's powerful closing line that night.

That revised, action-oriented slogan then remained front and center throughout the homestretch.

The presence of Tish James at the Washington Heights rally made headlines in both the *New York Times* and the *New York Post*. It was the AG's first public appearance since her indictment by the DoJ four days earlier. Tish called Zohran her "little brother," a far more endearing term than the president had been using to describe the Democratic nominee. Although the capacity crowd gave James a hearty reception, it was WNBA star Natasha Cloud who brought down the house. Echoing the moment in June when Alexa Avilés lit up Mamdani's rally with AOC, the New York Liberty point guard led the crowd in a chorus of "Free Palestine!"

*

Rather than participate in charity events or lead rallies, Andrew Cuomo visited TV studios. In his frequent interviews, he warned that a Mamdani win would result in a "Mayor Trump," with the president seizing control of City Hall. (How that process might work was not specified.) Despite stoking pro-Israel outrage during the primary, the veteran pol now insisted that Zohran's support for Gaza was "divisive." Along the way, Cuomo continued to mispronounce his rival's last name.

Trailing by double digits with three weeks to go, the second-place contender readied for two televised debates that provided his clearest opportunities to close the gap. Although he had several months to prepare for the October 16 showdown, the veteran campaigner nonetheless brought nothing new to 30 Rock that Thursday night. From the outset, he again tried to make experience the defining issue, reiterating his insistence that Mamdani needed "on-the-job training."[37]

After noting that Cuomo planned to "serve his billionaire donors," Zohran touted his work in more recent years, including helping win debt relief for taxi drivers and creating a free bus pilot program. A slugfest ensued. "On his resume, it says he interned for his mother," Mario's son sneered, warning that the Democratic nominee was unprepared "for a 9/11 or a health pandemic." That incendiary barb enabled the frontrunner to invoke Cuomo's nursing home scandal, with Mamdani charging that the former governor "sent seniors to their death."

The next-gen candidate then served up his most memorable statement of the night. "What I don't have in experience, I make up for in integrity," Mamdani said, turning towards Cuomo. "And what you don't have in integrity, you could never make up for in experience." As Zohran for NYC writing director Julian Gerson told me, campaign senior adviser Zara Rahim furnished the eloquent stinger, which the *New Yorker* and many other leading outlets highlighted.

---

[37] The 22 percent of respondents to a CNN general election exit poll listing "experience" as their foremost concern overwhelmingly supported Cuomo. By contrast, Mamdani received very strong support from the 28 percent that cited "change" and the 21 percent that selected "works for people like me." Had Cuomo paired invocations of his track record with coherent policy proposals, he likely would have done better in the latter category.

Only six minutes into the debate, the two main rivals were duking it out. Perhaps unusually for a frontrunner, Zohran stayed on the attack throughout the bout. Meanwhile, the third guy in the ring also made things entertaining.

"There's high levels of testosterone in the room," Curtis Sliwa observed in response to his opponents' sparring. The distinctly late twentieth-century Brooklyn character's comment sparked laughter at the large debate watch party hosted by OR Books at the Francis Kite Club on Avenue C. Although none of the gathered lefties shared the Guardian Angel's reactionary views, many respected Sliwa's sincerity and appreciated the fact that unlike Cuomo, he is often amusing.

Watched live by nearly 2.4 million viewers,[38] the event's opening half-hour saw extensive discussion of the utterly serious crisis in Gaza. Cuomo voiced no criticism of Israel, instead demanding that Mamdani "denounce" Hamas, Hasan Piker, and the phrase "globalize the intifada." In response, Zohran twice referred to the "genocide" of Palestinians and invoked international law. The frontrunner also stood his ground on the other main issue discussed in the first half of the debate: the future direction of the NYPD. Mamdani vowed to follow through on his pledge to create a new Department of Community Safety.

Cuomo failed to land any major blows in the most-watched portion of the event. During the latter part of the second, internet-only hour, he occasionally staggered—at one

---

38 WNBC and its partner Telemundo/WNJU reach audiences in New York, New Jersey and Connecticut.

point exhibiting Bidenesque confusion. As the dust settled, neither of the former governor's preferred local TV reporters advised their mostly older viewers that Cuomo won the debate. While WABC's N.J. Burkett scored Mamdani as the winner, WCBS mainstay Marcia Kramer gave the edge to Sliwa.

For a flickering moment, it appeared that Zohran might sail smoothly to victory on November 4. But Captain Ahab sharpened his harpoon—and now sought to slay the third-place challenger.

*

As of October 15, opinion polls provided only one plausible path for Cuomo. Checking in around 30 percent, the independent candidate needed to collect the roughly 15 percent of voters backing the Republican nominee. If he reeled in all of Sliwa's votes, Cuomo might surpass Mamdani, who was then hovering around 45 percent.

On the day after the 30 Rock debate, Cuomo launched a media blitz. "Sliwa cannot win the race," he advised WABC-TV reporters. "I believe the Republican Party bosses want to see Zohran Mandami [sic] win for their own political purposes."[39] As a *Times* headline that Friday put it, "Cuomo All but Begs Sliwa to Drop Out."

That same Friday afternoon, Zohran and Harlem City Councilman Yusef Salaam (one of the Exonerated Five)

---

39 As Liza Featherstone observed at the OR Books debate watch gathering, Mamdani's last name is "phonetic," and there was no good-faith explanation for Cuomo's repeated mispronunciation.

paid a visit to influential Brooklyn imam Siraj Wahhaj, who declared his support for Mamdani. The endorsement promised to yield many votes. As the frontrunner's close ally Asad Dandia stated on X, Wahhaj ranked "among the most beloved Muslim leaders in the US across all sects and schools of thought. By winning him over, Zohran has remade NYC's Muslim political map forever." Asad explained to me that he had known Wahhaj since the two had been among the lead plaintiffs in *Raza v City of New York*, a landmark case initiated in 2013 that resulted in restrictions on NYPD surveillance of Muslim communities.

Led by Bari Weiss's *The Free Press*, pro-Israel zealots quickly called attention to the fact that Wahhaj had been deemed an "unindicted co-conspirator" in the 1993 terrorist attack on the World Trade Center. That the feds' list included 169 other names did not diminish the outrage. "If Wahhaj was involved in a terrorist attack, why was he never charged, let alone convicted?" asked *Zeteo*'s Mehdi Hasan. The sensible question received scant attention.

On Sunday, October 19, the *New York Post* went for broke, with a front-page headline stating "Photobomb." The cover featured a picture of Mamdani smiling beside Wahhaj, who had his arm around Zohran. Elon Musk's pithy quote-tweet of the hit piece—"wow"—quickly garnered over 30 million views. That Wahhaj had joined with the *Post* in endorsing Eric Adams in 2021 meant little to Murdoch's forces.

While the fireworks went off, Curtis Sliwa held his ground. As he explained to next-gen MAGA YouTube host Nate Friedman, running as the Republican nominee obligated the candidate to represent the entire party, which also fielded down-ballot challengers for city council seats and judgeships. "Go out and get your own votes!" Sliwa advised Cuomo, who clashed regularly with city GOP leaders during his reign in Albany.

There was no doubt that Mamdani benefitted from Sliwa's persistence. In a quote-tweet of the Friedman interview, Zohran observed, "It's genuinely positive for our democracy that there's another candidate in this race who believes NYC voters should pick their next mayor, not billionaires who mostly live somewhere else." Leftist city councilman Chi Ossé—a newly declared member of the NYC-DSA—similarly urged the Republican nominee to resist the demands of "billionaires and establishment 'DEMOCRATS'." Cheekily channeling the sentiment of many Zohran supporters, Chi then advised Curtis: "NEVER BACK DOWN."[40]

Five days before early voting began, several leaders of the New York City GOP now took turns shanking Sliwa. On Monday morning, October 20, party figurehead John Catsimatidis went on WABC radio—Cats' own network, on which Sliwa had been a longtime host—to turn up

---

[40] Ossé's X post also suggested to Sliwa "YOU have a shot," which was also playful. For that to be the case, Cuomo would have needed to drop out, with Sliwa then trying to gain massive support from Democrats. In the 2021 general election, Eric Adams defeated Sliwa by 40 points.

the volume. Whereas he previously resisted pressure to call on Curtis to step aside, the billionaire now declared that the Republican nominee should "pull out right now" in order to prove that he "love[s] New York more than anything else." Rarely had the city's catchphrase sounded so threatening.[41]

Cats made his case to Sliwa's longtime radio colleague Sid Rosenberg (b. 1957), a MAGA diehard who spends plenty of time pumping iron. Since the spring, Sid—a militant Israel hawk with a large local listenership— had frequently referred to Mamdani as a "terrorist" on X. But until October 20, he remained solidly in Curtis' corner, recently clashing with far-right turncoat GOP activists who pressured him to throw his weight behind Cuomo.

Following the lead of his WABC boss, the shock jock now switched sides, telling the *Daily News* that "I love [Curtis], but I can't have Mamdani win. If that means Cuomo winning, God bless him."[42] The house organ of the New York City Republicans soon chimed in, amplifying Cats and Rosenberg's effort to circle the wagons.

"Swallow the bitter pill, Curtis Sliwa—quit the race to stop Zohran Mamdani," instructed the headline of a *New York Post* editorial posted at 3:55 p.m. on October 20. As seen in *RZR*, Murdoch's attack dogs hounded Cuomo from the

---

[41] Along with her four city counterparts, Andrea Catsimitadis (Cats' daughter)—leader of the Republican county organization in Manhattan—remained in Sliwa's camp.

[42] "I've hated Cuomo for the better part of ten years," Rosenberg acknowledged from the stage at the Republican Jewish Coalition in Las Vegas on the weekend before election day.

day he entered the race in March, when they labeled him as "New York's biggest liar." The ornery opinion-shapers now seemed nothing if not chagrined. It was difficult to believe that the order came from anywhere other than the uppermost sanctum of Rupert's empire.

"It burns to write this," began the short editorial, thereby assuming the tone of a desperate fundraising email. "Plenty of readers will erupt in fury at us, and we get it," the lament continued. "No one will confuse this page, or *The Post* as a whole, for Cuomo fans." To reaffirm their bona fides, the extreme-right crew hyperlinked the final three words of that sentence to a mid-March recap of their many beefs with Cuomo during his Albany tenure. Murdoch's opinion desk nonetheless warned that the clear and present danger was now Mamdani, an "oddball" whose win portended "major, *deadly* damage." The emphasis here was somewhat less than original.

The circuitous plug for Cuomo made no mention of Israel or socialism, but readers of the *New York Post* opinion page surely had their minds made up about such matters. Sliwa graced the tabloid's cover on Tuesday, beside an anachronistic headline reading, "Just Walk Away, Beret!"[43] Rosenberg's show that morning featured a chat with the host's new pal Andrew. Seeking a consolation prize for his old buddy Curtis, Sid got the would-be mayor to promise the Republican candidate a job in his administration. Invoking Mel Gibson's final scene in *Braveheart* (1995),

---

43   The reference to Left Banke's 1966 hit song "Walk Away Renée"—which features the refrain "Just walk away, Renée"—was not aimed at readers under 60.

Sliwa soon stated that he would rather be "impaled" than work for Cuomo. Note to readers: let that sink in.

While Cuomo's allies took victory laps on X, Sliwa valiantly clashed with Rosenberg on the latter's morning show two days later. The Republican nominee indignantly announced that "you will never see me at the studios of WABC again." Under no circumstances would he throw in the towel. Although his post-election future on the airwaves was unclear, Curtis seemed quite likely to patch things up with the *Post*, given that the tabloid had long kept him in the headlines.

Amid the Sliwa fireworks, Cuomo fanned the flames of pro-Israel outrage against Mamdani. On the evening of Monday, October 20, Bibi's volunteer counsel sat down with Elisha Weisel at Congregation Ohab Zedek, an Orthodox synagogue on W. 95th Street. Asked at the recent debate whether he considered Zohran to be antisemitic, the veteran pol served up the "what others are saying" routine. "I don't make those judgments about people," Cuomo stated, then added, "I know there are many Jewish people who believe he is antisemitic." Four nights later, the veteran pol changed his tune.

As witnessed in *RZR*, late in the primary Weisel launched an explosive Holocaust-themed attack on Mamdani, meaning that Cuomo clearly knew what the host wanted to hear. The second-place contender now told the W. 95 St. gathering that Zohran was "a candidate who r[an] based on his antisemitic stance." Worse yet, the former governor claimed, there had been widespread "complacency" throughout the city about his rival's "arrogance and antisemitism."[44] On social media, Cuomo touted Weisel's backing. For Mario's son, votes were all that counted.

*

While Cuomo and company cut deals, Zohran played a different sort of ballgame. In tandem with a recreational soccer league called NYC Footy, Mamdani's campaign hosted a "Cost of Living Classic" under the lights of a minor-league baseball stadium at Coney Island on Sunday, October 19. Favorable coverage in the *New York Times* featured a large photo of Zohran surrounded by scores of cheerful, multihued, mixed-gender, mostly 20-something participants.

"Soccer is a big part of what so many New Yorkers love about being in this city," the former Bronx Science varsity soccer captain observed. "I think to have this opportunity to celebrate the pride that we have in our own boroughs [provides] a glimpse of what politics can be in this city." In his video recap of the event, Zohran exchanged a warm embrace with the Latino goalie who made the tournament-ending save. Celebration of recreational sports seemed quite aligned with the spirit of Mamdani's grassroots campaign.

As the high-stakes showdown between Cuomo and Sliwa unfolded, Mamdani laid low during most of the run-up to the final debate on Wednesday, October 22. With the

---

[44] In the second primary debate (June 12), Cuomo explained that "I am not Mr. Mamdani. I'm not antisemitic." But until the last two weeks of the general election, he preferred to make indirect accusations.

Meet Mayor Mamdani

Republican nominee now on the ropes, the Fight and Deliver candidate now had one last chance to score points against the frontrunner. On NY1, anti-Mamdani political consultant J.C. Polanco likened the upcoming bout to the Thrilla in Manila, evidently forgetting the fact that Muhammad Ali prevailed in his final match with Joe Frazier.

In the run-up to the final debate of any campaign, it is usually the challengers, not the front-runner, who try to stir the pot. But about 90 minutes before showtime, *New York Times* reporter Nicholas Fandos delivered a big scoop. After months of pressure, Zohran announced that, if elected, he would ask current NYPD Commissioner Jessica Tisch to remain in the position. For the city elite that Tisch represents, it was a big concession from Mamdani. For criminal justice advocates, the announcement was a major blow. A leftist prospective mayor now vowed to keep a reactionary figure as the most prominent member of his administration. Why?

Since his triumph in the June primary, Mamdani faced a relentless stream of pressure to keep Tisch. The question appeared frequently in the *New York Times* and many other outlets' coverage of the race, serving as a litmus test for the next-gen nominee. As Elle Bisgaard-Church—Zohran's top adviser—told *Times* columnist Mara Gay in early October, she had been receiving "consistent, unsolicited advice" to retain Tisch from the city elite's many whisperers. On Sunday, October 19, Cuomo informed Marcia Kramer that if elected, he would keep the commissioner. Releasing their decision to follow suit just before the debate meant that Mamdani's team clearly wanted the political world to know their verdict.[45]

Patrick Gaspard, a veteran Democratic operative advising Mamdani, praised the move in the initial version of Fandos' story.[46] In an August chart showcasing the various circles influencing Zohran's decision-making since the primary, the *Times* uniquely dubbed Gaspard as a "Democratic wise man." Ambassador to South Africa under Obama, key ally to Mayor Bill de Blasio, and president of the liberal think tank Center for American Progress (2021-2025), Gaspard relished his backstage role as a progressive power broker. Amid post-election criticism from the left regarding Mamdani's decision to keep Tisch, Gaspard defended the commissioner.

Zohran was not quoted in the initial *Times* piece, meaning that his first comment came at the midway point of the debate. "Commissioner Tisch took on a broken status quo, started to deliver accountability, rooting out corruption and reducing crime across the five boroughs," Zohran told co-moderator Katie Honan of *The City*. The frontrunner then reaffirmed his intent to create a new Department of Community Safety that would address what he labeled a "mental health crisis." Although Tisch was not known for advancing progressive policy innovations, Mamdani

---

45 Although the matter was followed closely by the city's political class and criminal justice activists, the extent to which average voters cared about whether Tisch stayed on the job was not clear.

46 Gaspard's name did not remain in the subsequent version. Via email, Fandos told me that Zohran's comments in the debate eliminated the need for others to explain the move.

strongly suggested that she would agree to his proposal, which would involve the NYPD reducing its purview.[47]

The timing of Mamdani's offer was risky, especially given its potential to backfire if Tisch declined.[48] Until that point, the frontrunner had also repeatedly punted when asked staffing questions about his administration, keeping his focus on winning the election. In changing course just before early voting commenced, Zohran appeared to be making the announcement to reap political gain.

In the wake of his Tisch bulletin, Mamdani received some previously withheld high-profile support, although nothing qualified as a game-changer. In his belated, decidedly lukewarm endorsement of Zohran on the Friday afternoon before early voting began, Hakeem Jeffries praised the Democratic nominee's pledge to keep Tisch. As seen in the next chapter, the *New York Times*' re-assembled panel of experts now favored the newcomer, with their findings released one week after Mamdani's announcement. Tisch was not mentioned, but the commissioner's exalted reputation among the city elite no doubt influenced many panelists' newfound embrace of Zohran.

---

47 As Ray Kelly, the NYPD's hardline commissioner for the entirety of Mayor Bloomberg's tenure (2002-2013), told Sid Rosenberg, by reallocating resources away from the NYPD, Mamdani's DCS amounted to "defund" by another name.

48 If Tisch rejected the invitation before November 4, Cuomo definitely stood to gain because it would have bolstered criticisms regarding the leftist's wrongheaded approach to policing as well as lack of management chops.

Criminal justice activists were somewhat less than pleased with the move. Brooklyn College professor Alex Vitale, who had advised Zohran's campaign on policing issues and counseled against retaining Tisch, told me shortly after October 22 that his cellphone kept lighting up with alarmed messages. In her first year as commissioner, Tisch had repeatedly denounced progressive measures including bail reform and "raise the age" legislation, which moved 16- and 17-year-old defendants out of adult court. Mentored by Bill Bratton and Ray Kelly, Tisch stuck with the law-and-order playbook of the Giuliani and Bloomberg eras.

Ever since becoming a presence in New York City politics in 2018, the NYC-DSA was known for its often-radical criminal justice positions. As shown in *RZR*, Zohran was a committed participant in Tiffany Cabán's 2019 campaign for Queens DA, which advanced a decarceral platform. In his mid-October *New York Times Magazine* profile of Mamdani, Astead Herndon reported that local DSA co-chair Gustavo Gordillo did not support retaining Tisch. When the announcement came, the *Times* quoted DSA State Senator Julia Salazar's praise for the move. Although she is the group's most prominent figure on criminal justice issues, it was not clear that Salazar had first consulted with other NYC-DSA leaders.

Jessica ("Jessie") Tisch comes from an elite New York City family of leading Israel hawks[49] that provided substantial

---

49 As Substacker Jennifer Koonings explained (in a November 9 post), Jesse's grandfather Laurence Tisch took over CBS News in

funding for Fix the City, the main outside spending group attacking Mamdani on behalf of Cuomo. From October 14 through October 20, four members of the Tisch clan gave a combined $900,000 to the PAC, with Jessie's aunt Alice ponying up a half-million bucks. All told, the commissioner's close relatives gave just over $1.3m to help Fix the City smear the leftist Democratic nominee. Although the Tisch brigade generously turned off the spigot after Mamdani agreed to retain Jessie, their close ally Mike Bloomberg helped fill the void.

Did Zohran really think that the NYPD's current conservative commissioner was a good fit with his administration? Prior to announcing the move, he told Astead Herndon that the potential move would reflect his intent to create a "team of rivals," which sounded just a bit Obamaesque. Asked by MSNBC's Chris Hayes whether the Tisch invitation was a "calculated move to the center," Mamdani served up talking points including "this is not about polling" and "safety is the bedrock of an affordability agenda."[50] The former insurgent started to sound like a conventional pol.

When pressed specifically about Tisch's opposition to his various progressive positions—including Mamdani's support for disbanding the NYPD's Strategic Response Group, which polices protests and is known for hostility to pro-Palestine activism—Zohran insisted that the commissioner would change course. "I am confident that she will be alongside

---

1986. In a preview of recent actions by Bari Weiss, Laurence Tisch sought to squelch any negative coverage of Israel by the network.

50 In 2021, candidate Eric Adams frequently stated that "public safety is the prerequisite for prosperity," a notably different goal.

me," the frontrunner told WPIX11's Dan Mannarino. As Norman Finkelstein pointed out, Tisch seemed most unlikely to support Mamdani's call to arrest Netayanhu.

After taking over the department in December 2024, Tisch got rid of a few, but by no means all of Eric Adams' cronies in the top ranks, meaning that there was at least some substance to Zohran's repeated praise for her corruption crackdown. But elsewhere on the campaign trail, the Republican nominee was also fighting wrongdoing. Curtis Sliwa repeatedly denounced the attempts by billionaires to reward him with seven-figure sums if he dropped out. As *Indypendent* publisher John Tarleton told me, championing any political figure simply as a "corruption-fighter" set a "pretty low bar."

Meanwhile, the local media's oft-repeated claim that Tisch was popular with the NYPD rank and file was rejected by one of Mamdani's main law enforcement allies. The commissioner had been "making certain decisions that are demoralizing chiefs, inspectors and cops," Shamsul Haque, co-founder of the Bangladeshi American Police Association, informed *Politico* New York's Jeff Coltin at the October 22 debate.

A democratic socialist had opted to offer the most prominent position in his upcoming administration to the 1%'s clear choice. Kathy Hochul, Tish James and many other prominent local Democrats had made a strong push for Tisch. When the commissioner accepted the mayor-elect's invitation four weeks later, the party brass led the chorus of cheers. On at least one essential front, Mamdani was joining the establishment, not transforming it.

CHAPTER 21
Hot Seats

"I can tell you are clearly in the front-running position because they've gone 9/11 on you," Jon Stewart told Zohran at the outset of their *Daily Show* interview on Monday, October 27. The host dubbed the 9/11 card—i.e. a broad-brush smear associating Mamdani with the terrorist attacks on the World Trade Center—as the "closing argument" launched by the Andrew Cuomo-allied forces of reaction.

When shock jock Sid Rosenberg suggested to the former governor a few days earlier that in the event of a 9/11-style attack, Zohran would "be cheering," a snickering Cuomo replied, "That's another problem." Mamdani explained to Stewart that while his opponents lobbed grenades, Zohran for NYC's vast army of volunteers were knocking on voter doors and engaging in "conversations about how to build the city we want to live in."

Meet Mayor Mamdani

Five nights earlier, Cuomo unveiled a new ally. While Mamdani and Curtis Sliwa chatted with reporters after the debate in Long Island City, Cuomo raced across town to Madison Square Garden, where he joined Mayor Eric Adams in the first row at the Knicks' season opener. Although they had recently been at each other's throat, the former governor and outgoing mayor were now all smiles, united by their love for basketball and disdain for the youthful frontrunner.

"Corruption goes courtside," Zohran stated above a photo of the duo on X. It was not immediately clear who had paid for the premium seats. The next afternoon, Cuomo nodded along while Adams used an air horn instead of a dog whistle, with the mayor warning that a Mamdani victory would result in the terror attacks seen in Europe.[51] Although he had spent several weeks trying to court Muslim voters—making his first visits to mosques during his lengthy political career—the second-place contender now reversed course. Stoked by MAGA influencers, Islamophobic rage dominated the final days of the campaign.

Zohran, meanwhile, continued to build out the coalition that propelled his primary win, now adding local Democratic Party support. During the race's last laps, Mamdani hit the gas pedal, denouncing Islamophobia, visiting churches, popping up on stages and nightclubs, and marching

---

51 "New York can't be Europe, folks. I don't know what is wrong with people," Adams stated. "You see what's playing out in other countries because of Islamic extremism."

across the Brooklyn Bridge. With the finish line in sight, Zohran was ready to break the tape.

*

9/11 was not the only card that Team Cuomo played. In mid-October, Zach Sage Fox—whose X bio page characterized him as a CEO and comedian while featuring an Israeli flag—announced that he was handling the campaign's social media productions through election day. One of several millennial influencers who met with Bibi Netanyahu during his recent visit to the UN, Fox now churned out numerous hit posts against Zohran.

Shortly after the October 22 debate commenced, Fox's most sensational concoction went live on Cuomo's X account. It was 133 seconds of A.I.-generated racist slop, with characters including a Blaxploitation-era pimp and a keffiyeh-wearing young Black shoplifter declaring their support for Mamdani, who was shown eating rice with his hands. *Zeteo*'s Prem Thakker alertly downloaded the video before it was quickly taken down by the campaign. Fox's similarly incendiary output featured a group called "Muslims Against Mamdani," in which actual humans denounced the candidate's positions on crime; and a cringy Halloween post showing an A.I.-created Zohran frightening computer-spawned children and parents.

Six days before the election, Cuomo launched his own missiles, advising Fox host Maria Bartiromo that there was a "quiet civil war" inside the Democratic Party. The "far left" sought "destroy" the current regime, he warned. Why that might concern Fox viewers was not clear. That afternoon,

Cuomo turned it up a notch with popular sports talk figure Stephen A. Smith, declaring "I believe that Mamdani can kill New York City." Although Smith is known for his own verbal pyrotechnics, his statements don't usually involve mass extinction.[52]

Zohran called into Smith's radio show, likening his belligerent challenger to Trump. "What we heard from Andrew Cuomo was not leadership," the frontrunner stated. "It was him spending twenty minutes talking about me, because he has no vision left to actually offer New Yorkers." After seven months on the campaign trail, the agenda-deficient pol promised little more than 5,000 more cops and four more years of Cuomo wielding power.

As election day neared, the second-place contender insisted that Trump preferred a Mamdani win because it would create a leftist bogeyman for national Republicans. The relentless torrent of MAGA outrage against Zohran in late October soon undercut that argument, and the president ultimately dispelled any notion that he "wanted" the leftist to claim City Hall when he endorsed the former governor on the eve of the election. Trump's plug helped swing a sizable number of local Republican votes from Sliwa to Cuomo.

---

52 Cuomo's doomsaying continued the next day at a NYCHA senior center in Harlem, where he advised elderly folks that "I do not believe the city of New York has a future if Zohran Mamdani is elected mayor." Mayor Adams joined him in delivering the terrifying message.

On Thursday, October 23, the Muslim-baiting statements by Sid Rosenberg and Mayor Adams on Cuomo's behalf prompted immediate condemnation by many local Democratic leaders. "Imagine if this kind of bigotry was used against Jewish or Christian New Yorkers," Rep. Jerrold Nadler stated on X. "Would we roll over and accept it?" While most other party leaders echoed Nadler, Chuck Schumer and Kirstin Gillibrand seemed unperturbed.

That Friday afternoon, Zohran fought back tears while speaking to reporters outside of the Islamic Cultural Center in the central Bronx. Flanked by fellow Muslim women and men, Mamdani called out the recent comments by the Cuomo crowd, while also denouncing Sliwa's false charge at the recent debate that the frontrunner supported "global jihad." He further took aim at MAGA antagonists including Black conservative Larry Elder and extreme-right Queens councilwoman Vickie Paladino.[53]

"Growing up in the shadow of 9/11," Zohran observed, "I have known what it means to live with an undercurrent of suspicion in this city." That hostility led to a begrudging acceptance. "To be Muslim in New York is to expect indignity," he said, "but indignity does not make us distinct. There are many New Yorkers who face it." Mamdani argued that his co-religionists' "tolerance of that indignity" distinguished their experience from that of other groups, noting

---

53 On October 21, Elder posted a political cartoon that went viral on X showing a Soviet plane named "Mamdani" about to hit the World Trade Center. Meanwhile, continuing the xenophobic attacks she launched during the primary, Paladino's team sold "Deport Mamdani" t-shirts.

that like his elders, the candidate had advised younger Muslims not to make waves regarding mistreatment. But Zohran's campaign showed that those days were over.

"The dream of every Muslim," Mamdani insisted, "is simply to be treated the same as any other New Yorker." No longer would he and others in his community "feel like guests in our own home." Although he appreciated the outpouring of support he had received in the face of Islamophobic smears,[54] the aspiring mayor spoke for all those not in the spotlight, whose daily encounters with bigotry went unrecognized. His own progression could be mirrored by others. "I will no longer look for myself in the shadows," Zohran concluded. "I will look for myself in the light."

A video of Zohran presenting his remarks in front of the Islamic Cultural Center's library went viral, garnering over 25 million views on X during the next seven days. Speechwriter Julian Gerson, a former Jerrold Nadler staffer who is Jewish, teamed with the candidate in creating the landmark pro-Muslim statement. For a fleeting moment, Mamdani had elevated the discussion surrounding the mayoral campaign.

In a *Guardian* feature story published that same day, Moustafa Bayoumi connected Zohran's ascent to transformations within the city's Muslim communities seen since 9/11. In response to Islamophobia, Bayoumi explained, "Muslim New Yorkers spent years developing political

---

54 Among countless other groups, Jews for Racial and Economic Justice declared their "unbreakable solidarity with Muslim New Yorkers and all of our neighbors" on Instagram.

power in the city, building local political institutions, and leaning into a different kind of politics, one that embraces identity yet also moves beyond its sometimes shallow appeal." Mamdani's speech that day provided his first in-depth public account of his ascent as a pioneering mayoral candidate, marking another step forward in the progression Bayoumi described.

While Zohran critiqued Islamophobia, Musk's platform amplified it. Trump foot soldiers including J.D. Vance mocked Mamdani for invoking his loved ones' experience after 9/11 at the Islamic Cultural Center. Senator Ted Cruz repeatedly called Mamdani a "commie jihadist." At least one lesser-known MAGA figure garnered attention by joining the crusade.

Prior to fall 2025, Ellie Cohanim—a State Department apparatchik during Trump's first term—was not a particularly prominent figure on X. But her next-level tirade against Zohran soon gained widespread notoriety. On October 25, she wrote, "Never forget. Early voting begins today. Vote Andrew Cuomo & save our city" above two photos, one of the World Trade Center's Twin Towers in flames and the other of a person leaping to his death on 9/11 (a disturbing image known as "The Falling Man"). "Anyone flippantly posting images like this for clout is a fucking ghoul," City Councilman Justin Brannan responded. Cohanim was unapologetic in her reply.

Cohanim was joined by former Hollywood star James Woods, now known primarily as a MAGA megaphone and frequent butt of *Family Guy* jokes. Woods fanned the flames, calling New York City's prospective mayor an

"Islamist madman" and "smirking reptile." He, too, posted "The Falling Man" in reference to Mamdani. Like Cohanim, Woods evidently believed that bomb-throwing was fair game and that his attacks required no explanation.

On Monday, October 27, Fox News soon provided its own dubious addition to the crusade, releasing a 12-minute report called "Inside the Mamdani Machine: Soros cash, socialists and radical imams engineered Zohran Mamdani's path to power." Pakistan-born rightwing journalist Asra Q. Nomani led the investigation, which alleged that a network of 110 activist groups spurred the pro-Palestine candidate's ascent, with the conspiracy starting when Mamdani was at Bowdoin. Nomani made lots of insinuations about Zohran's Muslim allies Linda Sarsour and Imam Siraj Wahhaj.

That Mamdani prevailed with support from over 1.1 million city residents showed that a clear majority of the electorate did not embrace bigotry. An Associated Press exit poll recorded a whopping 92 percent of Muslim voters backing Zohran. But Islamophobic outrage drove MAGA turnout, which ultimately helped Cuomo reel in just over 900,000 votes.

Down the homestretch Pakistanis for Zohran, an Instagram account with nearly 12,000 followers, posted a much-shared clip of women singing in Urdu about their preferred candidate at a Jackson Heights debate watch party. "Everybody's talking about my dear Mamdani," went the up-tempo lyrics. "He wants to serve the people—he's not after power." As Pakistanis for Zohran stated below its post, "You're not relevant in Pakistani political culture until you have your own song." The city's Muslims of all origins shared the sentiment.

*

As election day approached, Fix the City (FTC) once again issued a multifaceted attack campaign against Mamdani on Cuomo's behalf. In October, Bill Ackman, Dan Loeb, the Lauder family and Barry Diller continued their charitable giving to FTC. New recruits including AirBnB co-founder Joseph Gebbia joined the cause, with the Trump appointee (to DOGE) pitching in $1 million. On the platform owned by Gebbia's pal Musk, Zohran highlighted Gebbia's stridently anti-immigrant statements, thereby yoking Cuomo to MAGA hatemongering.

FTC's largest expenditure during the final week of the campaign was a $1.7 million TV ad buy that included video footage of a 2022 Brooklyn subway attack during which the armed assailant set off two smoke bombs on the train, creating a mass panic. That the terrifying assault (which injured 29 passengers) occurred while retired NYPD Captain Eric Adams manned City Hall seemed beside the point. As "Mayhem" and "Terror" flashed across the screen, the narrator warned, "Sit this one out at your own peril."

"Vote like your life depends on it," similarly vowed one of FTC's numerous 11th-hour mailers, this one targeting Ultra-Orthodox Jewish voters in Crown Heights. To reinforce the threat, the last five words—*your life depends on it*—were in bright red. The flipside of the same piece referred to Cuomo as "The only one who can stop Mamdani." The mailer carried the endorsement of a "United Group of Crown

Heights Leaders," with 13 names listed (including three rabbis). Many of the figures were connected to the Chabad-Lubavitch organization, to which Cuomo first announced that he would join Netanyahu's legal team in late 2024.

In September, Cuomo briefly—and tepidly—criticized Israel's demolition of Gaza. Throughout October, he was squarely back in Bibi's camp. Cuomo aimed to shore up support from the city's large number of militantly pro-Israel voters. That one prominent local Orthodox Jewish leader remained allied with Curtis Sliwa posed a problem for the Fight and Deliver candidate.

A disciple of extreme-right figurehead Meir Kahane, former assemblyman Dov Hikind (b. 1950) initially championed the Republican nominee. On Thursday, October 9, Hikind brought Sliwa to a late-evening holiday celebration in Crown Heights. Photos in the Chabad-Lubavitch news outlet *COL Live* showed Sliwa receiving very warm greetings, with the candidate sporting his red beret while joining dance circles.

But on Sunday, October 26, Hikind suddenly shifted his support to Cuomo. Curtis "can't win," his former longtime ally told the *New York Post*, adding "Mamdani is a threat to the well-being of every New Yorker. He will destroy New York." Hamas "will celebrate," Hikind advised *The Forward*. The Ultra-Zionist firebrand has long served as an outspoken advocate of West Bank settlements.[55] Cuomo opted to quietly accept the 11th-hour plug.

---

55 For Hikind's track record of extremism, see Max Blumenthal's 2013 profile in *The Nation*.

Buoyed by FTC's billionaire backers, MAGA figureheads, and local right-wing power brokers, Cuomo remained in striking distance as early voting began. It was now Zohran's turn to fire up his base.

*

On Sunday night, October 26, Mamdani returned to the outdoor stage at Forest Hills Stadium in Queens for the second time during the fall campaign season. In late September, Lucy Dakus, a 30-year-old singer-songwriter, introduced Zohran as her special guest, with the candidate receiving a raucous welcome. With just over one week until election day, Mamdani was now the headliner, rolling in with a large entourage featuring Bernie, AOC and lots of (mostly) left-wing figureheads.

The "New York Is Not for Sale" rally was hosted by Sarah Sherman, a *Saturday Night Live* star from Long Island in her early 30s. The comedienne entertained the crowd of over 10,000 Mamdani enthusiasts who turned out on a chilly evening for an event that spanned over three hours. Like Zohran's June rally with AOC, the roster of speakers included a wide range of activists, labor organizers, and NYC-DSA elected officials, with Brooklyn State Senator Julia Salazar and Queens Assemblymember Claire Valdez stepping to the podium.

"As this race enters its final days," Zohran declared in his closing remarks, "we have witnessed levels of Islamophobia that shock the conscience." Rather than focus on the "affordability crisis that consumes New Yorkers' lives," Mamdani said, his opponents took aim at his faith and tried to "normalize hatred." The leftist candidate blasted the "robber barons," "oligarchs," and "Donald Trump's billionaire donors" who sought to take him down, then led the crowd in a passionate call-and-response rundown of his central campaign pledges.

Neither Zohran, AOC, nor Bernie furnished the most memorable lines at Forest Hills that Sunday evening. Instead, the honor belonged to the crowd. When Governor Kathy Hochul took the stage midway through the proceedings, loud chants of "Tax the rich!" rang throughout the stadium. The next day Hochul improbably claimed that the fans hollered "Let's go Bills!" The governor from western New York was out of her element in central Queens.

As seen in *RZR,* when Zohran surged in June, the *New York Times* editorial board desperately tried to sink him. With six days to go, the Gray Lady now issued a revised suggestion. A panel with fourteen "experts" (most of whom sat on a similar June iteration) had warmed to Zohran, with eleven members scoring Mamdani higher than Cuomo and Sliwa. *Times* mainstay Eleanor Rudolph furnished her seal of approval, calling the leftist candidate "smart and ambitious."

Because the announcement was not presented as a full-fledged endorsement, the panelists' backing did not generate much buzz. It was also difficult to imagine that many readers of the *Times* were undecided at that stage of the race. But the Gray Lady's change of heart suggested that the city establishment was now ready to work with Mamdani.

Until the final week of the general election, *Times* ally Michael Bloomberg stayed on the sidelines. With the clock running out, it appeared likely that the largest contributor to Fix the City would sit out the race. It was thus surprising that in the wake of the *Times* panel's nod, Bloomy reupped his support for Cuomo, touting the veteran pol's "experience and toughness."

To show that he meant business, the billionaire media mogul also contemporaneously delivered another $1.5 million to Fix the City, bringing Bloomy's total FTC contributions for the 2025 campaign to $9.8 million. That same day, the former mayor also gave $3.5 million to a different pro-Cuomo PAC called For Our City. That group's anti-Mamdani's spending included an ad released one week earlier that linked Zohran to "jihad" via his support from Imam Wahhaj.

An inveterate foe of Bernie Sanders and socialism, Bloomberg lent his influential backing to the incendiary campaign on behalf of Cuomo. Although he had reportedly been impressed by Zohran in their September meeting, the former mayor now condoned Islamophobic politicking against the Muslim frontrunner. Bloomberg's longtime aide Stu Loeser was a key player in FTC. It's not clear whether the team thought Cuomo might prevail on November 4. But reducing the size of Mamdani's mandate was a cause that Bloomy and his fellow billionaires could rally behind.[56]

*

---

56 By the end of the general election, outside spending on the 2025 race totaled over $64 million, with more than $52 million supporting Cuomo.

As election day neared, Zohran mobilized his supporters. On Thursday night, October 30, he canvassed with members of the Taxi Workers Alliance (TWA), then visited cab drivers at La Guardia Airport. He next greeted staffers—many belonging to the New York State Nurses Association, a leading union supporting Mamdani—at Elmhurst Hospital Center before walking over to Kabab King in Jackson Heights. There, the South Asian frontrunner cheerfully helped serve biryani with rice and naan to TWA members.

Over the weekend Mamdani also sought to mobilize long-time Democratic voters across the city. With its historically large number of party registrants, Brooklyn became a prime target. Tish James, a lifelong Brooklynite strongly backed by older Democrats, campaigned hard for Zohran down the stretch. That Trump's DoJ had recently targeted James galvanized the party faithful.

On Thursday night, October 30, Zohran was the star of the show at a Brooklyn Democratic Party gala in Red Hook. Somewhat surprisingly, the studious candidate invoked the American Revolution, specifically mentioning the Battle of Brooklyn, a rout by the British. Mamdani stated that the "spirit of refusing to abide by oppression" witnessed in August 1776 now could be found in the borough's support for "Brooklyn's very own Tish James." Although scholars may deem that to be a bit of a stretch, the audience loved it. Mamdani led the room in a loud chorus of "Hands off Tish!"

When Zohran exited the stage, the Democratic loyalists in attendance followed him. *City & State*'s Holly Pretsky posted a clip of Chuck Schumer's video address to the gala playing on a big screen that nobody in the room watched because they all sought to pat the party's mayoral nominee on the back. It was not a good look for Brooklyn's most powerful Democrat.

Zohran returned to the borough frequently over the next few days. Amid the large Halloween parade in Park Slope, he popped into Community Bookstore, a neighborhood mainstay for over 50 years. Mamdani was back the following day, joining Tish James at Hanson Place Seventh Day Adventist Church in nearby Fort Greene. A photo of the Muslim candidate joining a prayer circle with James and churchgoers spread across social media.[57] As returns soon showed, voters in both Park Slope and greater Fort Greene turned out in force for Zohran.

That Saturday night, the next-gen leader lit up Tik Tok after Cuco, a young Mexican American singer-songwriter, summoned him to the stage at the historic Kings Theatre in Flatbush. (Eight nights earlier, British alt-pop phenom Pink Pantheress similarly brought out Mamdani at the same venue, thrilling the capacity crowd of over 3,000 people.) After cutting a short clip with Cuco on November 1, Zohran made the rounds at several nightclubs in Williamsburg and Bushwick. His six-stop tour

---

[57] In one of the odder moments of the campaign, NY1's Courtney Gross reported that just before the Adventist service began, she spotted Hakeem Jeffries (who lives nearby) enter the church via a side door, then sit inconspicuously in a rear pew. According to Gross, Jeffries wanted to observe the congregation's response to Mamdani firsthand.

included an Afro-Caribbean venue, a Latin spot, and two queer dance parties.

Hell Gate's Adlan Jackson equated the excited Brooklyn clubgoers' response to their unexpected guest with Beatlemania. As Mamdani told Jackson, the campaign's focus on "affordability is also to ensure that New Yorkers can do more than just struggle. That also means that New Yorkers have time and room and space for joy." While Zohran thrilled youthful fans after midnight, Cuomo scheduled no campaign events after 3 p.m. that Saturday and wrapped things up on Sunday just after noon.

Mamdani's Sunday was full of sports, with stops to watch the New York City Marathon as it snaked through Greenpoint and later with Kathy Hochul and other top Dems to catch the governor's beloved Buffalo Bills at an Irish pub in Astoria. That evening the frontrunner joined Kid Mero for a Knicks game at Madison Square Garden. Unlike Cuomo and Adams, the comedian and would-be mayor sat far from courtside.

*

While Zohran watched the Knicks, audiences at home that Sunday evening saw Donald Trump tell *60 Minutes*, rather half-heartedly, that he wanted Cuomo to win. If the choice is between "a bad Democrat and a communist," the president advised interviewer Norah O'Donnell, he would opt for the former "all the time." While Mamdani's team highlighted Trump's plug, Cuomo insisted to reporters on Monday that the president had not, in fact, endorsed him.

At sunrise on Monday, November 3, Zohran and many of his key supporters assembled for the campaign's last big event: A large march across the Brooklyn Bridge to City Hall. Joined by elected officials including Tish James and Brad Lander, Muslim allies including Asad Dandia, and a wide range of labor leaders and community activists, Mamdani led the assemblage across the East River while holding a banner reading "Our Time Is Now." Outside City Hall, Zohran reiterated his pledge to fight Trump, with his supporters declaring "shame!" when the frontrunner mentioned the president's pro-Cuomo statement on *60 Minutes.*

Asked by WABC-TV's Phil Taitt to share his thoughts on the eve of election day, Zohran's response was anything but standard campaign stuff. "It has been the honor of a lifetime to run to lead the city that I love," Mamdani stated. It's "the city I grew up in," he continued. "The city that I got my citizenship in, where I got married." Without missing a beat, the frontrunner then circled back to the "cost of living crisis" before concluding that "our time is now." Even when reflective, Mamdani stayed on message.

Later that day, Trump forced Cuomo to revise his last-ditch pitch when the president clarified that yes, he wanted the city's MAGA voters to support the "bad Democrat." In a lengthy post on Truth Social that went up at 5:16 p.m., the president called Mamdani a "Communist" four times, stated that the White House would cut off federal funds to New York City if the leftist won, and declared that electing Zohran meant that the city had "NO CHANCE" to restore "its former Glory!" The crescendo ended with a Trumpian thud. "Whether you personally like Andrew Cuomo or not," he decreed, "you really have no choice. You must vote for him, and hope he does a fantastic job."

Trump's directive targeted city Republicans and Democrats who backed him in 2024, many of whom are older residents who prefer to cast their ballots on election day. Nine days of early voting had brought over 735,000 people to the polls, which ultimately produced one-third of the total ballots. Even though he could no longer claim to be "the anti-Trump candidate," Cuomo now stood to gain sizable support from MAGA loyalists. The second-place challenger promptly whistled a different tune. By instructing Republicans to shift their votes away from Sliwa, Trump's declaration "could be very helpful for me," Cuomo told *Fox & Friends* on election day morning. In not exactly Lincolnesque terms, the veteran pol characterized Mamdani's agenda as "all BS."

In June, Cuomo predicted that Trump would manhandle Mamdani, plowing through him like "a hot knife through butter." In August, the lifelong Democrat assured the Hamptons set that the Republican president was in his camp. From September through November 3, Mario's son claimed to be Donald's worst nightmare. On election day, he was excited to have Trump's blessing.

Shortly after the dust settled, the president had a very friendly meeting with the incoming mayor at the White House. Many in MAGA land now wondered what all the fuss had been about.

CHAPTER 22
Strange Bedfellows

At 11:19 p.m. on November 4 at the Brooklyn Paramount, Zohran kicked off his victory remarks with a line from Eugene Debs: "I can see the dawn of a better day for humanity."[58] He invoked the "calloused palms" of delivery workers and "burn-scarred knuckles" of kitchen staff. Mamdani denounced billionaires, rhapsodized about Yemeni bodega owners and Senegalese taxi drivers, used an Arabic expression, name-checked Fiorello La Guardia, and quoted 20th-century statesmen ranging from Jawaharlal Nehru to Mario Cuomo. The next-gen mayor

---

58 On November 3, Zohran paid tribute to socialist Vito Marcantonio (1902-1954) in the fifth (and final) episode of the campaign's "Until It's Done" series, this one shot initially in black and white. Seated at his traveling antique desk near the corner of 116th Street and Lexington Avenue (a stretch co-named "Vito Marcantonio Way"), Mamdani informed viewers about "Marc's" close relationship with Mayor Fiorello La Guardia. Calling Marc an "unapologetic socialist," Zohran (now in color) closed by asking voters, "Are we brave enough to believe in a city that benefits us all?"

bid farewell to his twice-defeated challenger, acerbically wishing Andrew Cuomo "only the best in private life."

The new face of New York City defiantly challenged a powerful older one. "If anyone can show a nation betrayed by Donald Trump how to defeat him," Mamdani declared, "it is the city that gave rise to him." Zohran addressed the president directly. "Since I know you're watching directly, I have four words for you: turn the volume up!" The new mayor then put bad landlords ("the Donald Trumps of our city"), tax evaders ("like Trump"), and exploitative employers on notice.

"New York City will remain a city of immigrants," Zohran vowed, which was "as of tonight, led by an immigrant." When Mira Nair, Mahmood Mamdani, and Rama Dujawi joined him on stage, the victorious quartet vividly showed that power had changed hands in the global capital.

Mamdani's celebration speech was far more fiery than standard conciliatory fare. Penned by campaign writing director Julian Gerson and the candidate (with input from strategist Morris Katz), the winner sought to settle a few scores. In addition to bidding adieu to Cuomo, the mayor-elect declared, "No more will New York be a city where you can traffic in Islamophobia and win an election." The passion from the podium flowed throughout the room. "I was bawling," Zohran's closest Albany comrade, Jabari Brisport, told me soon afterward.

Although the speech was widely lauded, and the *New York Times* would soon annotate it, CNN's Van Jones immediately denounced Zohran's performance. The commentator, who purports to speak for the national Democratic Party establishment, faulted Mamdani for sounding like an angry "class warrior." "The warm, open, embracing guy who is close to working people was not on-stage tonight," Jones insisted. "There was some other voice on stage." Like the national Democratic leaders who reside a short distance from the Brooklyn Paramount, Jones seemed more concerned about the reactions of the party's rich donors than its blue-collar voters.

According to Julian Gerson, Zohran intended to sound "defiant" on victory night. As the speechwriter told CNN host Laura Coates a few nights later, the mayor was speaking on behalf of city residents "whose voices do not echo in the halls of power." In response to Jones' claim that Mamdani "missed an opportunity to bring more people into the tent," Gerson called out the tone police. "Civility is often a one-way offer," he said. "It's given to a certain number of people in our society—and it's not extended to many more."

In his victory lap at the Paramount, Zohran reignited the radical fires of the June primary. But before the dust had settled on his landmark win, new blazes raged in different directions. While Mamdani clashed with fellow members of the NYC-DSA regarding whether the group should run a primary challenger against Hakeem Jeffries, pro-Palestine activists blasted his choice for NYPD commissioner. Meanwhile, just two-and-a-half weeks after mobilizing his ground troops against the "Communist" prospective mayor, Donald Trump gave Zohran a stunningly warm reception at the White House.

The post-election twists raised new questions. Rather than govern from the left, might Zohran simply become a more charismatic version of progressive Bill de Blasio? Would New York City's business leaders follow Trump's lead in warming up to Mamdani? The 2025 mayoral campaign had produced an earthquake, but it was not clear how much the landscape had changed.

*

On election night, initial returns showed Mamdani with over one million votes, putting him at just over 50 percent. Cuomo stood at 41 percent, with Sliwa collecting only seven percent. The Board of Elections' certified results released in early December produced the same percentages, with Zohran's tally of 1,114,184 votes the highest total number since John Lindsay (1,149,106) in 1965. The turnout of over 2.2 million New Yorkers nearly doubled the November 2021 mayoral contest.[59]

Results in the two other citywide races on the ballot shed light on the number of Democrats who stuck with Cuomo, whose final number was 906,614. Two Democrats—incumbent Public Advocate Jumaane Williams and comptroller candidate Mark Levine—captured over 350,000 more votes than Mamdani. A CNN exit poll's finding that one-third of Democrats casting ballots supported Cuomo thus roughly matched his yield.

---

59 In 2009, the most recent closely contested general election for mayor, Michael Bloomberg prevailed over Democrat Bill Thompson with just 585,466 votes (51%).

Meanwhile, backing from the Trump crowd provided Cuomo with over one-third of his total ballots, as evidenced by the returns for low-profile Republican challengers in the public advocate and comptroller contests. Both far exceeded Curtis Sliwa's total of just under 155,000, with one of the GOP candidates nearly reaching 500,000. Cuomo racked up his strongest returns in pro-Trump strongholds including Brooklyn's Borough Park and Brighton Beach, where Mamdani received close to zero votes in numerous precincts.

CNN's voter sampling revealed that Israel-Palestine was an important issue for voters on both sides of the divide. Although an equal number of the 4,744 respondents—67 percent—stated that the conflict was a factor in their vote, Mamdani prevailed by six points. Among those who did not view it as an important issue, the leftist candidate led Cuomo by twenty points. The attempt by Israel hawks to make support for the Netanyahu regime the defining conflict of the mayoral campaign clearly backfired.

On stage at the Paramount, a low-profile but pivotal figure in Mamdani's success took a turn in the spotlight. Tascha Van Auken, the campaign's field director, introduced the winning candidate, an honor illustrating the canvassing operation's importance in Zohran's victory. By election day, over 104,500 Mamdani volunteers had knocked on more than three million voter doors, doubling the totals from the June primary. By any measure, the numbers were eye-popping.

In a post-election discussion with *Jacobin* editor Micah Uetricht for *The Dig* podcast, Van Auken explained that before Mamdani's campaign, conventional wisdom held that the most successful field operation would only add "one to three points" to a candidate's vote total. But starting in December 2024, Zohran for NYC created a new playbook. Van Auken's apartment—in Brooklyn's Sunset Park, an NYC-DSA stronghold—served as the initial field headquarters. A group of around twenty DSA members began knocking on voters' doors in rent-stabilized buildings, testing out the campaign's "script."

By late January, Van Auken told Uetricht, the city's campaign finance program provided funding that enabled her to build the operation. She and her team organized Zohran for NYC's first major canvass, which fanned out from Brooklyn's Grand Army Plaza on Saturday, January 25. When more than 500 volunteers showed up, Van Auken sensed that they were on the right track.[60]

Inspired by the model that legendary community organizer Marshall Ganz (b. 1943) implemented during the 2008 Obama campaign, Van Auken and company recruited eager volunteers to become field leads. More than fifty became field coordinators. In addition to persuading voters, the extensive neighborhood outreach also provided a pipeline of information to Mamdani's campaign about what residents across the city wanted to hear.

---

60 On January 2, 2026, Mamdani named Van Auken as head of his newly created Office of Mass Engagement. The announcement came at Grand Army Plaza, with Mamdani highlighting the January 2025 canvass launch.

Many members of unions including those representing teachers (UFT), health-care workers (SEIU 1199), city government staffers (DC37), hotel workers (HTC), and building employees (32BJ) also knocked on doors and made phone calls for Zohran. In the campaign's final month, UFT headquarters in Downtown Manhattan hosted a dozen phone bank events led by retired teachers. Throughout the general election, Zohran met with union members on multiple occasions. "I look out and I see the leaders of this city," he told an early October gathering of 1,500 members of SEIU. "I see people who—whether we are speaking of your hospitals, your union chapters, your communities or your families—you are the ones who give faith back to those who have lost it in politicians."

Soon after winning the Democratic nomination in June, Mamdani received the backing of two major unions—HTC and 32BJ—which had supported Cuomo in the primary. The leaders of the Democrats' county organizations in Manhattan (Keith Wright) and Brooklyn (Rodneyse Bichotte Hermelyn) followed suit. Bronx Democratic boss Jamaal Bailey also threw his support behind the party nominee. Although Queens figurehead Greg Meeks withheld the organization's endorsement, Zohran won many of the precincts in the southeast portion of the borough controlled by Meeks.

Zohran racked up his highest vote totals in two Brooklyn assembly districts—one covering Brooklyn Heights through Park Slope, represented in the legislature by liberal Democrat Jo Anne Simon; the other spanning Fort Greene through Crown Heights, terrain controlled by NYC-DSA's Phara Souffrant Forrest. Spurred by both DSA-led canvassers and party leaders, the Democratic rank-and-file turned out for Zohran.

*

One prominent Mamdani supporter not at the Paramount on November 4 was Chi Ossé. Although the charismatic city councilmember from Bed-Stuy had been a prominent Mamdani backer since late in the primary, word circulated that Ossé had been "disinvited" from the victory party. The reason stemmed from his proposed bid to unseat Rep. Hakeem Jeffries. Ossé sought the backing of NYC-DSA, which had frequently clashed with the powerful Brooklyn Democrat.

As he embarked on the post-election phase of his victory, Zohran now spent a surprising amount of energy focused on a different campaign. With the NYC-DSA endorsement process playing out in November, the group's most prominent figure reversed his role from just over one year earlier. Mamdani was now the voice of cautionary realism, worrying about negative repercussions from an unsuccessful high-profile campaign.

That Ossé had only joined NYC-DSA in June—after previously distancing himself from the group— clearly troubled some local leaders besides Mamdani, including Van Auken. Although not an ally of Jeffries, AOC argued that primarying him was not "a good thing right now."[61] Ossé,

---

61 As *Current Affairs*' Alex Skopic argued in early December, the media's oft-stated claim that Jeffries remained "popular" in his

however, also had influential NYC-DSA backers, including Assemblymember Emily Gallagher, chapter co-chair Gustavo Gordillo, and Alvaro Lopez, the group's political director.

In order to drive home his message, Zohran attended a packed NYC-DSA endorsement meeting at the Church of the Village on Wednesday night, November 19. As reported by the *Daily News*' Chris Sommerfeldt, Mamdani told his comrades, "The choice is not whether to vote for Chi or Hakeem at the ballot box—the choice is how to spend the next year. Do we want to spend it defending caricatures of our movement, or do we want to spend it fulfilling the agenda at the heart of that very same movement?"

When the results of the Electoral Working Group rolled in that weekend, Zohran's position prevailed, albeit not resoundingly. While 626 of 1,205 members voted against a Jeffries challenge, 555 supported it (with 24 abstaining). Although the numbers showed plenty of enthusiasm, Ossé opted not to run without the NYC-DSA's blessing.

Why Zohran chose to lead the charge against the proposed effort against Jeffries merited explanation. When asked by *Majority Report* co-hosts Emma Vigeland and Sam Seder one week later, Mamdani essentially repeated his statement at the DSA forum about the need to "fulfill his agenda." On X, Canadian leftist Sana Saeed urged Zohran to explain precisely how "supporting primarying Jeffries

---

district is "suspect, because it's never been tested in a hard-fought election." As noted in *RZR*, Mamdani carried Jeffries' district by 12 points in the June primary.

[would] hurt the agenda." Mamdani never delineated. The soon-to-be mayor's concerns about Ossé seemed genuine, but the upshot was that the formerly insurgent candidate was now playing ball with Democratic Party leaders.[62]

On the same day that Zohran urged his comrades not to back Ossé, Jessica Tisch announced that she would accept Mamdani's offer for her to remain as NYPD commissioner. Led by Nerdeen Kirwani, founder of Within Our Lifetime (WOL), pro-Palestine activists blasted the move, connecting it to the Jeffries controversy. As Kiswani explained to journalist Briahna Joy Gray, Mamdani's "pragmatic" maneuvering in both cases benefited Israel allies, an alarming trend. Writers Against the War on Gaza, numerous DSA-affiliated groups, and multiple local campus chapters of Students for Justice in Palestine signed onto WOL's detailed denunciation of Tisch's pro-Israel actions. The commissioner's younger brother, Benjamin Tisch (in his early 40s, like Jessie) fueled the fire by calling Mamdani an "enemy" at a Jewish charity event in early December.

In a lengthy sit-down interview with the New York Editorial Board, Mamdani adviser Patrick Gaspard touted the new mayor's moves regarding both Ossé and Tisch. It

---

62 In mid-December, Brad Lander announced that he would primary Rep. Dan Goldman, a move supported by Zohran. Although she had been endorsed by NYC-DSA in mid-November, Alexa Avilés dropped her bid, sparking further criticism of Mamdani from within the group's ranks. Meanwhile, the incoming mayor threw his support behind DSA stalwart Claire Valdez in her bid to replace Rep. Nydia Velázquez, who announced her retirement.

was a "bold thing," the veteran Democratic operative maintained, for Zohran to speak out against the Jeffries challenge. After repeating the familiar talking points about Tisch "fighting corruption," Gaspard then uniquely insisted that the commissioner had been "incredibly thoughtful" in her approach to the city's mental health crisis. Although the consultant voiced pro-Palestine sentiments, he made no mention of Tisch's stridently pro-Israel track record.

*

On Friday morning, November 21, Zohran flew down to DC for a summit with the Don. The mayor-elect posted a selfie on X that showed him smiling while sitting in an airplane window seat. MAGA influencer Laura Loomer tried to stir up outrage, faulting the leftist for not taking Amtrak. By the end of the day, Trumpers everywhere would be grasping at straws.

Although Fox News previewed the mid-afternoon appointment as a "Showdown with Socialism," other MAGA voices predicted that it would be far less contentious. "Donald Trump is Donald Trump," the president's New York City pal John Catsimatidis told the *New York Times*. "He's going to do what he wants. But he doesn't want the city to go downhill." Based on Cats' comment, I suggested to BBC News host Ben Brown that Trump may indeed heed the advice of local business leaders who "don't want total chaos" in the nation's economic capital.

The lovefest that transpired nonetheless defied all predictions. "One of the things I would have loved to be someday is the mayor of New York City," the president told reporters while sitting at his desk at the Oval Office. "I think you really have a chance to make it great," the MAGA figurehead assured Zohran, standing at his side. When Trump said that "we agree on a lot more than I would have thought," right-wing provocateur Jack Posobiec exited the room in disgust. Although reporters highlighted criticisms voiced by Mamdani regarding Trump, the president brushed them off. "I don't mind," the Republican nonchalantly replied when asked about Zohran's references to him as a fascist.

Only slightly less improbable that afternoon was a cameo from Franklin Delano Roosevelt. As Zohran stated in the Oval Office, amid his visit he "appreciated" seeing a White House portrait of FDR, which brought to mind "the incredible work that was done with the New Deal [as well as] what it can look like when the federal government and New York City government work together to deliver on affordability." Uncritically noting that Roosevelt was a Democrat, Trump called it an "amazing portrait." On Truth Social, the now-avuncular figure shared a photo of himself with Mamdani standing in front of FDR.

"It was a productive meeting focused on a place of shared admiration and love, which is New York City," Mamdani assured reporters. The incoming mayor said that he and the president discussed the costs of rent, groceries, and utilities. Trump praised Mamdani for retaining Jessica Tisch, calling her "a good friend of some of the people in my family," specifically Ivanka. "They say she's really good and competent," the president said. "And he just retained her, so that's a good sign." The common ground here shifted to the right.

There seemed little dispute that by winning over Trump, Mamdani had (at least temporarily) deflated widespread fears that the White House would follow through on its threats to wreak havoc on New York City because of its leftward lurch. The *New York Post*'s next-day cover claim that Trump had "bulldoze[d] socialist Zo with kindness" sounded just a bit wishful.[63] Speaking from the other side of the political spectrum, Boston Mayor Michelle Wu declared that she was not "interested in a bromance with the federal regime."

Trump's dramatic mood-swing towards Mamdani appeared to spring from his hometown affinities, making it highly unlikely that any other major city would receive similar treatment. ICE raids along Canal Street one week later soon showed the feds still posed a major threat to the incoming regime. But other than diehard Zohran haters, it was difficult to find many locals upset about his White House rendezvous with Trump, which ended with the president stating "I'll be cheering for him" as he and Mamdani shook hands.

*

"I don't think he joined the race thinking he was going to win it," Mahmood Mamdani told Al Jazeera in late November regarding Zohran's mayoral run. "I think he joined wanting to make a point." Two things were "near and dear to him," Mahmood explained. In addition to

---

[63] Headlined "On your Marx, get set, Zo!" the *Post*'s November 5 cover depicting Mamdani holding a Soviet red sickle became a collector's item.

"social justice," Zohran believed strongly in the "rights of Palestinians." As his victory illustrated, over 1.1 million New York City voters echoed those views.[64]

"To believe in universal principles of freedom and justice is something I'm proud of," Zohran informed me in early April, responding to his *New York Post* front-page debut. That cover's headline only referred to him as "anti-Israel," but the charge soon morphed into "antisemitic." "One can criticize the Israeli state without being critical of the Jewish faith," Mamdani told me. "There are many who seek to weaponize a very real crisis of antisemitism for their own ends," he noted. "Andrew Cuomo is one of those people."

Soon after Zohran triumphed in the general election, Benjamin Netanyahu sought to reassert his influence in New York City. Outgoing Mayor Eric Adams visited Israel in mid-November, meeting with the prime minister at a military base in Tel Aviv. "I started my mayoralty here in Israel," Adams advised reporters. "And as I finish, I wanted to come back and let [Israelis] know that I served you as the mayor." Adams, who received a standing ovation during his visit to the Knesset, sported an NYPD baseball cap as he toured archeological sites below the Western Wall.

Israeli's far-right leader brushed off Mayor Mamdani's pledge to arrest him. In an early December video interview with the *New York Times*' Andrew Ross Sorkin, the accused war criminal stated, "I'll come to New York, OK? Of course I will." Sorkin asked how he would evade arrest.

---

64 Enthusiasm for the new mayor was also widespread among teens who will soon reach voting age.

"Why don't you wait and see?" Bibi sneered. He then conditioned a meeting with the new mayor upon Zohran's acceptance of "Israel's right to exist," a willful distortion of Mamdani's oft-stated position.

A mid-November protest by pro-Palestine activists at the Park East Synagogue, a leading Modern Orthodox center on E. 68th Street, portended future showdowns during the Mamdani era. The evening event was hosted by Nefesh B'Nefesh, an organization that promotes the migration of North American Jews to illegal West Bank settlements. Hundreds of demonstrators greeted event attendees with chants including "Death to the IDF," "Globalize the intifada," and "Free Palestine." No one was injured, but the fact that the confrontations occurred at a synagogue sparked several weeks of fallout.

In his response the following day, Mamdani—via press secretary Dora Pekec—stated that "every New Yorker should be free to enter a house of worship without intimidation, and that these sacred spaces should not be used to promote activities in violation of international law." Israel hawks wanted to hear only the first half of that statement. Three days after the protest, NYPD Commissioner Jessica Tisch addressed the Park East congregation during its Shabbat services, apologizing for the department's failure "to ensure that people could easily enter and leave shul."

Led by Governor Hochul, elected officials called for new restrictions on protests outside of houses of worship. In early December, 1,100 people attended a vigil outside of Park East. Comptroller-elect Mark Levine, an Israel hawk, assured the gathering that the recent demonstration "was

Meet Mayor Mamdani

unambiguously an effort to intimidate and threaten Jewish New Yorkers going into a synagogue." Cardinal Timothy Dolan soon echoed that claim, referring to it as a "terribly mean protest." Concerns regarding international law vanished into the ether.

*

On the day after his victory, Mayor-elect Mamdani hit the ground running, holding a press conference in front of the World's Fair Unisphere in Queens. There, he announced his team of five female transition leaders, four with extensive experience working in prior mayoral administrations.[65] The fifth, former chair of the Federal Trade Commission Lina Khan, added her expertise in corporate oversight. Six days later, Zohran announced that veteran government hand Dean Fuleihan (b. 1951) would serve as first deputy mayor and that his top adviser Elle Bisgaard-Church would become his chief of staff. Both Fuleihan and Bisgaard-Church made frequent public appearances with Mamdani over the next two months, with the latter attending the White House summit.

On the Monday following his DC visit, Zohran announced the appointment of over 400 prominent activists and practitioners to 17 separate advisory subcommittees. The roster featured several influential players in previous mayoral

---

[65] Maria Torres-Springer, who in February had resigned as a deputy mayor in response to Eric Adams' embrace of border czar Tom Homan, was the most familiar name among the group. Consultant Elana Leopold took on the role of transition director, with nonprofit executives Grace Bonilla and Melanie Hartzog joining Torres-Springer and Lina Khan as co-chairs.

administrations, including Dr. Mary Bassett, who served as public health commissioner under Bill de Blasio.[66] The presence of two CUNY criminal justice radicals, Lumumba Akinwole-Bandele and Alex Vitale, sparked right-wing condemnation, with a *New York Post* editorial calling both "anti-cop."

Although they captured less media attention, the presence of Cuomo-aligned figures on some of the transition committees was a bit surprising. Despite his firm's $250,000 contribution to Fix the City, Brooklyn real estate titan Jed Walentas joined the housing group. Masha Pearl, whose election-day engagement to prominent anti-Mamdani fundraiser Jeff Leb[67] was widely reported, sat on the social services committee. Because all members signed non-disclosure agreements, how much influence any figure wielded in the groups' deliberations was not immediately clear.

In early September, the *New York Times'* Dana Rubinstein reported that Jeff Blau, a leading Manhattan real estate developer, hosted an emergency summit in Midtown, raising substantial funds for Cuomo. On Tuesday morning, December 9, Blau joined a group of what the *Post* labeled as "real estate bigwigs" who met with the incoming mayor. Whether Zohran's door was just a bit too open for militant foes seemed a legitimate cause for concern.

---

66 Bassett's support for Palestinian rights led to her ouster from Harvard's School of Public Health in December 2025.
67 Leb, a staunch Israel ally, has an extensive track record of funding challengers to leftist candidates. In 2024, Leb named his PAC "Defeat the DSA."

Despite the outpouring of contempt for Mamdani during the campaign, city business leaders echoed his concerns about affordability. In mid-December, Kathryn Wylde, longtime spokeswoman for the city elite (and a member of the transition's economic development subcommittee), told *Inside City Hall*'s Bobby Cuza that the "business community totally shares the priorities of affordable housing and affordable, accessible childcare." The city's high cost of living meant that local employers were paying $20,000 to $30,000 more in salaries than elsewhere. Wylde stated that although some business titans still had "big issues" with Mamdani's stance towards Israel, the leftist incoming mayor no longer frightened the 1%.

Zohran's appointees faced scrutiny from Israel allies, however. On December 18, the new mayor's director of appointments resigned one day after being named to the position. The Anti-Defamation League had unearthed antisemitic posts that the nominee made in 2011, when she was in her late teens. That she was currently married to a Jewish deputy official in Brad Lander's office did not matter to Zohran critics including raging Islamophobe Vickie Paladino, who whipped up outrage about Mamdani and his team's misstep on X.

The *New York Post* was not pleased with Zohran's announcement one day later that Julie Su, acting labor secretary in the Biden administration (and a Lina Khan ally), would become the city's first-ever deputy mayor for economic justice. The new position will include oversight of consumer affairs[68] and for-hire car services. Citing her pro-labor record (particularly in fighting wage theft), Bernie Sanders applauded the move. In bringing Su aboard, Mamdani put exploitative city employers on notice.[69]

The final weeks of 2025 were a whirlwind for the incoming mayor. He attended a Lower East Side campaign fundraiser full of celebrities. Along with Bisgaard-Church and other members of his team, Mamdani spent twelve hours on Sunday, December 14 at the Museum of the Moving Image in Astoria chatting with everyday New Yorkers about ways to improve daily life. As he prepared to take office as the city's first Muslim mayor, Zohran celebrated Hanukkah at the home of Broadway legend Mandy Patinkin, who would perform at his inauguration.

Mamdani's meteoric ascent throughout 2025 meant that he was now an international sensation. As Liza Featherstone noted in her *Jacobin* election recap, in the process, the socialist and his comrades shared a new sensibility about politics throughout the city, a culture that invited everyone from A-list to Z. Whether riding the free Staten Island

---

[68] Mamdani also announced that Sam Levine, a Khan deputy at the FTC, would direct the Department of Consumer and Worker Protection, reporting to Su.

[69] Elon Musk took aim at Mamdani's December 23 appointment of Lillian Bonsignore as his fire department (FDNY) chief. The same figure who earlier in the year literally brought out a chain saw when announcing firings of federal workers now claimed that Bonsignore, who spent 31 years in the city's emergency medical system (EMS), lacked "proven experience" and would somehow endanger city residents. "You know, EMS addresses at least 70% of all calls coming into FDNY?" Zohran clapped back.

Meet Mayor Mamdani

Ferry, or playing soccer at Coney Island, Zohran and his campaign asserted that "Everyone deserves it all: love, leisure, pleasure, sport. For not only did Mamdani emphasize that you deserve to enjoy your life — he also made politics itself fun." The 2025 mayoral campaign was one hell of a ride.

Acknowledgements

Many thanks to Zohran Mamdani and members of his campaign team, particularly Andrew Epstein, Ali Najmi, and Julian Gerson, for their insights and cooperation. My lefty journalist comrades Liza Featherstone, Ari Paul, John Tarleton, and Ross Barkan were immensely helpful. My ace research assistant Urwah Ahmad helped steer social media promotion of *Run Zohran Run!* So, too, did my pals Shu-fy Pognon, Naeem Mohaimeen, Candis Davis, Tommy Gamba-Ellis, and filmmaker Daniel Solaris.

I was thrilled by the excellent media coverage of *Run Zohran Run!* The list includes podcast discussions with *Useful Idiots'* Katie Halper and Aaron Maté; *Turn Left*'s Curtis Daly; *Free State*'s Dion Fanning; *Scheerpost*'s Bob Scheer; *Consortium News*' Joe Lauria; *Payday Report*'s Mike Elk (et al.); and *Labour Left*'s Bryn Griffiths. I enjoyed my radio interviews with Randy Credico, Doug Henwood, Scott Harris, Michael Rowland, and Andrew McDonald; and my TV appearance with the BBC's Ben Brown. I appreciated attention to the book from Iker Seisdedos of *El Pais*, *L'Humanite*'s Christophe Deroubaix, Solveig

Godeluck of *Les Echos*, *Mediapart*'s Alexis Buisson, and Lorenzo Tijerina of the *Sunset Park Post*. Last but by no means least, I was quite honored that *The Progressive*'s Ed Rampell and *Novara Media*'s Rivkah Brown chose *Run Zohran Run!* as one of their best books of 2025.

I am grateful to the venues that hosted book talks throughout the fall of 2025. My itinerary included: Heritage Wines in Fort Greene (thanks to Charles McMickens), which was a Bookend event in the Brooklyn Book Festival (Stephan Herrera); Pete's Candy Store (Andy McDowell); John Jay College (Prof. David Brotherton); Sunset Stoop (Roberto Beltre); St. Joseph's University NY (Prof. Susan Nakley, Dean Phil Dehne); and the Brooklyn Society for Ethical Culture (Vandra Thorburn).

My longtime Brooklyn pals Williams Cole & Meghan McDermott, Diego Baraona & Susan Delamare, Donald Breckenridge & Johannah Rodgers, Ana Nery Fragoso & Luis Mallo, Sophie Gonick & Sander Hicks, Mark Chait, John Whitlow, and Chase Madar provided lots of encouragement. So did my Sunset Park neighbors including Peter Martin, Al Diaz, Heather von Rohr & Nick Dawson, Kate Hesler & Robert Minell, and Justin Jordan. I acquired lots of important perspective from the many members of Alex Vitale's criminal justice writers group, with particular thanks to Jeff Fagan, Andrew Case, Jayne Mooney, and Sergio Grossi. I also enjoyed chatting about the campaign with my Rutgers chums Alan Reeder, Denis Williams, Patrick Walsh, and Mike Crockford; my Bay Area buddies Rebecca Titcomb & Wayne de Jager, Denise Deslond &

Peter Doolittle, and John Smenk; as well as my Evanston loved ones Maddie Soglin, Rob Strom, and Anthony Rowe.

Colin Robinson and his crackerjack team at OR Books—led by Olivia Heffernan—once again deftly handled the production process. Special thanks to Sam Russek for editing as well as to Antara Ghosh for the book's design, Fatema Merchant for distribution, Zahra Khan and Georgie Carr for publicity, and Ana Ratner for project oversight.

–T.H.

Theodore Hamm is the author of *Bernie's Brooklyn: How Growing Up in the New Deal City Shaped Bernie Sanders' Politics*. He wrote about the 2025 race for *The Indypendent* and *Drop Site News*. Hamm is chair of journalism at St. Joseph's University, NY. He lives in Sunset Park, Brooklyn, a stronghold of the NYC-DSA.

www.ingramcontent.com/pod-product-compliance
Lightning Source LLC
Jackson TN
JSHW020238150326
99334JS00003B/639